The Death Penalty

The Death Penalty

*An American Citizen's
Guide to Understanding
Federal and State Laws*

by LOUIS J. PALMER, JR.

McFarland & Company, Inc., Publishers
Jefferson, North Carolina, and London

British Library Cataloguing-in-Publication data are available

Library of Congress Cataloguing-in-Publication Data

Palmer, Louis J.
    The death penalty : an American citizen's guide to understanding
federal and state laws / by Louis J. Palmer, Jr.
        p.   cm.
    Includes bibliographical references and index.
    ISBN 0-7864-0444-2 (library binding : 50# alkaline paper) ∞
    1. Capital punishment—United States.   I. Title.
KF9725.P35   1998
345.73'0773—dc21   98-27178
                                                                                    CIP

Manufactured in the United States of America

McFarland & Company, Inc., Publishers
  Box 611, Jefferson, North Carolina 28640

To the Honorable Chief Justice Robin Jean Davis,
a dear friend and one of our nation's most talented jurists

Acknowledgments

The present form of this book would never have been possible without the legal expertise and assistance of Xueyan Zhang, Esq. I must also recognize Leslie Anderson, Esq., for her moral support and confidence through the many revisions of this book.

Contents

PART IV. LAWS RELATED TO EXECUTION

List of Tables and Boxes

Introduction

Though possibly the most controversial subject in American law, the death penalty is not well understood by the public. The media provide little real information about how it operates, seizing for the most part on the sensationalistic: reports of capital felons being revived from suicide attempts so that they could be executed, instances of mentally retarded felons being executed, and an incident in which a capital felon's head caught fire during his execution. Confusion and alarm result more often than understanding. Adding to the death penalty confusion was a 1997 announcement by the American Bar Association which called for a halt to executions.

In all fairness, it must be pointed out that most of the misinformation the media feed to the public about capital punishment is unintended. Capital punishment is simply far too complex an area of law for the media to explain adequately to the public. The intent of this book is to unravel and make plain the laws of capital punishment as they exist in the United States.

There is one qualification to the general theme of this book. While some discussion will be given to death penalty issues that arise before a defendant is convicted of a capital offense, the primary focus of the book is upon issues that are resolved after a defendant has been convicted of a capital crime. The reason for greater treatment of the postconviction stage will become clear to the reader in subsequent chapters. It will suffice for now to say that the postconviction stage of capital punishment has undergone dramatic changes since the 1976 decision by the United States Supreme Court (hereinafter Supreme Court) to reinstate the death penalty.

The reader should keep in mind that the United States is comprised of 52 distinct legal jurisdictions (the 50 states, the federal government, and the District of Columbia). Much of the lack of understanding of the death penalty arises because the nation is comprised of autonomous legal jurisdictions. (Of course this autonomy is tempered by the Constitution.) Each jurisdiction has the authority, within the bounds of constitutional constraints, to design its own unique death penalty statutes. As a result of the majority of jurisdictions exercising their independent authority to create death penalty systems, no two death penalty systems are exactly the same in all particulars.

1

This book comprehensively examines the differences among death penalty systems throughout the United States. It not only enables the reader to see the various distinct aspects of each jurisdiction's death penalty system, but will also aid the reader in understanding why these differences exist.

In addition to a systematic treatment of the distinct aspects, this book will set out in detail those factors which are common to each jurisdiction's death penalty system. The reader will learn that many of these common factors exist because of decisions handed down by the Supreme Court.

In the final analysis, the one constant that the reader will find throughout this book is the role of the Supreme Court. Through its interpretation of the Eighth Amendment of the Constitution, the Supreme Court has established many death penalty legal principles that are binding in all capital punishment jurisdictions.

For the reader's convenience, the material in this book has been divided into four major parts. Part I lays out important foundational information. Chapter 1 provides a basic working knowledge of the common law origin of capital punishment in Anglo-American law. Chapter 2 builds on the previous chapter by exploring the impact of the Eighth Amendment on various specific death penalty issues. Chapter 3 rounds out Part I by setting forth a detailed but straightforward discussion of criminal conduct that triggers death penalty prosecutions.

Part II examines specific issues involving the governmental office responsible for enforcing death penalty statutes, i.e., the office of the prosecutor. This material has been set out in four chapters. Chapter 4 explores the general discretionary authority prosecutors have in seeking the death penalty. Chapter 5 contains a discussion of the charging documents used by prosecutors in death penalty cases. Chapter 6 looks at the type of information prosecutors must initially provide to defendants when the death penalty is involved. Chapter 7 culminates Part II with a discussion of the laws related to a prosecutor's ability to invoke death penalty statutes against defendants who have not actually inflicted death upon a murdered victim.

In Part III, which has been divided into six chapters, the reader is taken inside the courtroom for an examination of substantive issues involving primarily the sentencing phase of death penalty prosecutions. Chapter 8 provides a brief overview of how a capital felon's guilt is determined. Chapter 9 sets out a detailed discussion of the structure and nature of the penalty phase of a capital punishment prosecution. In Chapter 10 an exhaustive treatment is given to those factors which are used to permit a defendant to be sentenced to death. Chapter 11 takes a look at factors which may prevent the death penalty from being imposed upon a defendant who was actually found guilty of a capital offense. Chapter 12 provides a discussion of how the factors brought out in Chapters 10 and 11 are joined to determine whether a defendant will be sentenced to death. Part III is rounded out by a presentation in Chapter 13 of the mechanics involved in the review of a death sentence by appellate courts.

Part IV, which contains three chapters, outlines the laws involving implementation of the death penalty. In Chapter 14 a discussion is devoted to several factors that may temporarily or permanently delay execution of a sentence of death. Chapter 15 examines laws that regulate who may be present to observe executions. Chapter 16 terminates the book with a discussion of the methods of execution and the laws that control disposition of an executed capital felon's corpse.

This publication is designed to provide descriptive information pertaining to its subject matter. The publisher and author are not engaged in rendering legal or other professional service through this book. If legal advice or other expert assistance is required, an attorney should be consulted.

PART I

GENERAL
CONSIDERATIONS

CHAPTER 1

Common Law and Capital Punishment

Anglo-American jurisprudence owes its understanding and acceptance of the death penalty to the common law of England. For this reason it is prudent to undertake a cursory review of the punishment practices that were tolerated under the common law. Ultimately, as will be seen, many of the punishment practices of the common law have been rejected by Anglo-American jurisprudence.

The Meaning of Common Law

The phrase *common law* is often used without any understanding of its origin or meaning. It is important to note that the phrase *common law* and all of its implications stem from England. The actual use of the phrase has been traced back to the reign of Edward I in the thirteenth century.[1] During that period of time, two types of legal systems existed in England. The island nation had a temporal legal system and an ecclesiastical or religious legal system. The legal principles that fall under the phrase *common law* were developed in the temporal courts of England.

An explanation of the words *common* and *law* is also in order. As for the word *common*, it was indicated by an American court that "[i]n the context of English law, use of the word 'common' ... does not mean 'ordinary' or 'vulgar,' but rather 'uniform.'"[2] Legal principles that derived from temporal courts were thought of as customs or beliefs that were commonly or uniformly recognized and accepted by the people of England prior to being embraced by temporal courts.

The word *law* is generally associated with statutes and ordinances that are enacted by legislative bodies. For example, the United States Congress and the English Parliament are legislative bodies that enact laws. The creation of laws, however, is not restricted to legislative bodies. Courts, through judges, create what are referred to euphemistically as unenacted laws. (For constitutional reasons it is taboo in the United States to refer to judicial pronouncements as laws.) In the case of *Miranda v. Arizona*, 384 U.S. 436 (1966), for example, the Supreme Court developed a legal principle, that is, a law, which required all law enforcement agents to inform apprehended criminal suspects of certain constitutional rights before attempting to interrogate them. Although the legal system in America does not permit calling the *Miranda* warning a law, in the final analysis its application and effect are identical to that of a legislatively enacted law.

In putting the words *common* and *law* together, the legal profession is merely referring to principles that have the force and effect of law but were developed by judges in England's temporal courts.

As a final point in this area, it should be noted that the phrase *common law* is also traditionally used to refer to England's temporal courts. For example, to say that burglary is a common law crime is to say that burglary is a crime created by the temporal courts of England.

Offense Punishment
Under the Common Law

The common law recognized two types of criminal offenses: misdemeanor and felony. While numerous factors distinguished the two types of offenses, the ultimate difference resided in the fact that a convicted misdemeanant was not called upon to relinquish his life, but a convicted felon could be punished with death. A brief review of common law nonfatal corporal methods of punishment will precede the discussion of capital offenses and methods of capital punishment under the common law.

NONFATAL CRIMINAL PUNISHMENT

If one compares the nonfatal criminal punishments that are permitted by Anglo-American jurisprudence today with the nonfatal criminal punishments under the common law, the two appear as different as night and day. A proper perspective on this matter should be maintained, however, because the common law practices in question occurred between the thirteenth and eighteenth centuries. Attitudes have changed greatly since that period.

Some of the milder forms of nonfatal criminal punishment under the common law included confinement, hard labor, banishment, the pillory, stocks, and the dunking stool.[3] More drastic forms of punishment included plucking out eyes, castration,[4] cutting off feet, hands, noses, ears, and upper lips; and scalping.[5] Sometimes convicted prisoners were mercilessly whipped or were branded with hot irons on their cheeks or hands.[6]

COMMON LAW CAPITAL OFFENSES

The common law created only a few felony offenses, which included murder, arson, larceny, robbery, burglary, rape, treason, and petty treason. The limited number of felony offenses under the common law helps explain why the common law adopted the rule that all felony offenses were to be punished with death. Unfortunately for English citizens, however, the number of felony offenses in England expanded beyond what the common law created. As a result of parliamentary statutes, the number of felony offenses in England grew to 263 by the year 1822. Moreover, the common law rule that all felony offenses were to be punished with death was made applicable to each of the 263 felonies that developed in England.[7]

The great English jurist Blackstone commented sarcastically upon the tragedy of imposing the death penalty on all felony offenses. He pointed out that, as a result of misguided intentions by Parliament, it had become a capital offense to tear down the mound of a fish pond and allow fish to escape, to chop down a cherry tree that was in an orchard, or to be seen publicly with a gypsy for one month.[8]

COMMON LAW METHODS
OF CAPITAL PUNISHMENT

The methods by which the death penalty was carried out under the common law represent a journey through hell. The naked terror and devilish pain caused by common law methods of capital punishment shock and sober us today.

Many of the capital offenses under the common law had their own special execution methods. A male defendant convicted of treason or the felony crime of falsifying had to be dragged by a horse to the place of execution and hanged. A conviction for sodomy carried a penalty of death by being buried alive. A convicted heretic had to be burned alive. A conviction for a routine crime like murder, rape, arson, robbery, or burglary was punished by simple hanging. If any of the latter offenses was found to be especially vicious, however, the defendant was beheaded.[9]

The crime of treason by a female was punished initially under the common law by burning alive the defendant. However, in the year 1790 this method was halted and the punishment became strangulation and burning of the corpse.[10] For the crime of high treason (affecting the Crown directly), a defendant was punished by quartering, disemboweling, and beheading. In certain egregious murder prosecutions, a convicted defendant would be publicly dissected while alive.[11]

CHAPTER 2

Impact of the Eighth Amendment on Capital Punishment

Under the common law, capital punishment was carried out in a variety of painful ways. This fact, while important, is not the central issue here. The critical point to be gleaned is that 263 forms of human conduct could be punished with death, and under the common law, 99 percent of these offenses did not involve the taking of a human life.

The Eighth Amendment of the Constitution provides that: "Excessive bail shall not be required, nor excessive fines imposed, nor *cruel and unusual punishments* inflicted." (Emphasis added.) To what extent does the Eighth Amendment's Cruel and Unusual Punishment Clause affect capital punishment in the United States? Would the Cruel and Unusual Punishment Clause permit the death penalty to be imposed for the 263 offenses recognized by the common law? What, if any, limitation does the Cruel and Unusual Punishment Clause place on the ability of legislatures to enact laws mandating that certain offenses carry the death penalty?

The intent of this chapter is to address the above questions, as well as to bring out other aspects of the Supreme Court's interpretation of the Cruel and Unusual Punishment Clause. To this end, the material has been placed under two broad headings: (1) origin of the Eighth Amendment and (2) interpreting the Cruel and Unusual Punishment Clause.

Origin of the Eighth Amendment

The Eighth Amendment became a part of the Constitution in 1791.[1] The history of this amendment, however, does not begin with its insertion into the Constitution. The birth of the Eighth Amendment reaches back to the shores of England and the English Bill of Rights of 1689.

The tenth clause of the English Bill of Rights provided the following: "excessive bail ought not to be required, nor excessive fines imposed; nor cruel and unusual punishments inflicted."[2] It was pointed out by Supreme Court justice Thurgood Marshall that scholars debate "[w]hether, the English Bill of Rights prohibition against cruel and unusual punishments is properly read as a response to excessive or illegal punishments, as a reaction to barbaric and objectionable modes of punishment, or both[.]"[3] While there is no unanimous agreement as to why the English Rill of Rights included a clause prohibiting cruel and unusual punishments, there is no dissent to the assertion that the Eighth Amendment owes its existence to the English Bill of Rights.

The Eighth Amendment did not leap directly from the English Bill of Rights into the Constitution. "The precise language used in the [Eighth Amendment] first appeared in America on June 12, 1776, in Virginia's Declaration of Rights[.]"[4] A Virginia delegate named George Mason was responsible for taking the tenth clause of the English Bill of Rights and placing it into Virginia's Declaration of Rights. Mason was also a strong advocate at the Constitutional Convention for placing the tenth clause into the Constitution as the Eighth Amendment.[5] His foresight eventually paid off, and in 1791 the tenth clause, with slight modifications, became the Constitution's Eighth Amendment.

Interpreting the Cruel and Unusual Punishment Clause

In the case of *Trop v. Dulles*, 356 U.S. 86 (1958), the Supreme Court expounded upon the framework in which it viewed the Cruel and Unusual Punishment Clause. In succinct fashion the Supreme Court stated in *Trop*: "The basic concept underlying the [Clause] is nothing less than the dignity of man. While the State has the power to punish, the [Clause] stands to assure that this power be exercised within the limits of civilized standards. Fines, imprisonment and even execution may be imposed depending upon the enormity of the crime, but any technique outside the bounds of these traditional penalties is constitutionally suspect."

With the sweeping constitutional framework of *Trop* in view, this section of the chapter sets out to accomplish two things. First, to introduce specific principles that are used in interpreting the Cruel and Unusual Punishment Clause. Second, to provide a discussion of specific applications of the Cruel and Unusual Punishment Clause to death penalty issues.

THE BRENNAN PRINCIPLES

Trop v. Dulles sets out the general framework in which the Supreme Court views the Cruel and Unusual Punishment Clause, but this framework is a nullity without active principles to give it life. In his concurring opinion in *Furman v. Georgia*, 408 U.S. 238 (1972), Justice Brennan reviewed prior Supreme Court cases which had addressed the issue of cruel and unusual punishment. This examination was done for the purpose of discovering which principles of law the Supreme Court historically relied upon to decide whether a particular punishment was cruel and unusual. Justice Brennan determined that four basic principles were historically relied upon by the Supreme Court to make cruel and unusual punishment determinations.

The four principles that Justice Brennan found were as follows:
    (1) The punishment must not be so severe as to be degrading to the dignity of human beings.[6]
    (2) A government cannot arbitrarily inflict a severe punishment.[7]
    (3) A severe punishment must not be unacceptable to contemporary society.[8]
    (4) A severe punishment must not be excessive.[9]

Although it is not explicitly brought out in the material that follows, the Brennan principles were at play in the issues that are discussed.

THE DEATH PENALTY IS NOT CRUEL AND UNUSUAL PUNISHMENT PER SE

The Supreme Court did not squarely address the issue of whether capital punishment, per se, was a cruel and unusual form of punishment until it heard the case of *Gregg v. Georgia*, 428 U.S. 153 (1976).[10]

The Gregg ruling. The defendant in *Gregg* was prosecuted for committing two murders.[11] He was found guilty of both charges and was sentenced to die for both offenses. One of the primary arguments the defendant made to the Supreme Court was that the Cruel and Unusual Punishment Clause prohibited, under any and all circumstances, the imposition of death as a punishment for a criminal offense. In rendering its decision on this argument, the Supreme Court made the following observations:

> The death penalty is said to serve two principal social purposes: retribution and deterrence of capital crimes by prospective offenders.
> In part, capital punishment is an expression of society's moral outrage at particularly offensive conduct. This function may be unappealing to many, but it is essential in an ordered society that asks its citizens to rely on legal processes rather than self-help to vindicate their wrongs. ... Retribution is no longer the dominant objective of the criminal law, but neither is it a forbidden objective nor one inconsistent with our respect for

the dignity of men. Indeed, the decision that capital punishment may be the appropriate sanction in extreme cases is an expression of the community's belief that certain crimes are themselves so grievous an affront to humanity that the only adequate response may be the penalty of death.

Statistical attempts to evaluate the worth of the death penalty as a deterrent to crimes by potential offenders have occasioned a great deal of debate. The results have been inconclusive....

Although some of the studies suggest that the death penalty may not function as a significantly greater deterrent than lesser penalties, there is no convincing empirical evidence either supporting or refuting this view. We may nevertheless assume safely that there are murderers, such as those who act in passion, for whom the threat of death has little or no deterrent effect. But for many others, the death penalty undoubtedly is a significant deterrent....

The value of capital punishment as a deterrent of crime is a complex factual issue the resolution of which properly rests with the legislatures....

While the Supreme Court vacillated in *Gregg* on the issue of whether the death penalty was a deterrent, it pressed forward nonetheless and held that "the infliction of death as a punishment for murder is not without justification and thus is not unconstitutionally severe."

The Supreme Court's decision in *Gregg* must be held in its proper context. The decision did not address such issues as what method of execution is constitutional or under what circumstances imposition of the death penalty would be unconstitutional. *Gregg* merely held that, as a form of punishment, the death penalty does not violate the Cruel and Unusual Punishment Clause.

MANDATORY DEATH PENALTY
STATUTES ARE UNCONSTITUTIONAL

It is a common practice for legislatures to enact criminal offenses that carry mandatory penalties, that is, if a defendant is convicted of the offense, he or she must be sentenced according to the requirements of the statute. Mandatory sentencing statutes remove the discretion of trial judges to determine the appropriate punishment for defendants on an individualized basis.[12]

Mandatory death penalty statutes existed in all of the original 13 colonies prior to the Revolutionary War. Offenses that carried mandatory death sentences included: murder, arson, rape, robbery, burglary, sodomy, piracy, and treason. The acceptance of mandatory death penalty statutes by the colonists is attributed to the common law and its insistence upon imposing the death penalty on all felony offenses.

Acceptance of mandatory death penalty statutes by the colonists slowly faded after the Revolutionary War ended. Over time many states repealed all mandatory death penalty statutes, while others limited the number of offenses that were subject to mandatory death sentences. The Supreme Court did not squarely address this issue until it heard the case of *Woodson v. North Carolina*, 428 U.S. 280 (1976), where it noted: "The history of mandatory death penalty statutes in the United States ... reveals that the practice ... has been rejected as unduly harsh and unworkably rigid."

The Woodson ruling. The fact that some states rejected mandatory death penalty offenses, while others limited such offenses, does not address the issue of the constitutional legitimacy of mandatory death penalty statutes. This issue was put to rest with the Supreme Court's ruling in *Woodson*.

Woodson involved the prosecution of two defendants for the crime of first-degree murder. At the time of the defendants' prosecution, the state of North Carolina imposed a mandatory death penalty on anyone convicted of first-degree murder. After all the evidence in this case had been presented, a jury returned first-degree murder verdicts for both defendants.[13] As required by statute, the trial judge imposed a sentence of death on both defendants.

The issue presented to the Supreme Court by the *Woodson* defendants was whether North Carolina's mandatory death penalty statute violated the Cruel and Unusual Punishment Clause. The Supreme Court resolved the issue in the following manner:

> ...A process that accords no significance to relevant facets of the character and record of the individual offender or the circumstances of the particular offense excludes from consideration, in fixing the ultimate punishment of death, the possibility of compassionate or mitigating factors stemming from the diverse frailties of humankind. It treats all persons convicted of a designated offense not as uniquely individual human beings, but as members of a faceless, undifferentiated mass to be subjected to the blind infliction of the penalty of death.
>
> This Court has previously recognized that for the determination of sentences, justice generally requires consideration of more than the particular acts by which the crime was committed and that there be taken into account the circumstances of the offense together with the character and propensities of the offender. Consideration of both the offender and the offense in order to arrive at a just and appropriate sentence has been viewed as a progressive and humanizing development. While the prevailing practice of individualizing sentencing determinations generally reflects simply enlightened policy rather than a constitutional imperative, we believe that in capital cases the fundamental respect for humanity underlying the Eighth Amendment, requires consideration of the character and record of the individual offender and the circumstances of the particular offense as a constitutionally indispensable part of the process of inflicting the penalty of death.
>
> This conclusion rests squarely on the predicate that the penalty of death is qualitatively different from a sentence of imprisonment, however long.... Because of that qualitative difference, there is a corresponding

difference in the need for reliability in the determination that death is the appropriate punishment in a specific case.

For the reasons stated, we conclude that the death sentences imposed upon the [defendants] under North Carolina's mandatory death sentence statute violated the Eighth [Amendment] and therefore must be set aside.

It should be clearly understood that *Woodson* did not find mandatory sentencing per se unconstitutional. The decision narrowly held that mandatory death sentencing statutes are unconstitutional.[14] The Supreme Court affirmed the former point in the case of *Harmelin v. Michigan*, 501 U.S. 957 (1991), wherein it was held that a statute requiring a mandatory sentence of life imprisonment without parole for certain narcotic crimes did not violate the Cruel and Unusual Punishment Clause.

IMPOSING DEATH UNDER A FELONY-MURDER RULE CONVICTION

The felony-murder rule is a common law doctrine that makes it easier for a prosecutor to obtain a murder conviction when the victim is killed during the commission of a felony offense. "Under the felony-murder doctrine, a person who commits a felony is liable for any murder that occurs during the commission of that felony, regardless of whether he or she commits, attempts to commit, or intended to commit that murder. The doctrine thus imposes liability on capital felons for killings committed by co-felons during a felony."[15]

The common law did not make a distinction in punishment for codefendants convicted of felony-murder. That is, even though a victim's death may have actually been caused by a single defendant, under the common law all defendants involved in the underlying felony were subjected to the same punishment that was provided for the defendant who actually killed the victim.

The compact and simplistic punishment interpretation given to the felony-murder rule was fragmented and complicated as a result of decisions reached by the Supreme Court in two separate cases. Both cases involved the issue of whether the Cruel and Unusual Punishment Clause prohibited imposition of capital punishment for felony-murder convictions. In addressing this issue, the Supreme Court dissected the felony-murder rule into three distinct new doctrines: (1) felony-murder simpliciter, (2) felony-murder aggravatus, and (3) felony-murder supremus. All three doctrines are discussed in the context of the two cases that immediately follow.

The Enmund ruling. The first case to begin the dissection of the felony-murder rule was *Enmund v. Florida*, 458 U.S. 782 (1982). Under the traditional felony-murder rule, the defendant and a confederate in *Enmund* were convicted of committing two murders during the course of a robbery. The defendant was convicted of the two murders in spite of the fact that he did not actually kill the victims and was not present in the home at the time of the killings.[16]

In its analysis of the facts of *Enmund*, the Supreme Court was not disturbed by the fact that the defendant's convictions were based upon the application of the felony-murder rule. The Supreme Court viewed the defendant's role in the crime as driver of the get-away car to be sufficient to convict him for homicides committed during the course of the robbery.

The Supreme Court was disturbed, however, by the punishment the defendant received. In order to rescue the defendant from the death penalty, the Supreme Court created an exception to the punishment component of the common law felony-murder rule. The Court held in *Enmund* that the Cruel and Unusual Punishment Clause prohibits imposition of the death penalty upon a defendant "who aids and abets a felony in the course of which a murder is committed by others[,] but who does not himself kill, attempt to kill, or intend that a killing take place or that lethal force will be employed." This exception to the felony-murder rule is known as the felony-murder simpliciter doctrine.

The Tison ruling. Several years after the *Enmund* decision, the Supreme Court was asked to apply the felony-murder simpliciter doctrine to invalidate the death sentences imposed upon two brothers in *Tison v. Arizona*, 481 U.S. 137 (1987).[17] The defendants in *Tison* took part in killing four people during the course of helping their father escape from prison.

The defendants in *Tison* asked the Supreme Court to overturn their death sentences on the grounds that the sentences were an unconstitutional imposition of capital punishment for felony-murder simpliciter. The Supreme Court analyzed the conduct of the brothers under the elements of felony-murder simpliciter and concluded that their conduct fell outside of the felony-murder simpliciter doctrine.

The Supreme Court next analyzed the conduct of the defendants under the elements of felony-murder supremus, which it described as "[a] category of felony murderers for which *Enmund* explicitly finds the death penalty permissible under the Eighth Amendment." The elements of felony-murder supremus are (1) the felony-murderer actually killed, (2) attempted to kill, or (3) intended to kill. It was concluded by the Supreme Court that the conduct of the brothers in *Tison* did not fall within the elements of felony-murder supremus.

The Supreme Court then reduced the conduct of the brothers down to two factors: (1) their participation in the felonies was major and (2) their mental state was one of reckless indifference to the value of human life. Even though this conduct did not satisfy the elements of felony-murder simpliciter or felony-murder supremus, the Supreme Court determined that it was nevertheless a midrange level of felony-murder. This midrange felony-murder is the felony-murder aggravatus doctrine.

After reducing the conduct of the brothers to felony-murder aggravatus, the Supreme Court then concluded that the Cruel and Unusual Punishment Clause did not prohibit imposition of the death penalty for felony-murder aggravatus. However, since the defendants did not have a sentencing hearing based upon the elements of felony-murder aggravatus, the Supreme Court set aside their death sentences and remanded their cases for a sentencing hearing based upon felony-murder aggravatus.

CAPITAL PUNISHMENT AND CRIMES NOT INVOLVING DEATH

Current popular thinking associates the death penalty with a number of nonfatal crimes. Popular thought may or may not be an accurate barometer of what is constitutionally permissible.

It was pointed out earlier that under the common law all felonies were punishable by the infliction of death. The American colonies incorporated the common law's position in their criminal statutes. The first codified capital punishment offenses in the American colonies were drawn up in 1636 by the Massachusetts Bay Colony. The *Capital Laws of New England*, as they were called, provided the death penalty for the following crimes: rebellion, perjury, manstealing, rape, statutory rape, adultery, buggery, sodomy, murder, blasphemy, idolatry, witchcraft, and assault in sudden anger.[18]

All jurisdictions at some point in the past provided the death penalty for offenses that did not involve the death of a human being. For example, during the period 1930–1968, a total of 3,859 defendants were executed for criminal offenses; 3,334 executions were for murder, 455 executions were for the crime of rape, and 70 executions were for crimes other than murder or rape.[19] The constitutional issue of whether or not the death penalty could be inflicted for nonhomicide offenses, was not addressed by the Supreme Court until it heard the case of *Coker v. Georgia*, 433 U.S. 584 (1977).

The Coker ruling. The narrow issue presented to the Supreme Court in *Coker* was whether the Cruel and Unusual Punishment Clause prohibited imposition of the death penalty for the crime of rape of an adult woman. In addressing this issue, the Court observed that "Georgia is the sole jurisdiction in the United States at the present time that authorizes a sentence of death when the rape victim is an adult woman, and only two other jurisdictions provide capital punishment when the victim is a child." With this observation in sight, the Supreme Court concluded:

> Rape is without doubt deserving of serious punishment; but in terms of moral depravity and of the injury to the person and to the public, it does not compare with murder, which does involve the unjustified taking of human life. Although it may be accompanied by another crime, rape by definition does not include the death of or even the serious injury to

another person. The murderer kills; the rapist, if no more than that, does not. Life is over for the victim of the murderer; for the rape victim, life may not be nearly so happy as it was, but it is not over and normally is not beyond repair. We have the abiding conviction that the death penalty, which "is unique in its severity and irrevocability," is an excessive penalty for the rapist who, as such, does not take human life.

Interpretation of Coker. The *Coker* ruling established the proposition that it is unconstitutional to impose capital punishment for the offense of rape of an adult, without more. The issue of whether capital punishment may constitutionally be imposed for rape of a child was not directly addressed in *Coker*, but the opinion indicates that this too would be unconstitutional.

At this juncture in Anglo-American jurisprudence, it may be reasonably asserted that, with *Coker* as the barometer, capital punishment for any offense that does not involve the death of a victim would be found unconstitutional by the Supreme Court. This proposition is buttressed by the decision in *Cook v. State*, 251 S.E.2d 230 (Ga. 1978), where the Georgia Supreme Court interpreted *Coker* as invalidating statutes in that jurisdiction which had imposed the death penalty for armed robbery and kidnapping with bodily injury. Moreover, in *Buford v. State*, 403 So.2d 943 (Fla. 1981), the Florida Supreme Court interpreted *Coker* as invalidating a statute in that jurisdiction which had imposed the death penalty for committing rape of a minor. However, in *Upshaw v. State*, 350 So.2d 1358 (Miss. 1977), and *Leatherwood v. State*, 548 So.2d 389 (Miss. 1989), the Mississippi Supreme Court interpreted *Coker* as not invalidating a statute in that state which provided the death penalty for rape of a minor.

Notwithstanding *Upshaw* and *Leatherwood*, the consensus in capital punishment jurisdictions is in accord with the proposition that the Constitution prohibits imposition of the death penalty for crimes that do not involve death. (One qualification to the latter statement involves the federal crimes of treason and espionage. Both offenses are punishable with death, even though death may not result from the commission of either. The Supreme Court has not been called upon to determine whether treason and espionage are exceptions to the ruling in *Coker*.)

CHAPTER 3

Death-Eligible Offenses

As a result of the Supreme Court's interpretation of the Cruel and Unusual Punishment Clause, capital punishment today does not resemble its common law counterpart. A principal alteration of capital punishment has been the drastic reduction in the number of crimes that are punishable as capital offenses. Crimes that are punishable with death are called death-eligible offenses. The distinguishing feature of death-eligible offenses is that they are created by establishing what are called *special circumstances*. The intent of this chapter is twofold. First, to explain the significance of special circumstances. Second, to provide a detailed look at the death-eligible offenses that are used in capital punishment jurisdictions.

BOX 3.0
CAPITAL PUNISHMENT JURISDICTIONS 1997

Alabama	Illinois	Nevada	South Carolina
Arizona	Indiana	New Hampshire	South Dakota
Arkansas	Kansas	New Jersey	Tennessee
California	Kentucky	New Mexico	Texas
Colorado	Louisiana	New York	Utah
Connecticut	Maryland	North Carolina	Virginia
Delaware	Mississippi	Ohio	Washington
Florida	Missouri	Oklahoma	Wyoming
Georgia	Montana	Oregon	Federal System
Idaho	Nebraska	Pennsylvania	

21

The Nature of Special Circumstances

The Supreme Court has indicated that the Cruel and Unusual Punishment Clause requires "narrowing the categories of murders for which a death sentence may ... be imposed[.]"[1] In the case of *Jurek v. Texas*, 428 U.S. 262 (1976), the Supreme Court held that the constitutional narrowing requirement for the death penalty may occur at the guilt phase or penalty (sentencing) phase of a capital prosecution. Subsequent chapters will show that the vast majority of capital punishment jurisdictions impose the constitutional narrowing requirement at both the guilt phase and sentencing phase. As a result of this dual narrowing, special circumstances have taken on the role of merely creating death-eligible offenses. Special circumstances do not perform the task of actually imposing the death penalty. The decision of whether to impose death is controlled by statutory *aggravating circumstances* at the penalty phase. (In Chapter 10, special circumstances are distinguished from penalty phase statutory aggravating circumstances.)

An underlying premise of special circumstances is that not every murder justifies capital punishment consideration.[2] That is, in keeping with constitutional requirements, special circumstances seek to limit the class of murders that will be exposed to death penalty prosecution. In an effort to pull out a subclass of death-eligible murders from among all murders, legislators have singled out specific factors or conduct that may appear in some murders. These specific factors or conduct are called special circumstances and form the basis of all death-eligible offenses.[3] As a result of forming the basis of death-eligible offenses, a special circumstance actually constitutes an element of the capital offense. Because it is an element of an offense, the Constitution requires a special circumstance be proven at the guilt phase beyond a reasonable doubt.

A final point in this area. The crime of murder is the only offense that is punished with death. By applying special circumstances to murder, however, this single offense is transformed into numerous death-eligible offenses.

Death-Eligible Offenses

As previously pointed out, only one offense acts as the catalyst for the creation of all constitutionally valid capital crimes: murder. Capital punishment jurisdictions have taken the offense of murder and surrounded it with a variety of special circumstances that culminate in what are referred to as death-eligible offenses. A brief review of some of the current statutory death-eligible offenses follows.

TABLE 3.0
MURDER TIME CLOCK 1984–1995

Year	Frequency of Murder	Year	Frequency of Murder
1984	every 28 minutes	1990	every 22 minutes
1985	every 28 minutes	1991	every 21 minutes
1986	every 25 minutes	1992	every 22 minutes
1987	every 26 minutes	1993	every 21 minutes
1988	every 25 minutes	1994	every 23 minutes
1989	every 24 minutes	1995	every 24 minutes

SOURCE: U.S. Department of Justice, Federal Bureau of Investigation, Uniform Crime Reports *(1985–1996).*

MURDER-WITHOUT-MORE

The phrase *murder-without-more* refers to the killing of a single human being. A majority of capital punishment jurisdictions authorize death penalty consideration for the crime of murder-without-more.[4] A variety of names are used to describe this offense: first-degree murder,[5] murder,[6] deliberate homicide,[7] and aggravated murder.[8]

The special circumstance that is used to make murder-without-more a death-eligible offense is the mental state of a defendant at the time of the commission of the murder. Capital punishment jurisdictions differ on how they describe the mental state. The following words are found in various statutes: intentional, willful, deliberate, premeditated, malice, or prior calculation and design. Comments about each mental state will follow.

Intentional murder-without-more. To establish intent to kill, the prosecutor must do more than show an intentional act by the defendant, the prosecutor must establish that the defendant intended for his or her act to result in death.[9] In determining whether a defendant possessed the requisite intent to commit murder, relevant factors that are considered include any disparity in size and strength between the defendant and victim and the nature and extent of the victim's injuries.[10]

In proving intent to kill, it is not necessary to establish that a specific intent existed for any particular period of time before the homicide occurred.[11] The length of time during which intent to kill is needed varies with the individual defendant and circumstances, but need only be long enough to permit a defendant to contemplate maturely and meaningfully the gravity of his or her intended act.[12] Courts have held that, depending upon a given set of circumstances, intent to murder may occur as instantaneously as successive thoughts.[13]

A capital murder prosecution will be sustained provided the intent to kill is formed before the act is committed and not simultaneously with such act.[14]

Examples of how intentional murder-without-more may be established from the circumstances of the offense include the following. In *State v. McConnaughey*, 311 S.E.2d 26 (N.C.App. 1984), it was held that when a defendant intentionally fires a gun in the direction of a person, thereby causing the death of that person, the killing is intentional. In *Commonwealth v. Lacava*, 666 A.2d 221 (Pa. 1995), it was held that intent to kill may be inferred by the defendant's use of a deadly weapon on a vital part of the victim's body. The court in *State v. Golson*, 658 So.2d 225 (La.App. 2 Cir. 1995) indicated that intent to kill may be inferred from the fact that the defendant pointed the gun at the victim and fired three shots. In *People v. Deason*, 584 N.E.2d 829 (Ill.App. 4 Dist. 1991), however, it was said that the mere fact of beating a victim with a baseball bat does not support the conclusion that the defendant acted with intent to kill, as would the act of firing a gun at a person.

Willful murder-without-more. *Willful*, in the context of willful killing of a human being, simply means intentional.[15] To commit willful murder, the defendant must possess the intent to kill.[16]

Deliberate murder-without-more. In the context of capital murder, *deliberate* refers to something more than intentional but less than premeditated and represents a conscious decision that is greater than the mere will to cause the death of the victim.[17] For murder to be deliberate, there must be a full and conscious knowledge of the purpose to kill.[18] If a homicide results from a choice made as a consequence of thought, the offense is deemed deliberate murder.[19] Deliberation requires that the defendant consider the probable consequences of his act before doing it.[20] Factors that courts consider in determining whether a killing was done with deliberation include lack of provocation by the victim; conduct and statements of defendant before, during, and after the killing; ill will or previous difficulties between the parties; whether the victim continued to be assaulted after falling and being rendered helpless; and evidence that the killing was done in a brutal manner.[21]

More than a split-second of reflection is required to establish a homicide premised on deliberation.[22] Deliberation requires substantially more reflection than the mere amount of thought necessary to form the element of intent to kill.[23] Deliberation requires reflection and judgment but does not require a long period of time.[24] The deliberation required to support murder-without-more is found when the act done is performed with a cool and deliberate state of mind.[25]

Deliberate intent will not be sustained when the killing is the result of mere unconsidered and rash impulse, even though it includes intent to kill.[26] Deliberation is not negated, however, merely because the defendant was angry or emotional at the time of the killing, unless evidence establishes that the anger or emotion was strong enough to displace the defendant's ability to reason.[27]

Premeditated murder-without-more. For murder to be premeditated, the design to kill must have preceded the killing by an appreciable length of time.[28] In *Jackson v. Virginia*, 413 U.S. 307 (1979), the Supreme Court indicated that premeditation need not exist for any particular length of time and that the decision to kill may be formed at the moment of the commission of the homicide. The court in *DeAngelo v. State*, 616 So. 2d 440 (Fla. 1993), held that premeditation can be formed at any moment and need only exist long enough for a defendant to be conscious of the danger of his or her act and the probable result therefrom. It has been said that premeditation involves reflection, which is not so much a matter of time but logical sequence. In *State v. Martin*, 702 S.W.2d 560 (Tenn. 1985), it was held that the decision to kill the victim made during a struggle with the victim would support a finding of premeditation because only a moment of time was required between the plan to kill and execution of that plan.[29] In *State v. West*, 388 N.W.2d 823 (Nebr. 1986), however, it was held that no particular length of time was required for premeditation, provided that the decision to kill is formed before the act is committed and not simultaneously with it.[30] In *People v. Van Ronk*, 217 Cal.Rptr. 581 (1985), however, it was said that premeditation requires substantially more reflection than the mere amount of thought necessary to form the intent to kill.

To determine whether a defendant killed with premeditation, courts are obliged to determine whether the defendant had at the time of killing a settled and fixed purpose to take the victim's life.[31] Factors that may be considered in determining whether a defendant engaged in premeditation include the brutality of the attack, the number of blows inflicted, disparity in size and strength of the defendant and victim, concealment of the corpse, lack of remorse, motive and efforts to avoid detection.[32] Courts will also seek to determine any use of a deadly weapon, the conduct of the defendant before and after the killing, and the presence or absence of provocation.[33]

In the case of *People v. Pride*, 833 P.2d 643 (Cal. 1992), it was held that premeditation may be inferred from a violent and bloody homicide as a result of stab wounds. The court in *Hays v. State*, 599 So.2d 1230 (Ala.Cr.App. 1992), stated that the mere fact that a homicide was unskillfully and haphazardly conceived will not exclude a finding that it was premeditated. In *People v. Edwards*, 819 P.2d 436 (Cal. 1991), the court indicated that a homicide that is senseless and random but premeditated is capital murder. It was held in *Hays v. State*, 85 F.2d 1492 (11th Cir. 1996), that the mere fact that a defendant did not initially set out to kill the victim is irrelevant when the victim is beaten with a tree limb, dragged by a noose, and has his throat slit. Under such facts, premeditation can be found.

Malice murder-without-more. The term *malice* is not the same as, or interchangeable with, the phrase *malice aforethought*.[34] Malice aforethought may be defined as intentionally doing a wrongful act, without just cause or excuse, after thinking about it beforehand for any length of time.[35] Malice refers to hatred, ill will, or spite and may be appropriately used to describe the condition of mind which prompts a person to take the life of another intentionally without just cause, excuse, or justification.[36] Malice aforethought is not an essential element of the crime of murder.[37] Malice is an essential element of murder-without-more, and its presence, either directly or inferentially, must be established to sustain a conviction.[38]

Malice, as an element of murder-without-more, may be express or implied.[39] Proving express malice means establishing deliberate intent to kill, whereas proving implied malice requires establishing the commission of a wrongful act from which an abandoned and malignant heart may be inferred.[40] Malice may also be inferred from evidence showing wanton disregard for life and the subjective awareness of the risk created by the defendant's conduct.[41] It has also been held that malice may be implied when no considerable provocation appears.[42]

Implied malice may be regarded as constructive malice in that it has not been proven directly to have existed, but the law regards the circumstances of the defendant's act to be so harmful that the act is treated as malice. The circumstances must show the defendant's act was done willfully or purposefully.[43]

Implied malice has a physical and mental component. The physical component is met by performance of an act, the natural consequences of which are dangerous to human life. The mental component is met when an act is deliberately performed by a defendant who knows that the act endangers human life, but proceeds with conscious disregard.[44]

The term malice can be appropriately used to refer to the situation of having knowledge that there is a plain and strong likelihood, based upon the surrounding circumstances, that death will follow contemplated conduct. As a general rule, malice exists as a matter of law whenever there is an unlawful and intentional homicide without justification.[45] The mere fact that a defendant acted on an irrational motive does not preclude a finding of malice.[46]

Malice may be formed just prior to the commission of a homicide.[47] There is no particular length of time required for malice to be generated in the mind of the defendant, and it may be formed in a moment or the instant a mortal blow is given or fatal shot fired.[48] Factors which establish proof of malice in a homicide will vary depending upon the actual circumstances of each case.[49] Malice may be established by proof in one of three ways: (1) the defendant intended to kill the victim without justification or legal excuse, (2) the defendant intended to cause grievous bodily harm, or (3) the defendant acted in circumstances that a reasonably prudent person would know pose a plain and strong likelihood that death would follow the contemplated act.[50]

In *Crossley v. State*, 420 So.2d 1376 (Miss. 1982), it was held that a pistol, even if not loaded or capable of being fired, is a deadly weapon and, as such, its use supplied the element of malice in a murder-without-more prosecution. The court in *State v. Gandy*, 324 S.E.2d 65 (S.C. 1984), held that malice was inferred from the defendant's intent to kill a specific person by firing a gun through a door. In *Commonwealth v. Williams*, 650 A.2d 420 (Pa. 1994), it was held that malice may be established by showing the defendant used a dangerous weapon on a vital part of the victim's body. Malice may be shown by proof that, under circumstances known to the defendant, a reasonably prudent person would have known that there was a plain and strong likelihood that death would follow the contemplated conduct.

Prior calculation and design murder-without-more. It was said in *State v. Cotton*, 381 N.E.2d 190 (Ohio 1978), that in Ohio *prior calculation and design* replaced deliberation and premeditation in capital murder. The court in *Cotton* stated that prior calculation and design was a more stringent element, which meant that instantaneous deliberation was not sufficient to constitute this new element.

Prior calculation and design means that the purpose to kill was reached by a definite process of reasoning in advance of the killing, including a mental plan involving studied consideration of the method or instrument with which to kill.[51] Factors that are considered in determining whether homicide was the result of prior calculation and design include (1) whether the defendant knew the victim prior to the homicide and, if so, whether the relationship had been strained, (2) whether thought and preparation were given by the defendant to the weapon used and the site where the homicide occurred, and (3) whether the homicide was drawn out over a period of time or was an instantaneous eruption of events.

The mere fact that a defendant did not know the homicide victim is not conclusive on the issue of whether there was prior calculation and design if the evidence establishes the defendant planned to kill someone at random.[52] For murder committed with prior calculation and design, reflection need not be long, nor the plan elaborate, but both must have existed.[53]

HOMICIDE IN THE COMMISSION OF ANOTHER OFFENSE

A majority of capital punishment jurisdictions make it a death-eligible offense for anyone to cause the death of another during the course of committing a crime.[54] This offense, of course, is nothing more than felony-murder. A few capital punishment jurisdictions do not refer to the offense as such, though they adhere to the principles attendant to felony-murder. The following three statutes illustrate how this death-eligible offense is provided for.

Delaware Code Annotated 11 § 636(a)(6):
The person, with criminal negligence, causes the death of another person in the course of and in furtherance of the commission or attempted commission of rape, unlawful sexual intercourse in the first or second degree, kidnapping, arson in the first degree, robbery in the first degree, burglary in the first degree, or immediate flight therefrom.

Georgia Code Annotated § 16-5-1(c):
A person also commits the offense of murder when, in the commission of a felony, he causes the death of another human being irrespective of malice.

Indiana Statutes Annotated § 35-42-1-1(2):
Kills another human being while committing or attempting to commit arson, burglary, child molesting, consumer product tampering, criminal deviate conduct, kidnapping, rape, robbery, or carjacking.

Capital felony-murder statutes are not unconstitutional on the basis that they relieve the prosecutor of the burden of proving the mental element of murder because the mental element is established by the prosecutor's proof of intent in the underlying felony.[55] In *State v. McLoughlin*, 679 P.2d 504 (Ariz. 1984), the court said that it is constitutionally permissible to expose a defendant who causes death while seeking to accomplish one of several enumerated felonies, each of which requires a showing of intent or knowledge for a conviction, to the same criminal charge and punishment as a person who causes death with premeditation.

The justification for making homicide during the commission of a crime a death-eligible offense is to try to deter the taking of life when homicide is not the motive of a crime.

VICTIM-SPECIFIC MURDER

At present, 18 capital punishment jurisdictions provide that victim-specific murder is a death-eligible offense.[56] Victim-specific murder refers to the intentional killing of an individual in a category that has been officially recognized by a statute. The following statutory illustrations will help in understanding this type of capital crime.

Idaho Code § 18-4003(b):
Any murder of any peace officer, executive officer, officer of the court, fireman, judicial officer or prosecuting attorney who was acting in the lawful discharge of an official duty, and was known or should have been known by the perpetrator of the murder to be an officer so acting[.]

Arkansas Code Annotated § 5-10-101(a)(3):

With the premeditated and deliberated purpose of causing the death of any law enforcement officer, jailer, prison official, fire fighter, judge, or other court official, probation officer, parole officer, any military personnel, or teacher or school employee, when such person is acting in the line of duty[.]

Washington Revised Code § 10.95.020(12):

The victim was regularly employed or self-employed as a newsreporter and the murder was committed to obstruct or hinder the investigative, research, or reporting activities of the victim.

Victim-specific murder statutes seek to provide additional protection for the lives of individuals whose occupations expose them to potential revenge by criminals. Federal statutes provide such additional protection for the president and vice president,[57] members of Congress, and other federal officials.[58]

It will also be noted that victim-specific murder statutes are not confined exclusively to particular occupations. The statute that follows illustrates this point.

New York Penal Law § 125.27(1)(a)(V):

The intended victim was a witness to a crime committed on a prior occasion and the death was caused for the purpose of preventing the intended victim's testimony…, or the intended victim was an immediate family member of a witness to a crime committed on a prior occasion and the killing was committed for the purpose of preventing or influencing the testimony of such witness[.]

TABLE 3.1

MURDER CIRCUMSTANCES BY RELATIONSHIP 1994

Victim relation to murderer	Total victims	Victim relation to murderer	Total victims
Husband	346	Daughter	212
Wife	823	Brother	172
Mother	119	Sister	39
Father	189	Boyfriend	228
Son	326	Girlfriend	525

SOURCE: U.S. Department of Justice, Federal Bureau of Investigation, Uniform Crime Reports *19, Table 2.12 (1995).*

MURDER-FOR-HIRE

Eighteen capital punishment jurisdictions allow imposition of the death penalty for a homicide committed pursuant to a contract, that is, exchange of something of pecuniary value for killing another.[59] Murder-for-hire is generally thought of as conduct engaged in by organized crime. This is especially true after the 1992 trial and conviction of John Gotti, reputed former head of the largest Mafia organization in the United States, the Gambino crime family.[60] During the trial of John Gotti, one of his underbosses, Salvatore "Sammy the Bull" Gravano, testified that he had killed 19 people pursuant to contracts issued by John Gotti.[61]

Murder-for-hire is not, however, confined to organized crime. Husbands hire people to kill their wives, as in the case of *Parker v. State*, 610 So.2d 1181 (Ala. 1992), and wives hire people to kill their husbands, as in the cases of *Nunley v. State*, 660 P.2d 1052 (Okla. 1983), and *Coker v. State*, 911 S.W.2d 357 (Tenn. 1995). There are other nonspousal murder-for-hire crimes that are not related to organized crime, as in the cases of *Grandison v. State*, 670 A.2d 398 (Md. 1995), *State v. DiFrisco*, 662 A.2d 442 (N.J. 1995), and *State v. Kolbe*, 838 P.2d 612 (Ore. 1992). Two illustrations of death-eligible murder-for-hire statutes follow.

Kansas Statutes Annotated § 21-3439(a)(2):
[I]ntentional and premeditated killing of any person pursuant to a contract or agreement to kill such person or being a party to the contract or agreement pursuant to which such person is killed.

Oregon Revised Statutes § 163.095(1):
(a) The defendant committed the murder pursuant to an agreement that the defendant receive money or other thing of value for committing the murder.

(b) The defendant solicited another to commit the murder and paid or agreed to pay the person money or other thing of value for committing the murder.

LEN BIAS MURDER

On June 18, 1986, University of Maryland basketball standout Len Bias signed a lucrative contract to play professional basketball with the Boston Celtics. On June 19, 1986, Len Bias was found dead after allegedly ingesting cocaine. The nation was stunned over the way in which the basketball world had lost a promising superstar.[62]

Before national outrage reached its peak over the death of Len Bias, another senseless tragedy struck the sports world. On June 27, 1986, Cleveland Browns defensive back Don Rogers was found dead after allegedly ingesting cocaine.

After the death of Bias and Rogers, a national call rang out demanding special punishment for drug pushers if death resulted from the use of their drugs. All jurisdictions responded to this call in one way or another by toughening their drug laws. Three states, Colorado, Connecticut, and Florida, took the ultimate step by enacting specific death-eligible offenses for deaths that occur from the use of illegal drugs. Those statutes provide as follows:

Colorado Revised Statutes § 18-3-102(1)(e):
He commits unlawful distribution, dispensation, or sale of a controlled substance to a person under the age of eighteen years on school grounds ... and the death of such person is caused by the use of such controlled substance.

Connecticut General Statutes § 53a-54b:
A person is guilty of a capital felony who is convicted of ... the illegal sale, for economic gain, of cocaine, heroin or methadone to a person who dies as a direct result of the use by him of such cocaine, heroin or methadone.

Florida Statutes Annotated § 782.04(1)(a)(3):
The unlawful killing of a human being ... [w]hich resulted from the unlawful distribution of any ... cocaine ... or opium or any synthetic or natural salt, compound, derivative, or preparation of opium by a person 18 years of age or older, when such drug is proven to be the proximate cause of the death of the user[.]

DRIVE-BY-SHOOTING MURDER

At the height of the Prohibition Era, traffickers in illegal alcohol were famous for taking the life of competitors by firing machine guns and pistols from vehicles. This brazen public method of handling disputes lost its luster and subsided as a national problem in part because of the ironlike determination of law-enforcement folk hero Elliot Ness.[63]

Drive-by-shooting resurfaced as a national problem during the 1990s. The perpetrators of this deadly resurrection have not been bootleggers, however. Drug dealers have taken up this brazen method of handling disputes between themselves. An unfortunate side effect of the current drive-by-shooting problem is that innocent bystanders (too often children) have been gunned down in Los Angeles, Chicago, Atlanta, New York, and every major city in the nation.[64]

Seven capital punishment jurisdictions have responded to drive-by-shooting murder by making it a death-eligible offense.[65] Examples of drive-by-shooting murder statutes are as follows.

Alabama Code § 13A-5-40(a)(18):
Murder committed by or through the use of a deadly weapon fired or otherwise used within or from a vehicle.

Arkansas Code Annotated § 5-10-101(a)(10):
He purposely discharges a firearm from a vehicle at a person, or at a vehicle, conveyance, or a residential or commercial occupiable structure he knows or has good reason to believe to be occupied by a person, and thereby causes the death of another person[.]

SPECIFIC-DEVICE MURDER

A federal judge in Alabama opened a package received in the mail and the package exploded, killing him. A civil rights lawyer in Georgia opened a package he received at his office, and it exploded, killing him. These are two real and tragic illustrations of specific-device murders.

A strong and sturdy federal building sits placidly in the heart of America, holding children and the laughter of youth. Adults are in the building working toward their American dream. A van sits outside the building. The van explodes, and the strong, sturdy federal building falls. Death is everywhere. Oklahoma and the nation are brought to tears. This devastating crime involved specific-device murders.

In a hypothetical case, a police officer is in a shootout with a desperate drug dealer. The police officer is wearing a bulletproof vest. The drug dealer takes aim at the officer's heart and fires a shot, and the police officer falls to the ground, dead. The drug dealer was using special bullets designed to penetrate metal. This hypothetical represents a potential reality for every police officer in the nation, and would also be a specific-device murder.

Sixteen capital punishment jurisdictions have addressed specific-device murder by making this crime a death-eligible offense.[66] The following statute illustrates this offense.

Utah Code Annotated § 76-5-202(1)(l):
[T]he homicide was committed by means of a destructive device, bomb, explosive, incendiary device, or similar device ... planted, hid, or concealed in any place, area, dwelling, building, or structure, or mailed or delivered[.]

TABLE 3.2
MURDER WEAPON USED 1990–1994

WEAPON	Number of Victims				
	1990	1991	1992	1993	1994
Firearm	13,035	14,373	15,489	16,136	15,456
Knife	3,526	3,430	3,296	2,967	2,801

WEAPON	1990	1991	1992	1993	1994
Blunt object	1,085	1,099	1,040	1,022	912
Poison	11	12	13	9	10
Explosive	13	16	19	23	10
Fire	288	195	203	217	196
Narcotic	29	22	24	22	22
Drowning	36	40	29	23	25
Strangle	312	327	314	331	287
Asphyxiate	96	113	115	111	113

SOURCE:U.S. Department of Justice, Federal Bureau of Investigation, Uniform Crime Reports *18, Table 2.10 (1995).*

HOSTAGE/HUMAN-SHIELD MURDER

The offense of hostage taking must be distinguished from kidnapping. The traditional definition of kidnapping refers to the abduction or asportation of a person against his or her will for the purpose of holding the victim until a ransom has been paid.[67] Hostage taking, on the other hand, refers to the seizure or detention of a person against his or her will for the purpose of obtaining some political goal in exchange for the release of the hostage.[68] The two offenses are overlapping, but they are legally distinct forms of conduct.

The human-shield offense describes conduct that may occur in a kidnapping or hostage-taking situation. In the case of *People v. Casseus,* 606 N.Y.S.2d 21 (1993), the human-shield offense was described thus:

> On February 1, 1989, at approximately 12:30 p.m., a shooting erupted at the Cypress Hills Housing Projects in Brooklyn. While a mother and her two small children were seeking cover between two cars in a parking lot, the defendant grabbed one of the children and held the child up in front of him, using the child as a human shield to block the line of gunfire. The child was shot and seriously wounded.

One jurisdiction, Utah, has specifically provided that hostage-murder and human-shield murder are death-eligible offenses. The Federal System has made hostage-murder a death-eligible offense. The federal statute provides as follows.

Federal System 18 U.S.C.A. § 1203(a):
[W]hoever ... seizes or detains and threatens to kill, to injure, or to continue to detain another person in order to compel a third person or a governmental organization to do or abstain from doing any act as an explicit or implicit condition for the release of the person ... shall ... if the death of any person results ... be punished by death or life imprisonment.

In the case of *United States v. Yunis*, 681 F.Supp. 896 (D.D.C. 1988), it was stated that the federal hostage murder statute "imposes liability on any individual who takes an American national hostage irrespective of where the seizure occurs." *Yunis* further indicated that the purpose of the statute is to "demonstrate to other governments and international forums that the United States is serious about its efforts to deal with international terrorism," quoting the President's Message to Congress on the International Convention Against the Taking of Hostages, 20 Weekly Comp. Pres. Doc. 590, 592 (April 26, 1984).

MULTIPLE-VICTIM MURDER

In *State v. Copeland*, 300 S.E.2d 63 (S.C. 1983), three service station attendants were abducted and taken to a secluded area and shot to death. In the case of *State v. Pizzuto*, 810 P.2d 680 (Idaho 1989), two victims were beaten in the head until they were dead. In the case of *State v. Lavers*, 814 P.2d 333 (Ariz. 1991), a mother was shot to death and her daughter was stabbed to death.

The homicides committed in *Copeland*, *Pizzuto* and *Lavers* involved the killing of more than one victim. Eleven capital punishment jurisdictions provide that multiple-victim murder is a death-eligible offense.[69] (None of the jurisdictions in question have murder-without-more death penalty statutes.) The following are illustrations of multiple-victim murder statutes.

Virginia Code § 18.2-31(g):
The willful, deliberate and premeditated killing of more than one person as part of the same act or transaction.

Texas Penal Code § 19.03(a)(7):
[T]he person murders more than one person:
(A) during the same criminal transaction; or
(B) during different criminal transactions but the murders are committed pursuant to the same scheme or course of conduct.

New York Penal Code § 125.27(1)(a)(xi):
[T]he defendant intentionally caused the death of two or more additional persons within the state in separate criminal transactions within a period of twenty-four months when committed in a similar fashion or pursuant to a common scheme or plan.

DRUG-TRAFFICKING MURDER

During the period 1990 through 1994, an average of 1,300 murders per year occurred in the context of the illegal drug trade.[70] The staggering impact of drug-trafficking murder[71] may help illustrate why nine capital punishment jurisdictions have made this a death-eligible offense.[72]

The case of *United States v. Darden*, 70 F.3d 1507 (8th Cir. 1995), provides a gritty example of the violent context in which drug-trafficking occurs in the nation. There were seven defendants in that case, and they were charged with violating various federal drug laws and with committing several murders. The excerpt from the case centers on the murderous path of one of the defendants, Gerald Hopkins:

> The United States presented evidence at the appellants' trial tending to show that Jerry Lee Lewis participated in and became the leader of a powerful criminal racketeering enterprise that for over ten years controlled a large percentage of the market for ... heroin and cocaine in north St. Louis. Lewis obtained and maintained his position by murdering competitors and others who threatened his organization (the Jerry Lewis Organization or JLO). The profitable but bloody activities of the appellants in this case, all members of the JLO, were described by other JLO members who eventually cooperated with the government.... In essence, the investigation and prosecution of Jerry Lee Lewis and his associates produced evidence of a long-term, violent drug-trafficking enterprise....
>
> Jerry Lewis called Gerald Hopkins "my little hitman," and the evidence supports Lewis' conclusion. Earl Parnell testified that both he and [Gerald] Hopkins were involved in the 1985 murder of a deputy sheriff. The deputy, Antar Tiari, was attempting to evict Jerry Lewis ... from ... rented space in St. Louis ... from which JLO conducted operations. [Gerald] Hopkins and Jerry Lewis, dressed in army fatigues, met with Parnell ... to plan the murder.... Parnell testified that [Gerald] Hopkins said, "I shot that [expletive omitted]. Every time I hit him, he just jumped around and danced like this."
>
> Ruby Weaver testified that [Gerald] Hopkins participated in the planning of the 1987 killing of Harold "Court" Johnson, a rival drug dealer, and Ronnie Thomas testified that [Gerald] Hopkins helped to plan the 1988 killing of Ronald Anderson....
>
> Ronnie Thomas also testified that [Gerald] Hopkins participated in the JLO's March 28, 1988 surveillance of Billy Patton, a rival drug dealer who was eventually killed. Andrea Patton, Billy Patton's niece, was rendered a quadriplegic when the car she was driving was riddled with bullets. She had left her uncle's apartment in the car, and ... Thomas ... testified that JLO members shot at the car in the mistaken belief that Billy Patton was inside. [It was] testified that [Gerald] Hopkins fired the shots....

The drug-related killings by the JLO and Gerald Hopkins indicate why a minority of capital punishment jurisdictions have made drug-trafficking murder an independent death-eligible offense. The following statutes illustrate this offense.

Louisiana Revised Statutes 14 § 30(A)(6):
When the offender has the specific intent to kill or to inflict great bodily harm while engaged in the distribution, exchange, sale, or purchase ... of a controlled dangerous substance[.]

New Jersey Statutes Annotated § 2C: 11-3(c):
Any person ... who, as a leader of a narcotics trafficking network ... commanded or by threat or promise solicited the commission of the offense[.]

MURDER-ON-THE-RUN

During the 1980s, penal institution reformers were successful in their efforts to bring greater civility into correctional institutions. One such achievement in this area was that of allowing model inmates to work outside the grounds of institutions and to have weekend passes to leave confinement. Experience has shown, unfortunately, that many model inmates have taken advantage of release privileges by escaping from custody. Too often such escapes have ended with innocent people being killed by inmates on the run.[73]

Thus far 15 capital punishment jurisdictions have responded to homicides committed by escaped inmates by making murder-on-the-run a death-eligible offense.[74] Examples of this statutory offense follow.

Idaho Code § 18-4003(f):
Any murder committed by a person while escaping or attempting to escape from a penal institution is murder of the first degree.

Oregon Revised Statutes §163.095(2)(f):
The murder was committed after the defendant had escaped from a state, county or municipal penal or correctional facility and before the defendant had been returned to the custody of the facility.

GRAVE-RISK MURDER

It was held in *State v. Fierro*, 804 P.2d 72 (Ariz. 1990), that for a grave-risk murder to occur the person endangered by the conduct of the defendant must not have been the intended victim of the crime. The capital offense of grave-risk murder is triggered when unintended victims are endangered by a capital felon's conduct. Five capital punishment jurisdictions have made grave-risk murder a death-eligible offense.[75] The following are two statutory illustrations of this offense.

New Mexico Statutes Annotated § 30-2-1(a)(3):
Murder ... by any act greatly dangerous to the lives of others, indicating a depraved mind regardless of human life.

Utah Code Annotated § 76-5-202(1)(c):
[T]he actor knowingly created a great risk of death to a person other than the victim and the actor.

PERJURY/SUBORNATION OF PERJURY MURDER

The court in *State v. Crowder*, 123 S.E.2d 42 (W.Va. 1961), held that the offense of perjury may be defined as giving false testimony, while under oath, in a matter that involves a felony offense.[76] Subornation of perjury, on the other hand, involves inducing another person to testify falsely, while under oath, in a matter that involves a felony or misdemeanor offense.[77] Currently two capital punishment jurisdictions make perjury murder and subornation of perjury murder death-eligible offenses.[78] The statute that follows illustrates perjury and subornation of perjury murder.

Colorado Revised Statutes § 18-3-102(1)(c):
A person commits the crime of murder in the first degree if ... [b]y perjury or subornation of perjury he procures the conviction and execution of any innocent person.

FORCED-SUICIDE MURDER

The death-eligible offense of forced-suicide murder is distinguishable from the crime of assisted suicide, though both produce the same result. Assisted suicide involves intentionally or knowingly making an instrument available for someone who wants to voluntarily commit suicide. Forced-suicide murder, on the other hand, involves intentionally compelling someone to commit suicide when the victim does not want to die. One capital punishment jurisdiction, Delaware, has made forced-suicide murder a death-eligible offense. The statutory offense is provided for as follows.

Delaware Code Annotated 11 § 636(a)(3):
A person is guilty of murder in the first degree when ... [t]he person intentionally causes another person to commit suicide by force or duress.

GANG-STATUS MURDER

Organized crime flourishes in large part because of the existence of a hierarchy in each particular crime gang. The structural essence of any organizational hierarchy is tripartite—top, middle, and bottom. Those at the top wish to stay there. Those in the middle and bottom wish to move up. How does one at the bottom or middle move up in a criminal enterprise? Or how does one become a member of a criminal enterprise? There are, no doubt, numerous ways to advance in a criminal enterprise or become a member of a criminal enterprise. The concern here is with one method of advancement or entrance—murder.

Gang-status murder involves killing someone as a rite of passage into a criminal organization or killing someone in order to advance in the hierarchy of a criminal organization. At present, the state of Washington is the only capital punishment jurisdiction that makes gang-status murder an independent death-eligible offense. The following statute sets out this offense.

> **Washington Revised Code § 10.95.020(6):**
> The person committed the murder to obtain or maintain his or her membership or to advance his or her position in the hierarchy of an organization, association, or identifiable group.

Perpetrator-Status Murder

Not infrequently homicide is committed by someone who is on parole or probation, or has had a previous homicide conviction, or is incarcerated at the time of the commission of the homicide. In any of the latter situations, the perpetrator has a legally recognizable status, that is, parolee, probationer, ex-offender, or inmate.

The crime of perpetrator-status murder has as its focal point the particular status of the perpetrator at the time of the commission of a murder. The significance of status in this context is that it implies that the person is a threat to society.

Suppose, for example, that John Dillinger is a respected banker in Small Town, U.S.A. Mr. Dillinger for one reason or another shoots and kills a teller in his bank. At the time of the homicide, Mr. Dillinger's status was that of banker. This status does not convey or imply a threat to society. For all practical purposes, Mr. Dillinger's status is irrelevant in determining the offense to charge him with. The law is not concerned with how it should punish bankers, as opposed to anyone else who commits a homicide.

Fifteen capital punishment jurisdictions have, however, singled out particular statuses and created death-eligible perpetrator-status murder offenses.[79] The following statutes illustrate perpetrator-status murder offenses.

> **Kansas Statutes Annotated § 21-3439(a)(3):**
> [I]ntentional and premeditated killing of any person by an inmate or prisoner confined in a state correctional institution, community correctional institution or jail or while in the custody of an officer or employee of a state correctional institution, community correctional institution or jail.

> **Mississippi Code § 97-3-19(2)(b):**
> Murder which is perpetrated by a person who is under sentence of life imprisonment.

Oregon Revised Statutes § 163.095(1)(c):
The defendant committed murder after having been convicted previously in any jurisdiction of any homicide[.]

TORTURE-MURDER

The murder committed in *Penick v. State*, 659 N.E.2d 484 (Ind. 1995), provides some understanding of the death-eligible crime of torture-murder. The defendant in *Penick* and three other accomplices were satanic ritualists. On September 25, 1991, the defendant and his accomplices tricked a young man into going to a secluded area with them. The defendant wanted to kill the young man because the latter had knowledge that the defendant had previously killed someone.

Upon tying the young man up and putting him on the ground, the defendant and his accomplices did the following: "[T]he victim's chest and abdomen were cut open, [an accomplice] tried to cut out the victim's heart before he died.... [T]he victim remained conscious throughout this and responded to questions from the defendant. Only after [the] defendant slit the victim's neck did the torture end.... Finally [they engaged in the] dismemberment of [the] victim's head and hands."

The murder in *Penick* was not clean and quick. Death came only after the victim endured excruciating pain and suffering. The victim also sustained postdeath mutilation. It will be noted that torture and postdeath mutilation are legally distinct. Torture means the infliction of severe physical or mental pain upon the victim while he or she remains alive and conscious.[80] Postdeath mutilation refers to the dismemberment or disfigurement of a corpse.[81]

Nine capital punishment jurisdictions have isolated torture-murder and made it a death-eligible offense.[82] The statute that follows illustrates this offense.

New York Penal Law § 125.27(1)(a)(x):
[T]he defendant acted in an especially cruel and wanton manner pursuant to a course of conduct intended to inflict and inflicting torture upon the victim prior to the victim's death. As used [here], "torture" means the intentional and depraved infliction of extreme physical pain: "depraved" means the defendant relished the infliction of extreme physical pain upon the victim evidencing debasement or perversion or that the defendant evidenced s sense of pleasure in the infliction of extreme physical pain.

LYING-IN-WAIT MURDER

The elements of lying-in-wait murder were set out in the case of *People v. Sims*, 20 Cal.Rptr.2d 537 (1993), as follows: (1) concealment of purpose,

(2) substantial period of watching and waiting for an opportune time to act, and (3) immediately thereafter, a surprise attack on an unsuspecting victim from a position of advantage. In *Sims* two defendants were charged and convicted of lying-in-wait murder. The defendants rented a motel room for the purpose of committing the crime. The victim was a young man who worked for a pizza restaurant. The defendants called the restaurant and ordered pizza, knowing that the intended victim would make the delivery. Once the victim arrived he was attacked by the defendants and drowned in a prepared bathtub filled with water.

Six capital punishment jurisdictions have isolated lying-in-wait murder and made it a death-eligible offense.[83] The statute that follows illustrates this offense.

> **Nevada Revised Statutes § 200.030(1)(a):**
> Murder in the first degree is murder which is [p]erpetrated by ... lying in wait [or] torture[.]

VICTIM-AGE MURDER

The full force of the concern embedded in victim-age murder may be grasped by a review of the salient facts in the case of *State v. Simpson*, 462 S.E.2d 191 (N.C. 1995). The murder victim in this case was named Reverend Jean E. Darter. Most of the facts presented stemmed from a confession given by the defendant:

> Defendant confessed that ... he and his pregnant, sixteen-year old girlfriend, Stephanie Eury, went for a walk to look for some money. Stephanie went to the front door of Reverend Darter's house and rang the doorbell. She told Reverend Darter she was hungry, so he brought her a diet soft drink and gave the defendant a glass of milk. Stephanie asked if they could come inside, so the three went into the front living room. Stephanie told the Reverend that she and defendant were traveling to Florida and had gotten stuck in Reidsville. The Reverend suggested they contact the Salvation Army or the police. Stephanie asked [Reverend] Darter if he could give them some money, and Reverend Darter gave her four dollars, explaining that was all the money he had in cash.... Defendant told the police that before he and Stephanie left the house, the Reverend gave them some sponge cake and peaches to take with them....
>
> The next day ... defendant said that he and Stephanie "both talked about going back to preacher Darter's house to get some money. Stephanie and I decided we would go back to Darter's house and we would not come back empty-handed no matter what[.]" Once it was dark enough, the two walked to Reverend Darter's house, looking around to make sure no one saw them. They rang the doorbell, and when Reverend Darter answered the door, they forced their way inside. Reverend Darter

ran to the telephone, but defendant "pulled the preacher's hands off the telephone." Defendant told Stephanie to cut the telephone cords, and in the meantime, he was "struggling with Preacher Darter holding onto the preacher's arms to control him and force him back in his bedroom so he would tell me where some money was." Defendant held the Reverend down on the bed, with his hands around his neck, telling him he wanted money "or else," but the Reverend told defendant he did not have any money....

Defendant reached across the bed and got a belt and "looped it around his neck and tightened the belt.... Then I called Stephanie to bring me something in the bedroom to kill this preacher with."

When defendant did not receive any weapon to his liking, he called for Stephanie to come and hold the belt while he "went in the kitchen and looked for some device to beat the old preacher and finish him off." He picked up a full pop bottle and then decided to put it back and get an empty bottle. He returned to the bedroom, pulled tight on the belt, and "hit the old preacher hard three times with this bottle and on the third blow the soft drink bottle broke." Defendant then decided to tie the end of the belt to the bedpost, and he went into the bathroom and got a double-edged razor blade. "I held this double-edged razor blade between my right index finger and right thumb and then I sliced the preacher's arms from the biceps all of the way down the under side of the forearms to the wrist. I cut both of the preacher's arms." Stephanie gathered a bag of food, a porcelain lamp, a radio, and boxes of Kleenex and packed them in a plastic laundry bag. "The last thing we did before leaving the preacher's house was to turn off all the lights except the bathroom light[.]"

Pathologist Michael James Shkrum performed an autopsy on Reverend Darter and testified the Reverend sustained blunt-trauma injuries to his face causing swelling and bruising. The bone between the eye socket and the brain was fractured, the cheek and the jaw bone were broken, and the Reverend's tongue was torn.

The murder of Reverend Darter was, of course, torture-murder. The focus at this point, however, is not on torture-murder, but on victim-age murder. Should the fact that Reverend Darter was ninety-two years old be a factor in the decision to make his homicide a death-eligible offense?

In the case of *People v. Memro*, 47 Cal.Rptr.2d 219 (1996), the defendant slit the throats of two boys aged ten and twelve. In *Harrison v. State*, 644 N.E.2d 1243 (Ind. 1995), the defendant burned alive two children, one aged three and a half and one aged twenty-one months. Should the age of the victims be the determining factor in *Simpson*, *Memro,* and *Harrison* in deciding whether to hold the defendants under the pressure of death-eligible prosecutions?

Victim-age murder has begun to carve out a place as a distinct death-eligible offense. Six capital punishment jurisdictions currently have some form of a death-eligible victim-age murder statute.[84] The statute that follows illustrates this offense.

Louisiana Revised Statutes 14 § 30(A)(5):

First degree murder is the killing of a human being ... [w]hen the offender has the specific intent to kill or to inflict great bodily harm upon a victim under the age of twelve or sixty-five years of age or older.

PART II

PROSECUTORIAL ISSUES

CHAPTER 4

Charging Discretion of a Prosecutor

The legal system in the United States may be divided into two broad categories: civil and criminal. In civil litigation, individual citizens hire private attorneys to represent their interests. In criminal litigation, a defendant has a constitutional right to be represented by private counsel (appointed or retained). The victim of a crime, however, does not have a constitutional right to have a private attorney prosecute his or her case against a defendant. In criminal prosecutions, government attorneys called prosecutors represent the interests of a crime victim.

This chapter will provide a brief historical review of the development of the prosecutor in the United States. The emphasis in this historical review is on understanding why prosecutors have almost absolute discretion in criminal matters. The chapter will also provide a discussion on specific issues involving a prosecutor's discretion in capital punishment cases.

Historical Development of the Public Prosecutor

To understand properly the deference courts give to prosecutorial discretion, it is necessary to review the origin of the office of public prosecutor. This section will briefly trace the path that has given Anglo-American jurisprudence the public prosecutor.

THE PROSECUTOR UNDER COMMON LAW

The English Crown made criminal prosecution an unregulated for-profit business. All crimes in England were punishable by fine, in addition to the physical forms of punishment discussed in Chapter 1. Under the common law, a fine included cash, as well as other personal and real property. Depending upon the nature of the offense, a convicted defendant's land could be confiscated by the Crown, as well as everything else he or she might own.[1]

Although the English Parliament existed during the common law era, the Crown was the true sovereign authority. As the sovereign authority, it was the duty and responsibility of the Crown to maintain the peace and enforce the laws of the realm. This duty and responsibility meant apprehending and prosecuting lawbreakers. The Crown delegated, in large part, both its arrest and prosecution duties to the general public.[2] In other words, both the Crown and common citizens carried out criminal prosecutorial duties.

Prosecution by the Crown. The English Crown employed numerous legal advisers. Some of the legal offices created by the Crown included (1) King's advocate general, (2) King's attorney general, (3) King's solicitor general, and (4) King's serjeants.[3] Legal advisers employed by the Crown enjoyed the benefits of the inherent prerogative of the Crown because of their association with the Crown. This meant that, in practice, legal advisers of the Crown were viewed literally as being above all other attorneys and were treated with absolute deference in courts of law. It was said by one scholar that the Crown's attorney did not represent the Crown in court because the Crown was theoretically always present. The attorney merely followed a case on behalf of the Crown.[4] This framework of absolute deference to the Crown's attorneys laid the seeds of prosecutorial discretion that is present in Anglo-American jurisprudence today.

As pointed out, the Crown was the sovereign authority under the common law. In fulfilling its duty of prosecuting criminal offenders, the Crown relied primarily upon its attorney general, though King's serjeants are said to have played a minor role in this area of litigation as well.

The Crown's attorney general did not prosecute all crimes, although he had the authority to do so. Instead, the attorney general limited his attention to major felony crimes like treason, murder, outlawry, and robbery. The crime of murder and treason were of particular interest to the Crown because the real property of defendants convicted of either offense escheated to the Crown. Enormous fines were appended to other major felony offenses.

The attorney general's selection of the cases he would prosecute (those bringing the greatest bounty to the Crown) was a prerogative act of discretion that could not be challenged by the courts or anyone, save the Crown itself. The attorney general represented the Crown and, as one court put it, "[i]f the agent of the sovereign desired that a prosecution should [not occur], that was the end of the matter. The public subjects had no interest and could not be heard to complain."[5]

Further, if the attorney general began a prosecution and decided he did not wish to proceed further or if the prosecution was begun by a private citizen and the attorney general desired to terminate the action, he could do so by filing a *nolle prosequi*. The nolle prosequi was "a statement by the [attorney general] that he would proceed no further in a criminal case.... The discretion to discontinue prosecution rested solely with the [attorney general] and it was unnecessary to obtain the permission of the court to give legal effect to this decision."[6]

The underlying justification for permitting the attorney general to have absolute discretion in determining the fate of a prosecution anchored itself to the fact that the Crown, as sovereign authority, "was theoretically the only party interested in the prosecution."[7]

Prosecution by citizens. It was previously noted that criminal prosecution under the common law was an unregulated for-profit business. The validity of this assertion is nowhere more evident than in the Crown's relinquishment of its prosecutorial duties to all private citizens.

Under the common law, all citizens were permitted to prosecute criminal offenders in the name of the Crown. This privilege was monstrously abused because of the benefits that could be reaped by successful prosecutions. A citizen bringing a successful criminal prosecution could share in the proceeds of the fine that was invariably imposed.[8]

Private prosecutors were also able to take advantage monetarily of the common law's rule that an acquittal could be appealed (rejected by Anglo-American jurisprudence). A defendant who was acquitted of a crime could be confined in jail pending an appeal of the acquittal. This situation usually resulted in the defendant entering a settlement agreement with the private prosecutor. The private prosecutor would agree to forgo an appeal in exchange for a monetary payment by the defendant.[9]

EVOLUTION OF THE PUBLIC PROSECUTOR IN AMERICA

The common law did not have a public prosecutor as that term is understood today.[10] Instead, the common law tolerated gross selective prosecution by the Crown's attorney general and wholesale prosecution by private citizens. Unfortunately, this chaotic method of prosecuting criminals was transplanted to the American colonies. Fortunately, however, another method of prosecuting criminal defendants also took root in North America, but this second method did not come from England and the common law. When the Dutch founded the colony of New Netherland during the seventeenth century, they brought with them their system of prosecuting criminal defendants. A review of both methods of prosecution will follow.

Common law prosecution in the colonies. The Crown appointed an attorney general in all of the colonies. The first appointment was made in Virginia in 1643.[11] The primary task of a colonial attorney general was to promote and protect the financial interests of the Crown. This meant that the bulk of the legal work performed by the colonial attorneys general was civil in nature.

Colonial attorney generals were also responsible for prosecuting criminal defendants. However, this duty was neglected. Rarely did colonial attorney generals prosecute criminal defendants. They intervened in this area only when a notorious major felony occurred. A routine murder was not considered notorious unless it affected a colonial aristocrat.[12]

The attitude of colonial attorneys general was the same as that of their brethren in England—if the Crown did not obtain a substantial benefit from criminal prosecutions, there would be no prosecution by the sovereign authority whose duty it was to prosecute all crimes. Colonial judges did not challenge the discretion exercised by colonial attorneys general.

Two factors caused colonial judges to defer to the prosecutorial discretion of colonial attorneys general. First, the judges followed the legal principles of the common law. Under the common law, it was held that the Crown's prosecutors had absolute discretion in deciding what course, if any, to take regarding a criminal offense. This common law principle was echoed in modern times in the case of *Newman v. United States*, 382 F.2d 479 (D.C. Cir. 1967), in which it was said that "[f]ew subjects are less adapted to judicial review than the exercise by the [prosecutor] of his discretion in deciding when and whether to institute criminal proceedings, or what precise charge shall be made, or whether to dismiss a proceeding once brought."

The second factor which caused colonial judges to bow to the whim of colonial attorneys general was the Crown. Colonial attorneys general were not ordinary attorneys. The Crown's prerogative was vested in colonial attorneys general when they carried out their legal duties. No colonial judge could muster the courage to tell the Crown when it should prosecute a criminal case.

The fact that colonial attorneys general rarely prosecuted criminal defendants did not mean that vigorous criminal prosecutions were nonexistent in the colonies. Crime was routinely prosecuted, but it was the citizens of the colonies who prosecuted the vast majority of crimes.

The chaotic private prosecutorial method that existed in England was allowed to flourish in the colonies. The inducement used to encourage colonists to prosecute criminals was the same carrot used in England. Private prosecutors reaped monetary rewards for successfully prosecuting criminals. They also reaped rewards by intimidating defendants into settling criminal charges prior to trial by paying the private prosecutors monetary sums.[13]

Criminal prosecution in New Netherland. The Dutch ventured to North America in the seventeenth century and settled a colony called New Netherland. (This colony comprised parts of Delaware, New Jersey, New York, Pennsylvania, and Connecticut.)[14] As would be expected, Dutch colonists brought with them the Dutch culture, social norms, and system of government.

One aspect of the Dutch system of government that was brought with the colonists had a profound effect on Anglo-American jurisprudence. The legal system of the Dutch had an office called the *schout*. Although legal scholars rarely acknowledge the point, but it was the principles undergirding the office of schout which shaped the prosecutorial system that America would eventually adopt and utilize to this day.[15]

The schout was a public prosecutor. Unlike the chaotic system of prosecution tolerated by the common law, Dutch law intrusted the task of prosecuting criminals to a single office—the office of schout. Dutch colonists did not haul their neighbors into criminal courts on real or imagined charges for monetary gain. If a criminal offense occurred, the office of schout prosecuted the crime.[16]

When the English eventually took New Netherland from the Dutch, the term *schout* was buried, but the idea of entrusting a public prosecutor with the responsibility for prosecuting all crimes took root and blossomed in America. The public prosecutor of today is a distant cousin of the common law and the first cousin of the schout.[17]

Modern day public prosecutor. The nation's prosecutorial system is a hybrid of the common law and the schout. When the American colonists threw off the yoke of the Crown, they also tossed out the common law's ad hoc approach to prosecuting criminal defendants. The nation unanimously moved in the direction of imposing the duty of prosecuting criminal defendants upon individual governments. Neither the nation nor its legal system was prepared to continue depending upon private citizens to prosecute criminals. Crime would be prosecuted, but it would be under the schout model.

Today all jurisdictions have schouts, though they go by various names: district attorney, county prosecutor, state attorney, attorney general, or simply public prosecutor. A majority of jurisdictions provide for the election of prosecutors on a local, usually county, level.[18]

Although Anglo-American jurisprudence rejected the common law's method of prosecuting crimes, the judiciary continues to adhere to the common law principle that a prosecutor has broad discretion regarding the disposition of criminal cases. Although the nation is not governed by a Crown, the judiciary continues to allow prosecutors to have almost unassailable prosecutorial power and authority.

THE POWELL PROPOSITIONS

In the case of *Wayte v. United States*, 470 U.S. 598 (1985), Justice Powell articulated the modern day justification for adhering to the common law's deference to prosecutors. Justice Powell reasoned as follows:

> This broad discretion rests largely on the recognition that the decision to prosecute is particularly ill-suited to judicial review. Such factors as the strength of the case, the prosection's general deterrence value, the Government's enforcement priorities, and the case's relationship to the

Government's overall enforcement plan are not readily susceptible to the kind of analysis the courts are competent to undertake. Judicial supervision in this area, moreover, entails systemic costs of particular concern. Examining the basis of a prosecution delays the criminal proceeding, threatens to chill law enforcement by subjecting the prosecutor's motives and decisionmaking to outside inquiry, and may undermine prosecutorial effectiveness by revealing the Government's enforcement policy. All these are substantial concerns that make the courts properly hesitant to examine the decision whether to prosecute.

Justice Powell in effect offered five propositions for the modern day deference to prosecutors:
(1) the inability of the courts to systematically analyze the prosecutor's decision-making process
(2) oversight would be too costly
(3) wholesale review would clog up the system
(4) oversight would discourage prosecutions
(5) oversight could make public otherwise hidden agendas
The concerns expressed in the Powell Propositions have merit, but numerous commentators challenge the Powell Propositions and the unbridled prosecutorial discretion they permit.[19] At the core of arguments against deference to prosecutorial discretion stands one idea: prosecutors frequently abuse their discretion.

Death Penalty Charging Discretion

The determination of whether to charge a person with a capital offense rests with the prosecutor. The power vested in the prosecutor is almost without limit. In this section a review is given on specific issues related to a prosecutor's discretion in death penalty cases.

DISCRETION TO SEEK THE DEATH PENALTY

Traditionally the determination of what penalty a convicted defendant will receive is made by the presiding judge, based upon the penalty range provided by statute. For example, if a prosecutor obtains a conviction for rape and the penalty for the offense is from five to fifteen years imprisonment, the prosecutor cannot absolve the defendant from being subject to this penalty. At most, a prosecutor may recommend to the trial judge that the defendant receive probation or some other disposition. The court can accept or reject the recommendation.[20] In other words, once a prosecutor charges a defendant with a crime the penalty automatically attaches and the prosecutor cannot, *sua sponte*, remove the defendant from exposure to the penalty (short of dismissing the charge).

Tradition is abandoned, however, in capital murder prosecutions. In this context the prosecutor can invade the traditionally exclusive domain of the trial judge. All capital punishment jurisdictions except New Jersey give prosecutors statutory discretion to waive the death penalty, sua sponte, for any death-eligible offense. It was said by one appellate court that the exercise of this discretion does not violate "the separation of powers provision of [federal or state constitutions], in that the prosecutor is given power to exercise a part of the sentencing process, which should properly be a judicial function."[21]

A note of caution is in order with respect to waiving the death penalty. The fact that a prosecutor waives or gives up the right to seek the death penalty in a case does not mean that the case will not be prosecuted. The prosecution continues, but the maximum penalty a defendant would face upon conviction would be life imprisonment.

The McCleskey ruling. In the case of *McCleskey v. Kemp*, 481 U.S. 279 (1987), the defendant argued that the state of Georgia's capital punishment statute was unconstitutional because it gave unfettered discretion to prosecutors to determine when they would seek the death penalty for capital offenses. The defendant contended that the Constitution required that death penalty statutes set out guidelines to control the circumstances in which a prosecutor may seek, or decline to seek, the death penalty. The Supreme Court disagreed with the defendant as follows:

> ... [T]he policy considerations behind a prosecutor's traditionally wide discretion suggest the impropriety of our requiring prosecutors to defend their decisions to seek death penalties....
>
> ... Our refusal to require that the prosecutor provide an explanation for his decisions ... is completely consistent with this Court's long-standing precedents that hold that a prosecutor need not explain his decisions unless the criminal defendant presents a prima facie case of unconstitutional conduct with respect to his case....
>
> Similarly, the capacity of prosecutorial discretion to provide individualized justice is firmly entrenched in American law. As we have noted, a prosecutor can ... decline to seek a death sentence in any particular case. Of course, the power to be lenient [also] is the power to discriminate, but a capital punishment system that did not allow for discretionary acts of leniency would be totally alien to our notions of criminal justice[.]
>
> We have held that discretion in a capital punishment system is necessary to satisfy the Constitution.... Prosecutorial decisions necessarily involve both judgmental and factual decisions that vary from case to case. Thus, it is difficult to imagine guidelines that would produce ... predictability ... without sacrificing the discretion essential to a humane and fair system of criminal justice.

The import of *McCleskey* is that "the federal Constitution does not mandate guidelines for prosecutors in administering the death penalty statute[.]"[22] In fact, *McCleskey* pronounced, in dicta, that it would be unconstitutional for a prosecutor not to have discretion in determining whom to seek the death penalty against and whom to show mercy.

The broad sweep of *McCleskey* has been tempered by other Supreme Court cases, so that the decision to seek the death penalty cannot be made in a discriminatory manner that violates the constitutional rights of defendants. An example of the latter would be basing the decision to waive or not waive the death penalty on racial, gender, or religious grounds. Ultimately, however, the Supreme Court has indicated that "[a]bsent facts to the contrary, it cannot be assumed that prosecutors will be motivated in their charging decision by factors other than the strength of their case and the likelihood that a jury would impose the death penalty if it convicts."[23]

CONCURRENT JURISDICTION DISCRETION

The idea behind concurrent jurisdiction, in the context of capital punishment, is simply that more than one jurisdiction may prosecute a defendant for the same capital offense under certain circumstances. The discretion of prosecutors in this area is based upon the sovereignty of each jurisdiction. An extended excerpt from the case of *Heath v. Alabama*, 474 U.S. 82 (1985), will provide a realistic illustration of the issues involved when prosecutors in different jurisdictions seek to prosecute a defendant for the same capital crime.

As a preliminary to presenting the *Heath* opinion, a few remarks about the case will be given. The state of Georgia convicted the defendant of capital murder and sentenced him to life imprisonment. The state of Alabama also prosecuted the defendant for the same capital murder, but sentenced him to death. The defendant's argument to the Supreme Court was that Alabama's prosecution of him, for the same capital murder, was unconstitutional:[24]

> In August 1981, petitioner, Larry Gene Heath, hired [two men] to kill his wife, Rebecca Heath, who was then nine months pregnant, for a sum of $2,000. On the morning of August 31, 1981, petitioner left the Heath residence in Russell County, Alabama, to meet with [the two men] in Georgia, just over the Alabama border from the Heath home. Petitioner led them back to the Heath residence, gave them the keys to the Heath car and house, and left the premises in his girlfriend's truck. [The two men] then kidnapped Rebecca Heath from her home. The Heath car, with Rebecca Heath's body inside, was later found on the side of a road in Troup County, Georgia. The cause of death was a gunshot wound in the head. The estimated time of death [was] consistent with the theory that the murder took place in Georgia[.]
>
> Georgia and Alabama authorities pursued dual investigations in which

they cooperated to some extent. On September 4, 1981, petitioner was arrested by Georgia authorities. Petitioner waived his Miranda rights and gave a full confession admitting that he had arranged his wife's kidnapping and murder. In November 1981, the grand jury of Troup County, Georgia, indicted petitioner for the offense of malice murder.... On February 10, 1982, petitioner pleaded guilty to the Georgia murder charge in exchange for a sentence of life imprisonment, which he understood could involve his serving as few as seven years in prison.

On May 5, 1982, the grand jury of Russell County, Alabama, returned an indictment against petitioner for the capital offense of murder during a kidnapping. Before trial on this indictment, petitioner [filed a motion] arguing that his conviction and sentence in Georgia barred his prosecution in Alabama for the same conduct [under double jeopardy principles]. Petitioner also [contested] the jurisdiction of the Alabama court on the ground that the crime had occurred in Georgia.

After a hearing, the trial court rejected petitioner's double jeopardy claims....

On January 12, 1983, the Alabama jury convicted petitioner of murder during a kidnapping in the first degree. After a sentencing hearing, the jury recommended the death penalty [which was subsequently imposed by the trial judge].

Petitioner sought a writ of certiorari from this Court, raising double jeopardy claims....

Successive prosecutions are barred by the Fifth Amendment only if the two offenses for which the defendant is prosecuted are the "same" for double jeopardy purposes.... We [will] assume, arguendo, that, had [the offenses petitioner was convicted [of] arisen under the laws of one State ... the second conviction would have been barred by the Double Jeopardy Clause.

The sole remaining question ... is whether the dual sovereignty doctrine permits successive prosecutions under the laws of different States[.]

The dual sovereignty doctrine is founded on the common-law conception of crime as an offense against the sovereignty of the government. When a defendant in a single act violates the "peace and dignity" of two sovereigns by breaking the laws of each, he has committed two distinct offenses[.]

In applying the dual sovereignty doctrine, then, the crucial determination is whether the two entities that seek successively to prosecute a defendant for the same course of conduct can be termed separate sovereigns. This determination turns on whether the two entities draw their authority to punish the offender from distinct sources of power. [This] Court has uniformly held [in prior cases] that the States are separate sovereigns with respect to the federal Government because each State's power to prosecute is derived from its own "inherent sovereignty," not from the Federal Government....

The States are no less sovereign with respect to each other than they are with respect to the Federal Government. Their powers to undertake criminal prosecutions derive from separate and independent sources of power and authority ... preserved to them by the Tenth Amendment.

... Foremost among the prerogatives of sovereignty is the power to create and enforce a criminal code. To deny a state its power to enforce its criminal laws because another State has won the race to the courthouse would be a shocking and untoward deprivation of the historic right and obligation of the states to maintain peace and order within their confines.... [Conviction affirmed.]

SEEKING DEATH AFTER A REVERSAL OF A CONVICTION

Conviction of a capital crime does not mean that a sentence of death will be imposed. Life imprisonment is an option in capital prosecutions. Invariably a defendant convicted of a capital offense will seek to overturn the conviction, regardless of whether or not the death penalty was imposed. The issue presented now involves prosecutorial discretion to seek the death penalty at a retrial of a defendant, when the overturned sentence in the first trial was life imprisonment.

The Stroud ruling. In the case of *Stroud v. United States*, 251 U.S. 15 (1919), the defendant was convicted of the capital offense of first-degree murder and was sentenced to life imprisonment. The defendant appealed his conviction, and the appellate court overturned the conviction and granted him a new trial. At the second trial, the defendant was again convicted of first-degree murder, but this time he was sentenced to die. The defendant appealed his second conviction to the Supreme Court.

The defendant's argument to the Supreme Court was that the Double Jeopardy Clause of the Fifth Amendment prohibited imposition of the death penalty at his second trial because the first trial determined that the death penalty was inappropriate. This argument was rejected. The Supreme Court held that the death penalty may be constitutionally sought by a prosecutor at a retrial of a defendant, even though the punishment was not imposed at the first trial.

The Bullington ruling. The ruling in *Stroud* remained unchallenged law until the Supreme Court heard the case of *Bullington v. Missouri*, 451 U.S. 430 (1981). The relevant facts of *Bullington* are as follows.

The defendant in *Bullington* was indicted in 1977 for the capital murder of a woman during the commission of a kidnapping. After a lengthy trial, the jury returned a verdict of guilty of capital murder. The prosecutor indicated he would seek the death penalty, so a sentencing hearing was held to determine the penalty. The sentencing jury returned a verdict of life imprisonment.

Shortly after the sentencing verdict was returned, the defendant filed postverdict motions. In the motions he asked the trial court to set aside the guilty verdict and acquit him or set aside the guilty verdict and grant him a new trial. Because of a constitutional error at the trial, the presiding judge set aside the guilty verdict and granted the defendant a new trial.

Prior to the start of the second trial, the prosecutor filed a notice that he would again seek the death penalty. The defendant objected and filed a motion asking the trial court to quash the notice. The defendant argued that the Double Jeopardy Clause prevented the prosecutor from seeking the death penalty after the jury rejected this in the first trial.

The trial court agreed with the defendant and prohibited the prosecutor from seeking the death penalty in the second trial. The prosecutor thereafter made an interlocutory appeal of the trial court's ruling to the Missouri Supreme Court. The state high court agreed with the prosecutor that the Double Jeopardy Clause did not prevent him from seeking the death penalty in the second trial. The state high court then set aside the trial court's ruling.

Before the second trial began, the defendant made an interlocutory appeal of the state high court decision to the Supreme Court. The essence of the Supreme Court's response to the issue of seeking death in a retrial is as follows:

> It is well established that the Double Jeopardy Clause forbids the retrial of a defendant who has been acquitted of the crime charged. This Court, however, has resisted attempts to extend that principle to sentencing. The imposition of a particular sentence usually is not regarded as an "acquittal" of any more severe sentence that could have been imposed. The Court generally has concluded, therefore, that the Double Jeopardy Clause imposes no absolute prohibition against the imposition of a harsher sentence at retrial after a defendant has succeeded in having his original conviction set aside.
>
> The procedure that resulted in the imposition of life imprisonment upon [the defendant] at his first trial, however, differs significantly from those employed in any of the Court's cases where the Double Jeopardy Clause has been held inapplicable to sentencing. The jury in this case was not given unbounded discretion to select an appropriate punishment from a wide range authorized by statute. Rather, a separate hearing was required and was held, and the jury was presented both a choice between two alternatives and standards to guide the making of that choice. Nor did the prosecution simply recommend what it felt to be an appropriate punishment. It undertook the burden of establishing certain facts ... in its quest to obtain the harsher of the two alternative verdicts. The presentence hearing resembled ... the immediately preceding trial on the issue of guilt or innocence. It was itself a trial on the issue of punishment[.]
>
> In contrast, the sentencing procedures in [Stroud] did not have the hallmarks of the trial on guilt or innocence. In ... Stroud, there was no separate sentencing proceeding at which the prosecution was required to prove ... facts in order to justify the particular sentence. In [Stroud] the

sentencer's discretion was essentially unfettered[.]

By enacting a capital sentencing procedure that resembles a trial on the issue of guilt or innocence ... Missouri explicitly requires the jury to determine whether the prosecution has proved its case[.]

... Because the sentencing proceeding at [the defendant's] first trial was like the trial on the question of guilt or innocence, the protection afforded by the Double Jeopardy clause to one acquitted by a jury also is available to him, with respect to the death penalty, at his retrial. We therefore refrain from extending the reasoning of Stroud to this very different situation.

The judgment of the Supreme Court of Missouri is reversed[.]

Under *Bullington* a prosecutor is prohibited from seeking the death penalty in a retrial when the death penalty was rejected in the first trial. However, if a defendant is given the death penalty in the first trial, which is subsequently reversed, he or she is still exposed to capital punishment at a retrial.

It will be noted that *Bullington* did not expressly overrule *Stroud*. As a practical matter, however, *Stroud* is dead because of the nature of capital sentencing today.

CHAPTER 5

Capital Murder Charging Instruments

The intent of the chapter is to provide a review of the instruments prosecutors use to charge defendants with capital offenses. The chapter will also present material regarding specific issues that relate to capital charging instruments. In setting forth the discussion, the chapter has been divided into two major sections, based upon the two charging instruments used by prosecutors— the indictment and information.

The Indictment

Depending upon the requirements of a particular jurisdiction, capital murder is prosecuted by an indictment or an information. This section will explore prosecution of a capital felon under an indictment. The material starts out with a summation of the grand jury and its role with an indictment. Following that discussion the section will examine specific capital punishment indictment issues.

THE GRAND JURY

An indictment is an instrument that is drawn up by a grand jury. The origin of the grand jury is traditionally traced back to the reign of King Henry II of England. Legal scholars report that in the year 1166, King Henry II created an institution called the Assize of Clarendon. The assize consisted of 12 men who were given the duty of informing the local sheriff or an itinerant justice of the peace of any criminal conduct in their community. The assize operated in this fashion until the end of the fourteenth century.[1]

The assize split into two separate institutions by the end of the fourteenth century. One institution was called the petit jury and the other was called *le grande inquest* or grand jury.[2] The concern here, of course, is with the grand jury. At its inception the grand jury had two purposes: to prevent unjust prosecutions and to initiate just prosecutions.

The grand jury was incorporated into Anglo-American jurisprudence by the colonists. During the early development of the nation, all jurisdictions required that felony prosecutions be initiated by the grand jury. The document used by the grand jury to initiate a prosecution was called an indictment. The grand jury issues an indictment against a person only if it finds probable cause existed that a crime was committed and probable cause that a named person committed the crime.

As a result of a decision by the Supreme Court in *Hurtado v. California*, 110 U.S. 516 (1884) (discussed in the information section), only a minority of jurisdictions now require that felony offenses be prosecuted by a grand jury indictment.[3]

FATAL VARIANCE IN INDICTMENT

Allegations alleged in a capital indictment must be proven at trial. There are times, however, when a prosecutor will prove an essential issue at a trial that was not alleged in the indictment or fail to prove a matter that was alleged in the indictment. This situation is called a variance. Jurisdictions differ on how they treat specific capital indictment variances. Some variances are deemed fatal variances. A fatal variance in a capital indictment will result in a conviction being overturned. As a practical matter, most capital indictment variances are deemed nonfatal.

A few examples of fatal capital indictment variances are as follows. In *Borrego v. State*, 800 S.W.2d 373 (Tex.App.–Corpus Christi 1990), it was said that if an indictment alleged specific means of committing murder, failure to prove such means is a fatal variance. The court in *Alford v. State*, 906 P.2d 714 (Nev. 1995), held that when an indictment charged a defendant only with malice aforethought murder, the prosecutor could not pursue at trial the alternative theory of felony-murder. In *Fairchild v. State*, 459 So.2d 793 (Miss. 1984) it was held that the prosecutor must prove that the victim allegedly murdered is the same person named in the indictment as having been killed. The court in *Chavez v. State*, 657 S.W.2d 146 (Tex.Cr.App. 1983), said that when an indictment fails to recite use of a deadly weapon but proof at trial establishes a deadly weapon, a fatal variance occurs.

NONFATAL VARIANCE IN INDICTMENT

It was previously noted that in practice, courts tend to overlook capital indictment variances. The case-specific examples that follow represent indictment variances that were found to be nonfatal, that is, the convictions were not overturned.

The court in *People v. Nitz*, 610 N.E.2d 1289 (Ill.App. 5 Dist. 1993), found that there was no fatal variance in the indictment and proof at trial, where the indictment charged the defendant with shooting the victim to death, but the prosecutor did not present any evidence of a shooting. The *Nitz* court held that the indictment adequately informed the defendant that she was charged with murder and that the defendant was not prejudiced by the variance because her theory of defense was that she was not present during the murder. In *Battles v. State*, 420 S.E.2d 303 (Ga. 1992), the court held that there was no fatal variance in the indictment and proof at trial, where the indictment alleged the defendant struck the murder victim with a wrench, but the evidence proved that the victim was struck with a gun. It has also been judicially determined that a defendent is not deprived of a fair trial as a result of the indictment alleging that the murder victim died from a beating, while the evidence at trial revealed no beating took place. The court in *Manna v. State*, 440 N.E.2d 473 (Ind. 1982), held that where the indictment charged that murder occurred with a deadly weapon, the exact nature unknown, there was no material variance when evidence established that no deadly weapon was used. The *Manna* court reasoned that the allegation of a weapon was mere surplusage that did not mislead the defendant in preparation of a defense.

In *Stephens v. Borg*, 59 F.3d 932 (9th Cir. 1995), it was said that a jury may be instructed on felony-murder even though the indictment did not expressly set out such a theory. It has also been decided that there was no fatal variance in an indictment charging the defendant with malice murder merely because a felony-murder instruction was given to the trial jury. The courts in *People v. Wilkins*, 31 Cal.Rptr. 764 (1994), and *Dunn v. State*, 434 S.E.2d 60 (Ga. 1993), held that the defendants in those cases were not denied due process of law simply because the indictments alleged malice aforethought murder, but proof and convictions were based on felony-murder. In *Bush v. State*, 461 So.2d 936 (Fla. 1984), it was held that there was no material variance in charging the defendant with premeditated murder and proving felony-murder.

The court in *Williams v. Collins*, 16 F.3d 626 (5th Cir. 1994), found that there was no fatal variance in an indictment alleging the defendant killed the victim during a robbery of the victim and proof at trial that the victim was killed during the defendant's robbery of a convenience store where the victim worked. Courts have also made it clear that a defendant may be prosecuted as an accomplice even though the capital murder indictment indicated the defendant acted as a principal.

In *Crawford v. State*, 863 S.W.2d 152 (Tex.App.–Houston 1993), the court held that there was no fatal variance in an indictment charging the defendant with hiring a person to commit murder for remuneration "and" a promise of remuneration, while the jury was instructed that it could convict the defendant on a finding of remuneration "or" a promise of remuneration. The court in *McCall v. State*, 501 So.2d 496 (Ala.Cr.App. 1986), found that there was no fatal variance in an indictment alleging that a specific individual paid the defendant to kill the victim and the failure of the prosecutor to prove that a specific individual paid the defendant.

In *Turner v. State*, 406 So.2d 1066 (Ala.Cr.App. 1981), it was held that a variance in the middle name of the person named in the indictment as the victim and the actual middle name established at trial is not fatal. The court in *Johnson v. Estelle*, 704 F.2d 232 (5th Cir. 1983), found that there was no fatal variance in an indictment listing the victim's name as "Carol" and proof at trial that the victim was known as "Carlyn." In *Koehler v. State*, 653 S.W.2d 617 (Tex.App. 4 Dist. 1983), the court held that there was no fatal variance in an indictment calling the victim "Yolanda" and proof at trial that the victim was known as "Yolando."

In *Roberts v. State*, 314 S.E.2d 83 (Ga. 1984), it was held that there was no fatal variance in an indictment alleging the murder weapon was a .38 caliber handgun and proof at trial showing that it was a .38 special. The court in *Stevenson v. State*, 404 So.2d 111 (Ala.Cr.App. 1981), found that there was no material variance between an indictment charging murder with a pistol and proof at trial that the weapon used was a shotgun. In *Trest v. State*, 409 So.3d 906 (Fla.Cr.App. 1981), it was said that there was no material variance in an indictment charging murder by use of a .38 caliber pistol and proof at trial that the weapon was a .357 caliber. The court in *Weaver v. State*, 407 So.2d 568 (Ala.Cr.App. 1981), held that there was no fatal variance in an indictment alleging that death was caused by a .25 caliber automatic rifle and proof at trial that death resulted from a .25 caliber automatic pistol.

ALLEGING CAPITAL FELONY-MURDER

The issue of indicting a defendant on a capital felony-murder charge can be problematic, depending upon the dictates of the particular jurisdiction. The examples that follow illustrate issues defendants have argued regarding capital felony-murder indictments.

In *Davis v. State*, 782 S.W.2d 211 (Tex.Cr.App. 1989), it was said that a capital felony-murder indictment predicated on two underlying felonies does not require that the prosecutor prove both underlying felonies. The court in *State v. Jones*, 475 A.2d 1087 (Conn. 1984), indicated that an indictment may allege two underlying felonies in the alternative in a felony-murder prosecution. In *Gray v. State*, 441 A.2d 209 (Del. 1981), the court held that a felony-murder indictment is not defective in failing to recite the degree of the underlying felony. The court in *State v. Williams*, 292 S.E.2d 243 (N.C. 1982), held that an indictment for felony-murder is not defective in failing to charge the defendant with committing the underlying felony. In *Hogue v. State*, 711 S.W.2d 9

(Tex.Cr.App. 1986), it was determined that an indictment in a felony-murder prosecution that fails to set out the manner in which the underlying felony occurred is not vague or invalid for that reason.

The court in *Armstrong v. State*, 642 So.2d 730 (Fla. 1994), held that even though the indictment failed to provide notice of a felony-murder theory, a prosecution on that theory may proceed. In *State v. Bockorny*, 866 P.2d 1230 (Or.App. 1993), it was held that a felony-murder indictment need not set out all of the elements of the underlying crime nor the manner in which the crime occurred. In *State v. Flanders*, 572 A.2d 983 (Conn. 1990), the court said that a felony-murder indictment is valid even though it does not specify whether the defendant or a participant in the underlying felony caused the victim's death.

In *Stephenson v. State*, 593 So.2d 160 (Ala.Cr.App. 1991), it was held that an indictment which merely states that force causing physical injury was used against the murder victim in the course of committing theft was sufficient to charge the defendant with felony-murder predicated on first-degree robbery. The court in *Beathard v. State*, 767 S.W.2d 423 (Tex.Cr.App. 1989), held that an indictment for capital murder predicated on burglary did not have to set out the elements of burglary. In *Hunt v. State*, 659 So.2d 933 (Ala.Cr.App. 1994), the court held that a felony-murder indictment which erroneously alleged that sexual abuse in the second degree was a felony, when in fact it was a misdemeanor, did not invalidate the indictment in light of the fact that the aggravating component of the capital offense was burglary.

ALLEGING ALTERNATIVE THEORIES

A capital murder indictment is not infirm in setting out several ways in which the murder was committed.[4] An indictment may allege alternative means by which murder is alleged to have been committed, so long as the theories are not "stacked" to increase penalty phase aggravating circumstances.[5] Courts have held that even though an indictment alleges more than one theory of murder, the prosecutor does not have to prove all the theories alleged.[6]

EXCLUDED MATTERS FATAL TO INDICTMENT

In *State v. Clemmons*, 682 S.W.2d 843 (Mo.App. 1984), it was held that a capital murder indictment which fails to allege the element of deliberation is fatally defective. The court in *Brown v. State*, 410 A.2d 17 (Md.App. 1979), held that an indictment for murder is fatally defective when it omits the element malice aforethought. In *Peck v. State*, 923 S.W.2d 839 (Tex.App.–Tyler 1996), it was said that an indictment charging murder must allege the means used to commit the crime, if known by the grand jury. The court in *State v. Brown*, 651 A.2d 19 (N.J. 1994), held that a murder indictment must specify that the homicide resulted from the defendant's own conduct. In *Janecka v. State*, 823 S.W.2d 232 (Tex.Cr.App. 1990), the court indicated that an indictment is fatally defective if it charges a defendant with murder-for-hire but fails to include the name of the person providing the remuneration.

The court in *Ridgely v. State*, 756 S.W.2d 870 (Tex.App.–Fort Worth 1988), determined that an indictment was fatally defective in failing to allege the manner and means by which the victim was strangled because of testimony by a medical examiner that death could have occurred by choking with hands, suffocation with a paper towel, or by ligature. In *Crawford v. State*, 632 S.W.2d 800 (Tex.App. 14 Dist. 1982), the court held that a capital murder indictment was constitutionally defective in merely alleging the defendant committed murder in the course of committing rape when the statute required the underlying offense be "aggravated rape." In *King v. State*, 594 S.W.2d 425 (Tex.Cr.App. 1980), it was held that an indictment charging capital murder premised on rape is materially defective when it fails to recite the identity of the victim of the rape. The court in *Rougeau v. State*, 738 S.W.2d 651 (Tex.Cr.App. 1987), held that the indictment was defective in failing to provide the identity of the intended robbery victim in a prosecution of the defendant for murder predicated on robbery and attempted robbery. In *Welch v. State*, 331 S.E.2d 573 (Ga. 1985), the court held that the defendant's conviction for felony-murder could not stand, where the indictment charging him with two counts of malice murder did not charge him with committing the underlying felony of burglary.

EXCLUDED MATTERS NOT FATAL TO INDICTMENT

An indictment need not specify the theory of murder on which the prosecutor intends to rely.[7] Allegations as to the means used to commit murder are a formal, not an essential part of an indictment.[8] It has been held that the failure of an indictment to allege the means by which the murder occurred did not render it fatally defective when the defendant did not object to it until the prosecutor rested at the end of its case-in-chief.[9] An indictment is not fatally defective if it recites disjunctively phrased causes of death because allegations of the means used to cause death are not an essential part of indictment.[10] It is not required that an indictment charge the specific subsection of the murder statute identifying the mental state consistent with felony-murder.[11] In a prosecution for malice murder, an indictment does not have to set out facts the prosecutor will rely on to prove express or implied malice.[12]

A capital murder indictment does not have to specify the precise instrument used to cause the victim's death.[13] An indictment that alleges the defendant killed a police officer while the officer was lawfully discharging his or her official duties does not have to allege specific acts of the officer which constituted his or her official duties.[14] An indictment is not fatally defective because it does not allege which of two guns killed the victim.[15] A murder indictment is not fatally defective in failing to allege the cause of death when medical testimony establishes that decomposition of the victim's body made it impossible to determine the cause of death.[16]

An indictment charging the defendant with capital murder committed in the course of burglary of a habitation is sufficient even though it does not state burglarious intent.[17] A felony-murder indictment is not fatally defective in failing to allege the specific address of a burglarized dwelling in which the victim was killed.[18]

An indictment alleging the defendant murdered the victim while engaged in the commission of robbery is not fatally defective in omitting to allege an overt act for the robbery.[19] An indictment charging the defendant with committing murder during the course of theft of currency is not fatally defective in failing to specify the value or amount of the currency.[20] A capital murder indictment predicated on remuneration does not have to specify the object of value.[21] A capital murder indictment premised on homicide during robbery is not constitutionally defective in failing to allege the time of the offense.[22] An indictment charging capital murder premised on robbery is not defective in failing to allege the ownership of the property taken.[23]

An indictment charging the defendant with capital murder is not defective in failing to use the phrase "capital offense."[24] A capital murder indictment is not invalid in using the phrase "cause the death of" instead of the statutory word "kill" because the phrase is not misleading.[25] An indictment is not fatally defective in omitting the words "after deliberation upon the matter" when charging first-degree murder.[26] An indictment charging capital murder that fails to allege the defendant "knowingly" killed, is not fatally defective when the indictment contains words of similar import.[27] Although "malice" must be alleged in a capital murder indictment when required by the jurisdiction, that exact word need not be used.[28] An indictment failing to allege the murder was "premeditated" is not fatally defective in a capital murder prosecution when the essence of the term is conveyed through the use of other words.[29]

The fact that the an indictment only charges premeditated murder does not preclude the prosecutor from seeking a felony-murder conviction.[30] When a murder indictment recites the name of the victim, it need not state that the victim is a human being.[31] A murder indictment is not fatally defective in failing to allege that the defendant is a human being.[32]

An indictment charging the defendant with killing the victim by stomping and kicking is not invalid in failing to allege the defendant was wearing shoes at the time.[33] Failure of a murder indictment to allege that a rifle is a gun is not a fatal omission.[34]

ADEQUATE NOTICE

A capital murder indictment is not constitutionally invalid in failing to give notice that the charge carries the possibility of a death sentence.[35] Where an indictment charges the defendant with purposeful killing, it sufficiently apprises him or her that the charge includes specific intent to cause the victim's death.[36] The prosecutor has no obligation to give notice of the underlying felony that it will rely on to prove felony-murder.[37]

In the case of *Johnson v. State*, 815 S.W.2d 707 (Tex.Cr.App. 1991), the court held an indictment alleging the defendant caused the victim's death by striking him with his feet and hands gave the defendant adequate notice that the prosecutor would seek an affirmative finding that the defendant's feet and hands were deadly weapons. In *Long v. State*, 820 S.W.2d 888 (Tex.App.-Houston 1991), it was said that although the indictment did not state explicitly that the named weapon used in the murder, a knife, was a deadly weapon, the defendant was not deprived of adequate notice that the prosecutor would seek an affirmative finding of the use of a deadly weapon in killing the victim.

The Information

This section examines issues involving prosecution of a capital felon under an information. The material begins with a brief comment on how the information came into use in felony prosecutions generally. The remainder of the section reviews specific issues related to an information charging capital murder.

THE HURTADO RULING

Utilization of the grand jury and indictment to prosecute felony offenses began to lose favor by the mid–1800s. It has been reported that in 1859 Michigan became the first jurisdiction to permit felony prosecutions without a grand jury handing down an indictment. The path taken by Michigan was followed initially by only a few jurisdictions. The trend started by Michigan, however, picked up steam after the decision of the Supreme Court in *Hurtado v. California*, 110 U.S. 516 (1884).

In *Hurtado* the defendant was prosecuted and convicted of murder based upon a charging document, an information, drawn up by the prosecutor. The defendant argued to the Supreme Court that the Fifth Amendment guaranteed him the right to be prosecuted by a grand jury indictment and that the prosecutor's information was therefore unconstitutional. The Supreme Court disagreed with the defendant. The *Hurtado* opinion made clear that the requirement under the Fifth Amendment that all felony prosecutions be initiated by a grand jury indictment was applicable only to federal prosecutions. Utilization of the grand jury and indictment was thus a discretionary matter for each state to determine. This ruling permitted use of a prosecutor's information to prosecute felony offenses generally. Today a majority of jurisdictions utilize the information exclusively in all felony prosecutions.

FATAL VARIANCE IN INFORMATION

If an information alleges a named murder victim, the prosecutor must prove the victim's identity.[38] Where an information states the means in which a homicide occurred, the prosecutor must prove that death occurred through those means.[39] An information charging the defendant with malice afterthought murder only is fatally defective in sustaining a conviction for felony-murder.[40]

ALLEGING CAPITAL FELONY-MURDER

It is not necessary in a felony-murder prosecution to place in the information the elements of the underlying felony nor the specific means of committing that felony.[41] A prosecutor is required to charge felony-murder and its attendant facts, however, if he or she chooses to pursue a felony-murder conviction.[42] An information is not constitutionally vague because it recites two underlying felonies in a felony-murder prosecution without identifying which underlying felony would be relied upon.[43]

ALLEGING ALTERNATIVE MATTERS

An information charging premeditated murder or felony-murder is sufficient without specifically referring to either theory.[44] A prosecutor is required to charge felony-murder and its attendant facts as an alternative theory if he or she chooses to pursue a felony-murder conviction.[45]

EXCLUDED MATTERS FATAL TO INFORMATION

An information is fatally defective if it does not charge a defendant with felony-murder explicitly and the prosecutor obtains a conviction for felony-murder.[46] An information is fatally defective in charging a defendant with felony-murder if it fails to recite facts that allege every element of the capital murder offense and every element of the underlying felony.[47] When an information fails to set out a mental state in a homicide charge, it is fatally defective.[48] An information is constitutionally inadequate when it charges a defendant with murder by torture but fails to provide the defendant with notice that the prosecutor has to prove he acted for the purpose of revenge, extortion, or persuasion.[49] It has been held that an information is invalid when it purports to charge murder during the course of an armed robbery but fails to allege facts constituting armed robbery.[50]

Excluded Matters Not Fatal to Information

Courts have held that an information need not specify the theory of murder on which the prosecutor intends to rely.[51] An information need not recite cause or manner of death.[52] It has been determined that an information need not recite method of murder if it states the elements of the offense with sufficient clarity to apprise the defendant of what he or she must defend against.[53] Courts have held that an information is not fatally defective in failing to narrate the mental state of the defendant when allegedly committing the underlying offense in a felony-murder prosecution.[54] It has also been held that an information charging felony-murder does not have to charge the underlying felony.[55]

An information charging a defendant as a principal includes a charge as an accessory, therefore the information does not have to explicitly charge the defendant as an accessory in order for a conviction as an accessory to occur.[56] Courts have said that an information charging malice murder does not have to recite facts that will be used to prove malice.[57]

Where probable cause affidavits apprised defendant of the means and manner in which the murder occurred, the information is not fatally defective in failing to specify how the murder occurred.[58] An information charging the defendant as an aider and abettor in felony-murder is not fatally defective in not explicitly stating that the victim died.[59] The failure of an information to allege the caliber of weapon used in a murder does not require dismissing it because the matter is not an element of the offense.[60] A capital murder information is not fatally defective because it failed to recite the exact place of the victim's death.[61]

CHAPTER 6

Death Penalty
Notice Requirements

In the case of *In re Oliver*, 333 U.S. 257 (1948), the Supreme Court held that the Due Process Clause of the Constitution demands that a defendant be given "reasonable notice of a charge against him, and an opportunity to be heard in his defense[.]" The constitutional notice requirement is generally satisfied at the arraignment stage of a prosecution. At an arraignment a defendant is formally given a copy of the charging instrument and is informed by the trial court of the nature of the accusation against him or her.

In the context of a capital prosecution, a charging instrument will inform the defendant that he or she is accused of an offense that may be punished with death. As a general matter, the Constitution does not require death penalty notice beyond that which is provided in the charging instrument and explained during an arraignment. The intent of this chapter is to show that some capital punishment jurisdictions have death penalty notice requirements that are not constitutionally required.

Two types of notice requirements are discussed below: notice that the death penalty will be sought and notice involving aggravating circumstances. (Chapter 10 explores the meaning of aggravating circumstances.)

Notice of Intent to
Seek the Death Penalty

This section looks at three aspects of providing notice that the death penalty will be sought: (1) statutory notice, (2) notice in multiple death cases, and (3) the Lankford notice exception.

STATUTORY NOTICE REQUIREMENT

Eight capital punishment jurisdictions statutorily require that prosecutors provide defendants notice of the intent to seek the death penalty prior to the trial and independent of the notice provided at the arraignment in the charging instrument.[1] Several justifications have been proffered for the stringent statutory notice requirement: (1) it is an acknowledgment that the death penalty is unlike any other form of punishment in its finality, (2) it insures that the plea bargaining process is effectively and fairly carried out, and (3) it enables a defendant to make in a timely fashion a more intelligent determination of what evidence to present at trial.[2]

NOTICE IN MULTIPLE MURDER PROSECUTION

In the case of *Grandison v. State*, 670 A.2d 398 (Md. 1995), the court addressed the issue of notice to seek the death penalty in a multiple murder prosecution. The defendant in *Grandison* was prosecuted for committing two homicides. The prosecutor provided the defendant with statutory notice that the death penalty would be sought, but the notice did not state that the death penalty would be sought for each homicide.

Subsequent to the defendant's convictions for multiple homicides, he appealed the convictions on the basis that the statutory death penalty notice he received was inadequate. The defendant contended that he should have received notice that the death penalty would be sought for each murder. The *Grandison* court disagreed with the defendant in a cautious way. The court indicated that the record in the case revealed that the defendant was aware before the trial started that the death penalty would be sought for each murder. The court did not indicate what its decision on the issue would have been if the record did not show that the defendant was aware before the trial that the death penalty was going to be sought for each murder.

THE LANKFORD NOTICE EXCEPTION

The Supreme Court had an opportunity to address the issue of death penalty notice in the case of *Lankford v. Idaho*, 500 U.S. 110 (1991). The defendant in *Lankford* was convicted and sentenced to death for committing two murders. The record revealed that "[a]t the [defendant's] arraignment, the trial judge advised [him] that the maximum punishment that [he] may receive if … convicted on either of the two charges [was] imprisonment for life or death."

Subsequent to the defendant's double murder convictions, his penalty phase hearing was postponed until after the trial of a codefendant in the case. During this hiatus the defendant asked the trial judge to order the prosecutor to disclose whether the death penalty would in fact be sought at the sentencing hearing. The trial court issued the requested order, and the prosecutor responded that it "will not be recommending the death penalty as to either count of first-degree murder for which the defendant was earlier convicted."

When the sentencing hearing was finally held, no discussion or evidence was presented in contemplation of the death penalty. The prosecutor recommended a sentence of life for each conviction, to run concurrently. The defendant put on evidence to support concurrent life sentences. To the surprise of both parties, the trial court imposed two death sentences on the defendant.

The defendant appealed the death sentences to the Supreme Court. In the appeal the defendant argued that he did not have notice that he would be subject to the death penalty. In responding to this issue, the Supreme Court initially noted that "the advice received at [defendant's] arraignment, provided such notice." The Court went on to point out, however, that subsequent conduct in the prosecution nullified the notice given at the arraignment. The Court ultimately held that:

> Notice of issues to be resolved by the adversary process is a fundamental characteristic of fair procedure.... If notice is not given ... the adversary process is not permitted to function properly [and] there is an increased chance of error, and with that, the possibility of an incorrect result. [The defendant's] lack of adequate notice that the judge was contemplating the imposition of the death sentence created an impermissible risk that the adversary process may have malfunctioned in this case.

The opinion in *Lankford* established two things.[3] First, a properly conducted arraignment will constitutionally satisfy the notice requirement in capital murder cases. Second, if subsequent to an arraignment a prosecutor explicitly indicates he or she will not seek the death penalty, such a punishment may not be imposed, absent a timely notice that the punishment will in fact be sought.

Notice of Aggravating Circumstances

As a general matter, the phrase *aggravating circumstances* refers to factors that a prosecutor must prove at a penalty phase hearing in order for the death penalty to be imposed. This section addresses the issue of providing a defendant notice of aggravating circumstances before the trial starts and before the penalty phase hearing begins.

NOTICE BEFORE TRIAL

In response to the critical role of aggravating circumstances in death penalty cases, 11 capital punishment jurisdictions statutorily require that prosecutors provide defendants with pretrial notice of the aggravating circumstances that will be used against them.[4] In the case of *People v. Arias*, 913 P.2d

980 (Cal. 1996), it was held that pretrial notice of aggravating circumstances is adequate if it gives a defendant a reasonable understanding of what to expect and prepare for at the penalty phase hearing.

Two primary concerns are addressed by the requirement of giving pretrial notice of aggravating circumstances.[5] First, the requirement provides a defendant with sufficient time to prepare a penalty phase defense to the aggravating circumstances. Second, this requirement can facilitate the plea bargaining process by letting the defendant know the strength of the prosecutor's penalty phase evidence.[6]

NOTICE PRIOR TO PENALTY PHASE

The penalty phase of a capital offense prosecution is the sentencing hearing. This proceeding follows the guilt phase of a prosecution. (Chapter 9 provides a detailed discussion of the penalty phase.)

Four capital punishment jurisdictions statutorily require that prosecutors provide defendants with notice of aggravating circumstances prior to the start of the penalty phase of a capital murder prosecution.[7] This requirement means that the notice does not have to be given until after the trial.

CHAPTER 7

Prosecuting
a Nontriggerman

Determining under what circumstances a convicted nontriggerman may be sentenced to death is not at issue in this chapter (see Chapter 2). The material in this chapter is narrowly confined to exploring circumstances that allow a prosecutor to charge a nontriggerman for capital murder and obtain a conviction. Various legal theories are available which permit a prosecutor to charge and convict a defendant for capital murder, even though he or she did not actually perform the act which resulted in the victim's death. The legal theories in question include law of parties, accomplice liability, theory of accountability, felony-murder, common design rule, and joint venture theory. Some discussion regarding each theory follows.

Law of Parties

Under the law of parties, it is immaterial that the actual murder was not participated in by the defendant.[1] Even when the actual killer is only convicted of a lesser included offense of murder, a co-felon may be prosecuted for murder on the theory that he or she aided, abetted, counseled, or procured the actual perpetrator to commit the homicide.[2]

The law of parties is circumscribed by the limitation that the lethal force act must be (1) in furtherance of a crime, (2) in prosecution of a common design, or (3) an unlawful act the parties set out to accomplish.[3] In determining whether a defendant should be prosecuted for murder as a party to a homicide, courts look at events occurring before, during, and after the offense and also consider the conduct of the parties that shows an understanding and common design to kill the victim.[4] The law of parties consists of four types of actors: (1) principal in the first degree, (2) principal in the second degree, (3) accessory before the fact, and (4) accessory after the fact. Remarks about each follows.

Principal in the First Degree

A principal in the first degree is the actor who, with the requisite mental state or *mens rea*,[5] actually performs the act which directly inflicts death upon a victim.[6] Some examples of the application of the principal in the first-degree rule follow.

In the cases of *Smith v. Farley*, 59 F.3d 659 (7th Cir. 1995), *Ex Parte Simmons*, 649 So.2d 1282 (Ala. 1994), and *People v. Pock*, 23 Cal.Rptr.2d 900 (1993), it was held that a prosecution for murder may be sustained against the defendant as a principal when the defendant and a co-felon both shot the victim, but it is not known which of the two actually fired the bullet that killed the victim. The courts in *Strickler v. Commonwealth*, 404 S.E.2d 227 (Va. 1991), and *People v. Vernon*, 152 Cal.Rptr. 765 (1979), held that when two or more persons take direct part in a fatal beating of the victim, each participant is a principal for capital murder prosecution. In *Purifoy v. State*, 822 S.W.2d 374 (Ark. 1991), it was held that even though a co-felon fired the shot which killed the victim that would not preclude the defendant's liability as a principal for murder, when the defendant and co-felon both had guns and both fired at the victim. The court in *Darden v. State*, 758 S.W.2d 264 (Tex.Cr.App. 1988), ruled that when a defendant intentionally took arms to a police station to engage in a gun battle with the police, he may be prosecuted for capital murder as a principal even though the officer killed was shot by a fellow officer. It was held in *State v. Forrest*, 356 So.2d 945 (La. 1978), and *State v. Thomas*, 595 S.W.2d 325 (Mo. App. 1980), that a defendant who drives a co-felon and the victim to the murder scene and gives the co-felon the weapon used to kill the victim is a principal in the first degree to murder.

Principal in the Second Degree

To be a principal in the second degree, an actor must (1) be present at the scene of the crime and (2) aid, abet, counsel, command, or encourage the commission of the offense.[7] The general rule is that one who aids and abets murder with the intent to assist the murder to completion may be prosecuted for capital murder.[8] An aider and abettor can be said to share the principal's intent to murder when he or she knowingly intends to assist the principal in the commission of a crime and the murder is a natural and probable consequence of that crime.[9] The Constitution does not prohibit jurisdictions from making aiders and abettors equally responsible, as a matter of law, with principals.[10]

A defendant may be convicted of first-degree murder premised on aiding and abetting, even though no other party was convicted of first-degree murder.[11] To establish a murder charge premised on aiding and abetting, the prosecutor must show that (1) the defendant knew the crime was occurring,

(2) the defendant associated himself or herself with the effort to murder, (3) the defendant took part in the murder as something he or she wished to bring about, and (4) the defendant committed some overt act to make the murder a success.[12]

To prosecute a defendant for murder as a principal in the second degree, it is not necessary to prove an agreement between the defendant and another in advance of the criminal act or even at the time of the act.[13] A defendant may be found constructively present and acting in concert with the principal murderer if the defendant shared the criminal intent with the principal and the principal knew it.[14] The fact that a prosecutor cannot prove with certainty who pulled the trigger of the gun that killed the victim will not preclude prosecution of a defendant as an aider and abettor.[15] While the mere presence of a defendant at a murder scene, without more, is insufficient to deem him or her a party to crime, when combined with other incriminating evidence, presence at the murder scene may be sufficient to sustain a murder prosecution.[16]

Where the evidence does not establish the defendant was present at the time of the killing and aided and abetted the crime, a charge of being a principal in the second degree fails.[17] Liability for a homicide will not attach to a defendant who becomes an aider and abettor to robbery after the victim has already been killed.[18] In *State v. Raines*, 606 A.2d 265 (Md. 1992), it was held that if there was no evidence (1) that the driver of a car knew or believed that the passenger intended to shoot and kill from the car or (2) that the driver himself acted with such intent or (3) that the victim was shot in furtherance of the commission of a criminal offense which the driver and passenger had undertaken, then the driver could not be convicted of murder as a principal in the second degree. The case of *Rogers v. Commonwealth*, 410 S.E.2d 621 (Va. 1991), held that a principal in the second degree cannot be prosecuted for capital murder when the principal commits capital murder willfully, deliberately, and with premeditation while in the commission of armed robbery or while in the commission of or subsequent to rape.

ACCESSORY BEFORE THE FACT

The general rule is that an accessory before the fact to murder may be prosecuted for murder.[19] To be prosecuted as an accessory before the fact to murder, (1) the defendant must have counseled, procured, commanded, encouraged, or aided the principal in killing the victim, (2) the principal must have murdered the victim, and (3) the defendant must not have been present when the killing occurred.[20]

To successfully prosecute a defendant for murder as an accessory, the prosecutor must show the defendant had the intent to aid the principal and therefore must have intended to commit the offense.[21] A charge of accessory before the fact of murder will be sustained when the defendant counseled, procured, or planned a robbery during the course of which the victim is killed.[22] A defendant may be prosecuted for first-degree murder as an accessory before the fact even though the principal pled guilty to second-degree murder.[23] The mere fact that the defendant was in jail when the murder occurred will not preclude his or her conviction for murder when it is shown that he or she was involved in planning the murder.[24] A person who procures another to commit murder is an accessory before the fact of murder.[25]

ACCESSORY AFTER THE FACT

To sustain a charge of accessory after the fact, the prosecutor must show that (1) the principal committed murder, (2) the defendant aided the principal in evading arrest, punishment, or escape, and (3) the defendant knew that principal committed the murder.[26] An accessory after the fact may not constitutionally be punished with death. However, the common law rule that an accessory after the fact cannot also be a principal in the same crime is inapplicable when the defendant is charged as an accessory after the fact to the murder of one victim and as a principal on a charge of assault with intent to murder a second victim because the two offenses represent separate felonies.[27]

Accomplice Liability

For all practical purposes, accomplice liability is nothing more than a legal phrase that describes the conduct of a principal in the second degree and accessory before the fact without distinguishing presence or absence at the crime scene. As a general matter, a person is liable as an accomplice if he or she provided assistance or encouragement or failed to perform a legal duty with the intent thereby to facilitate or promote the commission of a crime.

A defendant can be an accomplice to murder even though his or her participation in the killing is relatively passive when compared to that of the principal.[28] To hold a defendant liable as an accomplice for a homicide committed by another, the prosecutor need only show that the defendant intended to promote or facilitate a crime, and there is no need to show that the defendant specifically intended to promote or facilitate a murder.[29] A murder prosecution under the accomplice liability theory does not require that the defendant participate in the actual murder.[30]

Where an accomplice purposely aids in the commission of murder, he or she is said to have the same intent as the principal.[31] In determining whether murder is the appropriate charge against an accomplice to a homicide, however, it is necessary to look at his or her state of mind and not only that of the principal.[32] Moreover, under the accomplice liability theory, it is not necessary that the defendant be shown to have the intent to commit murder after deliberation and premeditation; it is enough to establish that the defendant had the intent purposely to promote the commission of murder.[33]

In *State v. Gordon*, 915 S.W.2d 393 (Mo.App. 1996), it was said that proof that a defendant fired the fatal shot which killed the victim is not essential where the defendant is prosecuted under the theory of accomplice liability. The court in *State v. Langford*, 837 P.2d 1037 (Wash.App.Div. 3 1992), held that by assisting in promoting a fist fight between the victim and principal, the defendant could be held liable as an accomplice to murder, even though he alleged not be to aware that the principal was carrying the knife used in the killing. In *State v. Dees*, 916 S.W.2d 287 (Mo.App. 1995), it was said that a defendant who aided and encouraged a co-felon to hire a third party to kill the victim could be held liable for murder, even though she did not personally perform each act constituting the elements of murder.[34]

Theory of Accountability

The theory of accountability is nothing more than a restatement of the liability theories of principal in the second degree and accessory before the fact, without a distinction being made as to presence or absence at the crime scene. To sustain a murder charge under the theory of legal accountability, the prosecutor must show (1) the defendant solicited, aided, abetted, agreed, or attempted to aid another person in planning or committing murder, (2) the defendant's act or conduct occurred before or during the commission of murder, and (3) the defendant acted with concurrent specific intent to promote or facilitate the murder.[35] In *People v. Watts*, 525 N.E.2d 233 (Ill.App. 4 Dist. 1988), it was said that under legal accountability principles it is not necessary that the defendant be shown to have had the specific intent to kill or that he took part in a preconceived plan to commit murder. The court in *People v. Richards*, 413 N.E.2d 5 (Ill.App. 1980), held that when individuals conspire to commit a crime wherein they contemplate violence may be necessary to carry out the plan, all such felons are liable for acts done in furtherance of the plan, so that if death occurs all are liable for murder whether present or not during the commission of the crime.

To sustain a prosecution for murder premised on legal accountability principles, it is not necessary to have a disposition against the principal.[36] The fact that the actual killer of the victim is acquitted will not preclude prosecution of the defendant under the theory of accountability when it is shown the defendant cooperated in planning the felony which resulted in the victim's death and was an active participant in the felony.[37] Liability may attach for murder under the theory of accountability even though the criminal act committed does not result from a preconceived plan if evidence indicates the defendant was involved in the spontaneous act of the group.[38] Mere presence, without more, will not sustain liability under the theory of accountability.[39] However, it was said by the court in *People v. Taylor*, 646 N.E.2d 567 (Ill. 1995), that under the theory of accountability, if a defendant is a passenger in a vehicle and knows that one of its occupants has a weapon and is looking for the victim for the purpose of killing the victim and the defendant remains in the vehicle with such knowledge, as well as remains with the occupants after the killing, such a defendant may be prosecuted for murder even though he or she did not actively participate.

The theory of accountability will sustain a charge of murder when a defendant and a co-felon enter a common design to commit battery and the co-felon kills the victim during the course of battery.[40] The theory of accountability permits a defendant to be convicted under a capital multiple-victim murder statute, regardless of whether the defendant personally killed more than one person.[41] When the defendant knew that a co-felon intended to rob a victim and the defendant acted as a lookout, he or she can be held accountable for intentional murder of the victim.[42] Even though evidence is not definite that a defendant intended for co-felons to kill the victim, clear proof that the defendant played an integral role in the plan to harm the victim by bringing the victim to the co-felons will support a murder charge under the accountability theory.[43]

Felony-Murder

The law of parties and the felony-murder doctrine merge in order to make a defendant liable for the acts of his co-felons. Both doctrines are circumscribed by the limitation that the lethal force act must be (1) in furtherance of the crime, (2) in prosecution of a common design, or (3) an unlawful act the parties set out to accomplish.[44] The Supreme Court's ruling in *Enmund v. Florida*, 458 U.S. 782 (1982) (discussed in Chapter 2), applies only to the penalty phase of a capital prosecution, not the guilt phase; therefore a non-triggerman who is a major participant in the underlying felony may be prosecuted for murder under a felony-murder theory.[45] When a conspiracy is formed to commit a crime and any of the conspirators commits murder in perpetration or attempted perpetration of the crime, all conspirators actually or constructively present, aiding and abetting the actual perpetrators of the crime, may be prosecuted for murder under the felony-murder theory.[46] In order to hold a defendant liable for murder as an aider and abettor in a felony-murder prosecution, the prosecutor must show that the defendant either had the intent to kill or acted with reckless indifference to human life while participating in the underlying felony.[47] Under the felony-murder doctrine, all participants in the underlying crime are regarded as principals, irrespective of whether they can be classified as aiders, abettors, or principals.[48]

Application of the felony-murder rule occurred in the situations that follow. In *State v. Littlejohn*, 459 S.E.2d 629 (N.C. 1995), it was held that when the defendant accompanied his confederate to commit armed robbery, he could be prosecuted for felony-murder even though he opposed killing and was not in the room when the victim was stabbed. The court in *Hagood v. State*, 588 So.2d 526 (Ala.Cr.App. 1991), said that the defendant may be prosecuted for capital murder even though he did not stab the victim if he had the intent to aid in the murder of the victim during the course of robbery. In *State v. Johnson*, 365 So.2d 1267 (La. 1978), the court held that when the defendant is responsible for providing escape from a robbery by accomplices, he may be held liable for a homicide committed during the course of the robbery or attempt of the same. In *Wallace v. Lockart*, 701 F.2d 719 (8th Cir. 1983), the court said that evidence showing the defendant was an accomplice to kidnapping the victim is sufficient to sustain a capital felony-murder prosecution, even though the codefendant actually caused the victim's death.

Common Design Rule

The common design rule (also known as concert of action theory) is merely an adaptation of the felony-murder rule. Under the common design rule, when two or more persons act in concert in the commission of a felony and a victim is killed by one of the felons, that felon's intent is transferred to the other felon(s) as principal(s) in the second degree.[49] The court in *Price v. State*, 362 So.2d 204 (Miss. 1978), addressed the matter by stating that when two or more individuals act in concert, with a common design to commit a crime of violence against another and a homicide is committed by one of them as incident to the execution of the common design, all participants are criminally liable for the homicide. The court in *State v. Blankenship*, 447 S.E.2d 727 (N.C. 1994), however, held that criminal liability for murder under the common design rule will not attach unless the defendant has the requisite specific intent to commit murder.[50]

In general, proof of a common design to commit an unlawful act which results in death may be inferred from circumstances such as: (1) presence at the scene of crime without opposition or disapproval, (2) continued close association with the perpetrator after the criminal act, (3) failure to inform authorities of the incident, or (4) concealment or destruction of evidence after the crime.[51]

Joint Venture Theory

The joint venture theory is nothing more than a version of the felony-murder rule. To convict a defendant for murder under the joint venture theory, the prosecutor must prove (1) the defendant was present at the scene of the crime, (2) the defendant had knowledge another intended to commit a crime, and (3) by agreement the defendant was willing and available to help the confederate if necessary.[52] The theory of joint venture murder requires more than mere knowledge of planned criminal conduct or a failure to take affirmative steps to prevent it; a defendant must intend that the victim be killed or know that there is a substantial likelihood of the victim being killed.[53] A joint venturer may be prosecuted for murder if he or she intended that the victim be killed or knew that there was a substantial likelihood that the victim would be killed.[54] Unlike a felony-murder theory prosecution, the joint venture theory requires that each participant share the requisite *mens rea* or mental state of the principal.[55]

To sustain a charge of felony-murder premised on the joint venture theory, the prosecutor must show (1) the defendant was a joint venturer with another, (2) the defendant intentionally assisted the principal in the underlying felony, (3) the defendant shared the principal's mental state regarding the underlying felony, (4) the homicide occurred in the commission or attempted commission of the underlying felony, and (5) the homicide flowed naturally from carrying out the joint enterprise.[56]

Murder by joint venture does not require that the defendant have an unwavering intent to commit murder; it will suffice if the purpose of murder was a conditional or contingent one.[57] To sustain a joint venture theory of murder in which another person carried and used the weapon, the prosecutor must establish that the defendant knew the other person had the weapon with him.[58] A defendant who takes part in a robbery as a joint venturer is responsible for the natural and probable consequences of the robbery and will not escape liability when a homicide results therefrom by asserting that he or she was unaware that violence was preplanned by his or her accomplices without his or her knowledge.[59] Courts have been firm in holding that a defendant will not escape liability for murder under the joint venture theory when the defendant planned the murder with another but did not actually kill the victim.

PART III

COURT
PROCEEDINGS

CHAPTER 8

Determining Guilt
Before Sentencing Hearing

The Constitution prohibits imposing capital punishment upon any defendant without there first being a lawful determination that he or she is guilty of committing a capital offense. This determination is made at the guilt phase of a capital prosecution. A capital felon's guilt may be determined in one of three ways: (1) verdict by plea, (2) verdict by the court, or (3) verdict by jury. This chapter examines the legal devices that are used to determine whether a defendant has committed a capital offense.

Verdict by Plea

The Fifth Amendment protects a capital felon from being compelled to confess to committing the offense charged against him. Under the Sixth Amendment, a capital offender has the right to have his guilt determined by a jury. Although the constitutional right against self-incrimination and the right to trial by jury are unshakable rights when invoked, a capital felon may constitutionally waive both.

A capital felon who waives the right against self-incrimination and the right to trial by jury usually intends to enter an adverse plea. The Supreme Court has held that in order for a defendant to enter an adverse plea, he or she must knowingly, voluntarily, and intelligently waive the guarantees provided by the Constitution.[1] It is only after the latter three elements have been judicially determined that a trial court may accept an adverse plea from a capital felon.

A capital offender does not have a constitutional right to enter an adverse plea. In the case of *North Carolina v. Alford*, 400 U.S. 25 (1970), the Supreme Court pointed out emphatically that "[a] criminal defendant does not have an absolute right under the Constitution to have his ... plea accepted by the court[.]" The privilege of entering an adverse plea is a matter determined by the laws of each jurisdiction.

Up to now the phrase "adverse plea" has been used without distinguishing its components. There are two types of adverse pleas: a nolo contendere plea and a guilty plea. A few comments about each follows.

NOLO CONTENDERE PLEA

The essence of the plea of nolo contendere is an acceptance of the punishment for an offense without technically resolving the innocence-guilt issue. Six capital punishment jurisdictions statutorily permit a capital offender to enter a plea of nolo contendere.[2]

The purpose of a nolo contendere plea is to shield a capital offender from having a plea of guilty used against him or her in a civil law suit. Unlike a guilty plea, evidence of a nolo contendere plea generally is not admissible against a defendant in a civil suit.

GUILTY PLEA

The plea of guilty ends all discussion concerning who did what, when, where, and how. A capital felon who enters a plea of guilty terminates the adversarial essence of the prosecutorial system. Such a plea, figuratively speaking, places a defendant on his or her knees in supplication for mercy. In the context of a plea of guilty to a capital offense, mercy means a sentence to life imprisonment.

A majority of capital punishment jurisdictions statutorily permit a plea of guilty to a capital offense.[3] Statistics show that while over 90% of all noncapital prosecutions are resolved by pleas of guilty, less than 50% of all capital offense prosecutions terminate by guilty pleas. Obviously this disparity is reflective of the finality incident to a sentence of death.

Verdict by the Court

A capital offender may waive the right to trial by jury but nonetheless have a trial. A trial without a jury is called a bench trial. The factfinder in a bench trial is the presiding judge. All capital punishment jurisdictions afford a capital offender the privilege of waiving the right to trial by jury and having a bench trial instead.[4] Two jurisdictions, Connecticut and Ohio, require that a capital punishment bench trial be presided over by a three-judge panel. In all other jurisdictions, a single judge sits as factfinder in a bench trial.

A bench trial usually will not occur unless three factors are met: (1) the capital felon validly waives his or her right to trial by jury, (2) the prosecutor consents to trial by the bench, and (3) the judge agrees to holding a bench trial.

Verdict by Jury

No capital offender may be prosecuted without a jury unless he or she validly waives the constitutional right to trial by jury. The right to trial by jury may be understood more clearly in the context of petty offenses, that is, offenses that carry a maximum incarceration punishment of six months. In *Baldwin v. New York*, 399 U.S. 66 (1970), and *Codispoti v. Pennsylvania*, 418 U.S. 506 (1974) the Supreme Court held that the Sixth Amendment did not require use of a jury for offenses that carried no more than six months confinement. Any offense carrying a penalty greater than six months incarceration must be presided over by a jury unless a defendant validly waives the right to trial by jury (*Duncan v. Louisiana*, 391 U.S. 145 [1968]).[5] Capital offenses are punishable by life imprisonment or death.

Number of Jurors

All capital punishment jurisdictions require that capital offense juries be composed of 12 members. This privilege is crucial in light of the Supreme Court's pronouncement that the Sixth Amendment does not require use of a 12-person jury in felony prosecutions (*Williams v. Florida*, 399 U.S. 78 [1970]). The Supreme Court has also held, however, that a jury composed of fewer than six persons violates the Constitution (*Ballew v. Georgia*, 435 U.S. 223 [1978]).

Voting Requirement

The Supreme Court has been firm in holding that there is no constitutional right to have a 12-person jury return a unanimous verdict (*Johnson v. Louisiana*, 406 U.S. 356 [1972]). In the case of *Burch v. Louisiana*, 441 U.S. 130 (1979), however, the Court held that the Constitution required verdict unanimity when a six-person jury is used. The majority of capital punishment jurisdictions require a unanimous verdict in capital offense prosecutions.

Death-Qualified Jury

Two unique legal principles have developed and become a part of the process of selecting a petit jury to decide the facts in a capital offense prosecution. The two legal principles in question were developed for the purpose of having a death-qualified jury preside over the trial of a capital punishment prosecution.[6] A death-qualified jury is one that can fairly and impartially hear the evidence of a capital offense prosecution and return a verdict that serves the interests of justice.[7]

The first death-qualified jury principle was developed by the Supreme Court in *Witherspoon v. Illinois*, 391 U.S. 510 (1968), and refined in *Wainwright v. Witt*, 469 U.S. 412 (1985). The *Witherspoon-Wainwright* principle holds that a trial court may exclude from a venire panel any potential juror who has acknowledged that he or she is opposed to the death penalty. The second death-qualified jury principle was announced by the Supreme Court in *Morgan v. Illinois*, 112 S.Ct. 2222 (1992). Under the *Morgan* principle, a trial judge may exclude from the venire panel any potential juror who has made known that he or she would automatically vote for imposition of the death penalty, regardless of the evidence in the case.[8]

CHAPTER 9

Structure and Nature
of Capital Penalty Phase

The intent of this chapter is to provide a review of the structure and nature of a capital penalty phase hearing. The material is presented in three sections. The first section looks at the impact of two Supreme Court cases that changed the structure and nature of capital prosecutions in the nation. In the second section, an examination of the basic structural components of the penalty phase is provided. The third section provides a general review of the evidentiary nature of a penalty phase proceeding.

Impact of Furman and Gregg

Capital punishment was fundamentally altered in the nation as a result of decisions by the Supreme Court in two cases. This section looks at both cases individually.

FURMAN ABOLISHED UNITARY CAPITAL TRIALS

The Supreme Court decision in *Furman v. Georgia*, 408 U.S. 238 (1972), repudiated almost 200 years of American capital punishment jurisprudence.[1] In the final analysis, *Furman* voided and invalidated every capital punishment statute in the nation. The decision itself was a per curiam opinion that consisted of only one paragraph containing six sentences. Never in the history of criminal law have there been six sentences more powerful and revolutionary. *Furman*, in a manner of speaking, woke up and traumatized the nation.

The decision in *Furman* implicated only one capital punishment issue: the constitutionality of the method used by capital punishment jurisdictions to impose the death penalty.[2] *Furman* did not address the issue of whether an offense could have death as a penalty or whether the method of executing the death penalty was valid. *Furman*'s challenge was confined exclusively to the decision-making process that was used to determine who would be sentenced to death and who would be spared death.[3]

Furman concluded that the capital punishment decision-making process used in the nation, which was in substance unitary, violated the Cruel and Unusual Punishment Clause of the Eighth Amendment. This conclusion was narrowly reached by a 5–4 vote.[4]

Factually, *Furman* involved three separate death penalty cases, two from Georgia and one from Texas. Two of the capital felons involved were sentenced to die for committing the crime of rape, and the third defendant was given the death penalty for committing the offense of murder. All three defendants were poor, extremely limited in education, and African-Americans.

The *Furman* decision put an end to the death penalty in the nation. In doing so, the opinion only held that the arbitrary and capricious method by which all capital punishment jurisdictions imposed the death penalty violated the Cruel and Unusual Punishment Clause. As a result of this narrow holding, the door was left open for a rebirth of capital punishment if a method could be found that would impose death in a constitutionally fair and impartial manner.[5]

BIFURCATION UNDER GREGG

Perhaps it was only appropriate that the state of Georgia developed a new method of imposing capital punishment which resurrected the death penalty. Georgia devised a scheme which called for a bifurcation of the guilt and penalty phases of a capital offense prosecution. Under this approach, a capital offender's guilt would first be determined. Once the guilt of a capital felon was determined by the factfinder, a totally separate proceeding would be held wherein aggravating and mitigating circumstances would be presented for consideration by the factfinder in determining whether the death penalty was the appropriate punishment.

Georgia's new bifurcated scheme was challenged in the case of *Gregg v. Georgia*, 428 U.S. 152 (1976). The Supreme Court held in *Gregg* that Georgia's new method of imposing the death penalty passed constitutional muster. With this monumental ruling the death penalty took on new life and once again became an active part of Anglo-American jurisprudence. Georgia's bifurcated death penalty procedure with its guilt phase–penalty phase has become the model for all capital punishment jurisdictions.[6]

Penalty Phase Structure

The decisions of the Supreme Court have fashioned a unique capital punishment penalty phase. This section explores the basic skeleton of the penalty phase.

TIME BETWEEN GUILT PHASE AND PENALTY PHASE

The guilt phase of a capital prosecution can last for several weeks. Following the guilt phase, of course, is the penalty phase. At present no jurisdiction provides by statute for a specific time between the end of the guilt phase proceeding and the start of the penalty phase hearing.[7] As a general matter, a recess occurs between the two phases in order to allow the parties to review their notes and strategies, as well as to allow the factfinder to take a breather.

A recess between the guilt phase and penalty phase is not the equivalent of a continuance. A continuance involves a relatively long period of time. An exceptional and prejudicial circumstance must present itself before a trial court grants a continuance between the two phases. For example, in *State v. Hines*, 919 S.W.2d 573 (Tenn. 1995), the issue of continuance was addressed. The defendant in *Hines* argued on appeal that the trial court abused its discretion in not allowing him a continuance between the two phases. The defendant wanted the continuance in order to arrange for material out-of-state witnesses to appear and testify at the penalty phase hearing. The appellate court rejected the argument that the trial court should have granted a continuance because prior to the guilt phase the trial court had granted the defendant time to have the witnesses appear.

BASIC OUTLINE OF THE PENALTY PHASE

The format for conducting a penalty phase hearing generally follows that of a trial: opening statements, case-in-chief, rebuttal, closing arguments, and charge to the jury. A few remarks regarding each stage in the hearing follows.

Opening statements. The prosecutor and defense counsel are afforded an opportunity to make opening statements to the penalty phase factfinder. The opening statement is a nonargumentative summary presentation of the type of evidence each party intends to present to the factfinder. The prosecutor's opening statement generally is given first.[8] The capital felon will usually give his or her opening statement immediately after the prosecutor concludes. For strategic reasons, however, a capital felon may delay giving his or her opening statement until after the prosecutor's evidence has actually been presented.

Case-in-chief. Once opening statements have been given, the actual evidence of both parties will be presented. This stage is called case-in-chief. Generally the prosecutor will present its case-in-chief first.[9] The prosecutor's case-in-chief will consist of testimonial and physical evidence on the issue of aggravating circumstances. The prosecutor's examination of witnesses that it calls will be through direct examination. What this means is that the questioning must generally be open-ended and not leading. The capital felon will be afforded an opportunity to cross examine all witnesses called by the prosecutor. Leading questions are permitted on cross examination.

At the conclusion of the prosecutor's case-in-chief, the capital felon will be allowed to put on his or her case-in-chief. The evidence presented by the capital felon will consist of testimonial and physical evidence on the issue of mitigating circumstances. The capital felon's questioning of witnesses called by him or her will be through direct examination. The prosecutor will be given an opportunity to cross examine witnesses called by the capital felon.

Rebuttal. In the event that an issue was brought out during the capital felon's case-in-chief that was not addressed during the prosecutor's case-in-chief, the trial court has the discretion to allow the prosecutor to present rebuttal evidence.[10] Rebuttal evidence refers to evidence that is proffered to explain, repel, counteract, or disprove facts given in evidence by the opposing party.[11]

The court in *Johnson v. State*, 660 So.2d 637 (Fla. 1995), noted as a general matter that when a defendant proffers evidence of his or her good character, the prosecutor may rebut such evidence with other character evidence, including collateral crimes that tend to undermine the defendant's character evidence.[12] It was said in *People v. Bounds*, 662 N.E.2d 1168 (Ill. 1995), that a defendant is not denied a fair penalty phase hearing because the prosecutor is permitted to present rebuttal evidence. The court in *State v. Murray*, 906 P.2d 542 (Ariz. 1995), held that a prosecutor may call rebuttal witnesses who did not testify at the guilt phase if such witnesses are timely disclosed to the defendant.

In *State v. Barrett*, 469 S.E.2d 888 (N.C. 1996), it was held that when the defendant's mother testified to his good character, the prosecutor could offer as rebuttal testimony evidence of rumors that the defendant had killed two other people and wounded a third. In *State v. Sepulvado*, 672 So.2d 158 (La. 1996), it was said that when the defendant offered evidence to show that he was a deeply religious man, the prosecutor could rebut the same with evidence concerning details of the defendant's past relationships with women and physical abuse of his stepson. The court in *People v. Medina*, 906 P.2d 2 (Cal. 1995), held that when a defendant proffered evidence that he had a loving relationship with his family, the prosecutor could rebut such testimony with evidence that the defendant had threatened his father when confronted about a stolen truck.

The court in *Greene v. State*, 469 S.E.2d 129 (Ga. 1996), held that when the defendant called a sheriff to testify that he acted as a model prisoner while in jail, the prosecutor was permitted to show in rebuttal that the defendant's model prisoner conduct was merely a ploy to avoid the death penalty. In *Jenkins v. State*, 912 S.W.2d 793 (Tex.Cr.App. 1993), the court held that when a defendant proffers evidence that he would not pose a danger in the future if given a life sentence because drugs would be unavailable to him in prison, the prosecutor may rebut such testimony by calling a prison narcotics investigator to testify to the availability of drugs in prison.

In *State v. Roscoe*, 910 P.2d 635 (Ariz. 1996), the court held that while a prosecutor may offer as rebuttal evidence testimony from the victim's father that focused on the impact of the victim's death, it would be improper rebuttal for the prosecutor to solicit the recommendation for punishment offered by the victim's father. It was said in *People v. Medina*, 906 P.2d 2 (Cal. 1995), that when a defendant proffers evidence that his violent acts began when he was released from prison, it is improper rebuttal for the prosecutor to introduce evidence that the defendant was arrested for violent conduct before he was released from prison.

Closing arguments. At the conclusion of the presentation of all evidence, both sides are given an opportunity to give closing arguments. The purpose of the closing argument is to allow both parties to offer reasons why the factfinder should reject the evidence of the other party. The general rule is that the prosecutor gives his or her closing argument last, but four jurisdictions statutorily require that the capital felon give his or her closing argument last.[13]

Charge to the jury. If a jury presides over the penalty phase, the trial judge will read jury instructions to the jury before it retires to deliberate. The charge to the jury informs it of the law that must be applied to the facts presented during the penalty phase proceeding.

Retrial of a penalty phase proceeding. Not infrequently a capital defendant sentenced to death will have his or her sentence reversed by an appellate court and the case remanded to the trial court solely for a second penalty phase proceeding. Defendants have argued against being subjected to a second penalty phase hearing when the initial penalty phase proceeding is invalidated. In the case of *People v. Davenport*, 906 P.2d 1068 (Cal. 1995), it was pointed out that subjecting a defendant to retrial of the penalty phase hearing does not violate his or her constitutional rights to due process, equal protection, fair trial, or proportional sentencing in view of the fact that a defendant has an opportunity to present a significant portion of his or her guilt phase evidence during the second penalty phase proceeding.

JURY PENALTY PHASE HEARING

The penalty phase of a capital offense prosecution is a distinct, trial-like proceeding that allows aggravating and mitigating factors to be introduced and argued. The arguments presented at the penalty phase may be heard by a jury or the court. The brief remarks here concern issues involving participation by a jury at the penalty phase.

Nature of right to have penalty phase jury. The Constitution guarantees a capital felon the right to trial by jury at the guilt phase of a capital offense prosecution. With that point in mind, it would seem logical that the Constitution would guarantee a capital felon the right to have a jury determine at the penalty phase whether the death penalty should be imposed.[14] The

Constitution is not, however, always interpreted in a logical manner. In several cases, *Walton v. Arizona,* 497 U.S. 639 (1990), *Clemons v. Mississippi,* 494 U.S. 738 (1990), and *Spaziano v. Florida,* 468 U.S. 447 (1984), the Supreme Court has been adamantly consistent in holding that a capital felon does not have a constitutional right to have a jury determine the issues presented at the capital penalty phase. Notwithstanding the Supreme Court's insistence that there is no constitutional right to a capital penalty phase jury, a majority of capital punishment jurisdictions utilize a 12-person jury at the penalty phase.[15]

It was held in *Odle v. Calderon,* 919 F.Supp. 1367 (N.D.Cal. 1996), that there is no constitutional bar to having the jury that presided at the guilt phase also preside at the penalty phase of a capital prosecution.[16] In *United States v. Walker,* 910 F.Supp. 837 (N.D.N.Y. 1995), the court held that a capital felon does not have a right to have a non-death-qualified jury for the guilt phase and a separate death-qualified jury for the penalty phase.

The defendant in *People v. Lucas,* 907 P.2d 373 (Cal. 1995), contended that he was entitled to a separate penalty phase jury because the trial court had informed the guilt phase jury that he would put on mitigating evidence at the penalty phase, when in fact he did not put on any evidence at the penalty phase. The *Lucas* court acknowledged that it may have been error for the trial court to inform the guilt phase jury that the defendant was going to introduce mitigating evidence at the penalty phase, but the error did not warrant a separate penalty phase jury because the trial court purged any prejudice from the error by instructing the jury that the defendant was not obligated to put on mitigating evidence.

Jury unanimity. The Constitution does not require jury unanimity at the guilt phase of a capital prosecution. For the sake of consistency, if nothing else, the Constitution does not require jury unanimity at the penalty phase. In spite of the position of the Constitution, a majority of capital punishment jurisdictions that utilize penalty phase juries statutorily require jury unanimity in the decision to impose the death penalty.[17] One jurisdiction, Alabama, requires that at least 10 jurors must concur in the decision that the death penalty is appropriate. Another jurisdiction, Florida, requires only that a "majority" of jurors agree that the death penalty is appropriate.

Jury deadlock. It is not uncommon for a penalty phase jury to be hopelessly deadlocked, that is, unable to render a verdict based upon the requirements of the jurisdiction. The Supreme Court has not declared that the Constitution requires a particular procedure be used or disposition rendered when a penalty phase jury is deadlocked. The Constitution's silence on this issue means that capital punishment jurisdictions have the discretion to determine this issue as they deem fair.

A majority of capital punishment jurisdictions that utilize penalty phase juries require that a capital felon be sentenced to prison for life by the trial judge if the jury is deadlocked.[18] Alabama and California depart from the above majority position, as shown by the statutes below.

Alabama Code § 13A-5-46(g):

If the jury is unable to reach [a] verdict recommending a sentence ... the trial court may declare a mistrial of the sentence hearing. Such a mistrial shall not affect the conviction. After such a mistrial or mistrials another sentence hearing shall be conducted before another jury, selected according to the laws and rules governing the selection of a jury for the trial of a capital case.

California Penal Code § 190.4(b):

If [the] defendant was convicted by the court sitting without a jury the trier of fact at the penalty hearing shall be a jury[.] If the ... jury ... has been unable to reach a unanimous verdict as to what the penalty shall be, the court shall dismiss the jury and shall order a new jury impaneled[.] If such new jury is unable to reach a unanimous verdict ... the court ... shall either order a new jury or impose a punishment of confinement in state prison for a term of life without the possibility of parole.

Two other jurisdictions do not follow the majority rule on disposition of a capital case when the penalty phase jury is deadlocked. Under Indiana's death penalty statute, the trial judge is required to determine the punishment when a penalty phase jury is deadlocked. The capital offense statutes of Nevada require that a three-judge panel be selected to determine a capital felon's punishment when a penalty phase jury is deadlocked.

Binding/nonbinding jury verdict. The Supreme Court held in the case of *Baldwin v. Alabama*, 472 U.S. 372 (1985), that the Eighth Amendment was not violated by a judge's decision to override an advisory jury recommendation of life imprisonment and impose the death penalty. In the case of *Hildwin v. Florida*, 490 U.S. 638 (1989), the Supreme Court stated that the Sixth Amendment was not violated by the trial court's decision to override an advisory jury recommendation of life imprisonment and impose the death penalty.[19]

The *Baldwin-Hildwin* decisions stand for the following legal principle: There is no constitutional right to have a penalty phase jury return a binding recommendation at the penalty phase. The *Baldwin-Hildwin* principle has created two categories of capital penalty phase jury verdicts: binding and nonbinding.

Notwithstanding the *Baldwin-Hildwin* principle, a majority of capital punishment jurisdictions that utilize penalty phase juries require that judges impose the sentence recommended by the jury.[20] These jurisdictions are called binding jurisdictions. Five jurisdictions utilizing penalty phase juries statutorily permit judges to override the recommendation of the jury.[21] These jurisdictions are called nonbinding jurisdictions.

NONJURY PENALTY PHASE HEARING

It was previously pointed out in this chapter that based upon the Supreme Court's decisions in *Walton v. Arizona, Clemons v. Mississippi*, and *Spaziano v. Florida*, there is no constitutional right to have a jury preside over the penalty phase of a capital prosecution. On the other hand, as was pointed out in *People v. Membro*, 905 P.2d 1305 (Cal. 1995), there is no constitutional right to have a judge act as factfinder in a penalty phase hearing. As will be seen below, however, under certain circumstances a bench penalty phase hearing is a requirement.

Jury prohibited per se. In capital punishment jurisdictions that allow participation of penalty phase juries, a capital felon can waive the jury and have the trial judge preside over the penalty phase. In several jurisdictions the jury waiver privilege is meaningless because participation of the jury is prohibited per se. Under the statutes of four capital punishment jurisdictions, a capital offender cannot have a jury participate at the penalty phase under any circumstance.[22] These jurisdictions adhere to common law principles that vest all sentencing decisions in the trial judge.

Three-judge panel. Nebraska allows a three-judge panel to preside over the penalty phase if the presiding judge makes a request that two additional judges participate in the proceeding. Nevada and Ohio require that a three-judge panel preside over the penalty phase if a capital felon's guilt was determined by a plea or at a bench trial. The death penalty may not be imposed in the three-judge panel jurisdictions unless the judges' verdict is unanimous.

Guilt by plea or bench trial. Six capital punishment jurisdictions which utilize capital penalty phase juries require that the trial judge alone decide a defendant's punishment if his or her guilt was determined by a plea or at a bench trial.[23]

RIGHT TO COUNSEL AT PENALTY PHASE

It was not until the case of *Gideon v. Wainwright*, 372 U.S. 335 (1963), that the Supreme Court held that criminal defendants in all jurisdictions have a Sixth Amendment right to counsel at criminal trials. The right to counsel at trial means that if a defendant cannot afford to retain counsel, the prosecuting jurisdiction must provide an attorney to the defendant. *Gideon*, however, addressed only the guilt phase of a prosecution.

It was not until the case of *Mempa v. Rhay*, 389 U.S. 128 (1967), that the Supreme Court addressed the issue of a defendant's right to counsel during sentencing by the trial judge. (*Mempa* was not decided in the context of bifurcated death penalty proceedings.) In *Mempa* the Court eloquently reasoned that "the necessity for the aid of counsel in marshaling the facts, introducing evidence of mitigating circumstances and in general aiding and assisting the defendant to present his case as to [the] sentence is apparent." The *Mempa* opinion went on to hold that the Sixth Amendment guaranteed a defendant a right to counsel during the sentencing hearing of any criminal prosecution.

Under the *Mempa* precedent, a capital felon has a constitutional right to have an attorney represent him at a capital penalty phase proceeding.[24] This right requires appointment of an attorney for the penalty phase by the prosecuting jurisdiction if the capital felon is indigent.

Appointment of co-counsel. All capital punishment jurisdictions provide trial courts with discretion to appoint co-counsel for indigent capital felons (a few jurisdictions require this by statute).[25] It was pointed out, however, in *Hatch v. Oklahoma*, 58 F.3d 1447 (10th Cir. 1995), and *United States v. Chandler*, 996 F.2d 2083 (11th Cir. 1993), that the Constitution does not require the appointment of more than one attorney for an indigent capital felon. Notwithstanding *Hatch* and *Chandler*, trial courts will in fact appoint co-counsel for an indigent capital felon if the prosecution involves complex factual and legal issues.[26]

Nature of Evidence at Penalty Phase

The common law developed a body of rules that were used to determine the type of facts that could be introduced as evidence at an actual trial. The common law evidence rules served the purpose of reasonably assuring that a defendant's guilt or innocence would be determined fairly and justly. The rules were not developed to give the prosecutor an advantage at trial, nor were they developed to give the defendant a trial advantage. Fundamental fairness and basic justice were the twin engines that drove common law evidence rules.

The common law evidence rules were adopted, developed, and modified by Anglo-American jurisprudence. Presently a majority of jurisdictions have taken the common law evidence rules and, with varying degrees of modification, compiled them into what are known today as rules of evidence. A minority of jurisdictions continue to utilize evidentiary rules that are not in a systemic compilation.

Prior to the Supreme Court's monumental decision in *Furman v. Georgia*, 408 U.S. 238 (1972), the rules of evidence had no real significance outside of the guilt phase of a capital prosecution. This was because the capital sentencing hearing in most jurisdictions involved nothing more than the formality of the trial judge imposing a previously determined sentence. In other words, the pre–*Furman* sentencing hearing was not adversarial. It was because of the nonadversarial nature of the pre–*Furman* sentencing hearing that the rules of evidence had no real application.

Part of the Supreme Court's acceptance of Georgia's penalty phase proceeding in *Gregg v. Georgia*, 428 U.S. 153 (1976), arose from the adversarial nature of the proceeding. As a result of the adversarial nature of the penalty phase, the rules of evidence have now been extended to some degree from the guilt phase to the capital penalty phase. The rules of evidence generally are relaxed at the penalty phase, however, and evidence is admissible if it is relevant and reliable.[27]

Capital punishment jurisdictions are split down the middle on the issue of application of the rules of evidence at capital penalty phase proceedings.[28] Half of the jurisdictions do not apply the rules of evidence (at least by statute) to the penalty phase.[29] The remaining half have addressed the issue in three different ways. First, in eight jurisdictions the rules of evidence apply only against the prosecutor.[30] In these jurisdictions the defendant can introduce any evidence, but the prosecutor's evidence must comply with the rules of evidence. Second, two jurisdictions apply the rules of evidence to both the defendant and prosecutor.[31] Finally, in ten jurisdictions the prosecutor is prohibited from introducing evidence that was obtained in violation of the federal or respective state constitution.[32]

PHYSICAL EVIDENCE

For purposes here, physical evidence is limited to documents and photographs. Examples of decisional law on the admissibility of such evidence follows.

Documentary evidence. In *Barbour v. State*, 673 So.2d 461 (Ala.Cr.App. 1994), the appellate court sustained the trial court's exclusion of a letter proffered by the defendant at the penalty phase. The letter was written by the murder victim's brother and requested that the defendant be sentenced to life imprisonment instead of death. In *Grandison v. State*, 670 A.2d 398 (Md. 1995), it was held that a trial court may exclude court docket entries and an indictment against a co-felon involving an unrelated crime that was proffered by the defendant as mitigating evidence because such evidence had no relevancy and did not concern the defendant's character or background or the circumstances of his offense.

In *Ballenger v. State*, 667 So.2d 1242 (Miss. 1995), the appellate court held that the trial court could exclude as irrelevant a psychological report alleging that it was probable that a confederate, rather than the defendant, masterminded the plan in which the victim was killed. In *Johnson v. State*, 660 So.2d 637 (Fla. 1995), the court upheld exclusion of medical records pertaining to the defendant's psychological problems on the grounds that the records were not authenticated, were incomplete, and required interpretation to be understood by the factfinder. The court in *McKenna v. McDaniel*, 65 F.3d 1483 (9th Cir. 1995), held that excluding defendant's autobiography from evidence did not violate his constitutional right to individualized sentencing because witnesses testified as to the substance of the facts contained in the autobiography, thereby making the autobiography cumulative evidence.

Photographic evidence. In *State v. Williams*, 468 S.E.2d 626 (S.C. 1996) the appellate court held that in determining whether to admit photographs of a murder victim's body, a trial court should perform a balancing test to ascertain the prejudicial effect of the pictures against their probative value, with an understanding that probative value has a greater scope at the penalty phase than at the guilt phase. In *Cargle v. State*, 909 P.2d 806 (Okl.Cr. 1995), it was held that a photograph showing the victim holding one of his art works was not admissible, though arguably relevant, because its probative value was substantially outweighed by its prejudicial effect. The back of the photograph had the victim's date of birth and death inscribed on it.[33]

The appellate court in *Pennington v. State*, 913 P.2d 1356 (Okl.Cr. 1995), held that the trial court properly excluded as irrelevant mitigating evidence the defendant's proffer of a photograph of himself while in military uniform. In *Johnson v. State*, 660 So.2d 637 (Fla. 1995), it was said that the trial court properly excluded as mitigating evidence a photograph of the defendant's stillborn daughter because the photograph was of little relevance, had the potential to disturb the jury unduly, and was cumulative in light of the fact that the jury was told of the photograph's existence. In *Cargle v. State*, 909 P.2d 806 (Okl.Cr. 1995), the court held that for the purpose of showing victim impact evidence by the prosecutor, a photograph of two murder victims was irrelevant and inadmissible because it did not show financial, psychological, or physical impact of the deaths on the family or any particular information about the victims.

Video recording. In *Cave v. State*, 660 So.2d 705 (Fla. 1995), it was held that a video recording which dramatized the route taken by the defendant when the victim was kidnapped and the location where the victim was killed was irrelevant, cumulative, and unduly prejudicial because the defendant's guilt was unquestioned and witnesses had testified to the distance between the scene of the abduction and murder, as well as the time it took to travel the distance. In *Whittlesey v. State*, however, 665 A.2d 223 (Md. 1995), it was said that the trial court properly admitted a video recording of the murder victim playing a piano because this evidence provided relevant information not already in evidence such as the victim's appearance near the time of death and the victim's skill at playing the piano.

TESTIMONIAL EVIDENCE

It was articulated in *People v. McDonald*, 660 N.E.2d 832 (Ill. 1995), that only evidence having a direct impact on statutory prerequisites for imposing the death penalty should be admitted at the penalty phase. In *Commonwealth v. Stevens*, 670 A.2d 623 (Pa. 1996), it was said that testimony regarding one victim's status as an off-duty police officer and a pathologist's testimony regarding his examination of all the victims and medical conclusions were admissible because the evidentiary value of such evidence (1) clearly outweighed any likelihood of inflaming the minds and passions of the factfinder, (2) assisted the factfinder in understanding the circumstances surrounding the victims' deaths and (3) formed the history and natural development of events for which the defendant was being sentenced. In *State v. Sepulvado*, 672 So.2d 158 (La. 1996), it was said that the general rule which prohibits the prosecutor from initiating character evidence about the defendant at the guilt phase is inapplicable at the penalty phase because the defendant's character is the central focus at the penalty phase.

Hearsay testimony. It was noted in *Whittlesey v. State*, 665 A.2d 223 (Md. 1995), that it would be error for a trial court to rule that all hearsay evidence is inadmissible at the penalty phase. The proper course, instead, is for a trial court to make individual determinations of the reliability of proffered hearsay.

The court in *People v. Moore*, 662 N.E.2d 1215 (Ill. 1996), considered hearsay testimony by a deputy sheriff that a correction officer had told him that the defendant had attacked two correction officers and had threatened a third officer and that other law enforcement officers had informed him that while the defendant was being escorted back to the state for trial he threatened to grab a gun and escape. The court decided this evidence was properly admitted at the penalty phase because such hearsay was sufficiently reliable and the information was compiled for security precautions for those officers who had to guard the defendant. The court in *Moore* also approved of hearsay testimony by police officers that the defendant committed the uncharged crimes of rape and attempted rape on the grounds that the officers had actually investigated the offenses, the victims had immediately reported the incidents, and the officers were thoroughly cross examined.[34]

The court in *Russell v. State*, 670 So.2d 816 (Miss. 1995), held that when prosecution witnesses testify at the guilt phase but are unavailable to testify during the penalty phase, their guilt phase testimony may be introduced into evidence at the penalty phase under the former testimony exception to the hearsay rule.[35] The court in *Miles v. State*, 918 S.W.2d 511 (Tex.Cr.App. 1996), held that statements made by a deceased declarant which implicated the defendant in the murder were not admissible at the penalty phase under the exception to the hearsay rule for statements against penal interest, when the declarant had maintained that he was not a participant in the crime.

CHAPTER 10

Statutory Aggravating Circumstances

This chapter will provide a review of statutory aggravating circumstances. The material on statutory aggravating circumstances is divided initially under three broad headings: (1) criminal offense statutory aggravators, (2) identity of victim statutory aggravators, and (3) other statutory aggravators. Before presenting this material, some preliminary discussion is required in order to place statutory aggravating circumstances in the proper perspective.

The Meaning of Statutory Aggravating Circumstances

The phrase "statutory aggravating circumstances" refers to unique factors created by legislators which, if found to exist by the penalty phase factfinder, will constitutionally permit the death penalty to be imposed upon capital offenders.[1] In the case of *Zant v. Stephens*, 462 U.S. 862 (1983), the Supreme Court held that no capital felon may validly be sentenced to death unless at least one statutory aggravating circumstance is proven against him or her. The statutory aggravating circumstance requirements have replaced the pre–*Furman* arbitrariness in imposing the death penalty and are the sole criteria that permit the death penalty to be imposed.

In the case of *Tuilaepa v. California*, 114 S. Ct. 2630 (1994), the Supreme Court established two conditions that must be satisfied in order for a statutory aggravating circumstance to be constitutionally valid.[2] First, the statutory aggravating circumstance must not be a factor that could be applied to every defendant convicted of murder. For example, the mere fact that a victim died could not be a constitutionally valid statutory aggravating circumstance that allows imposition of the death penalty because in every murder the victim dies. A statutory aggravating circumstance must be some factor that would have application to only a subclass of murders.[3] The second requirement announced

TABLE 10.0
MURDER TOTAL 1990–1995

Year	Total Murders	Year	Total Murders
1990	23,440	1993	24,530
1991	24,700	1994	23,330
1992	23,760	1995	21,600

SOURCE: U.S. Department of Justice, Federal Bureau of Investigation, Uniform Crime Reports 106, Table 7 (1996).

in *Tuilaepa* is that a statutory aggravating circumstance cannot be set out in a manner that makes it vague; it must have a commonsense meaning that a jury would understand.[4]

DISTINGUISHING SPECIAL CIRCUMSTANCES AND STATUTORY AGGRAVATORS

Special circumstances and statutory aggravating circumstances are factors that are created by legislators. The purpose of special circumstances and statutory aggravating circumstances are the same. Both seek to narrow the class of murders subject to death penalty treatment. The function of special circumstances and aggravating circumstances are different. The function of a special circumstance is that of merely triggering death penalty consideration for those whose conduct fall within its sphere of proscriptions. The function of a statutory aggravating circumstance, on the other hand, is that of causing the death penalty to be imposed.

Special circumstances are elements of capital offenses and, as such, are constitutionally required to be proven beyond a reasonable doubt at the guilt phase. If a special circumstance is not so proven at the guilt phase, then a defendant cannot be subject to capital sentencing for a homicide. Statutory aggravating circumstances are not elements of capital offenses. They are not constitutionally required to be proven beyond a reasonable doubt, and the proof of their existence is made at the penalty phase.

Many special circumstances are also duplicated as statutory aggravating circumstances. Most jurisdictions utilize only a few special circumstances that are the same as some of their statutory aggravating circumstances. Four capital punishment jurisdictions, however, duplicate all of their special circumstances as statutory aggravating circumstances.[5] Notwithstanding such duplication, each of the four jurisdictions requires proof of both types of "circumstances" at the guilt phase and penalty phase.

DISTINGUISHING SPECIAL STATUTORY ISSUES
AND STATUTORY AGGRAVATORS

Four capital punishment jurisdictions do not utilize statutory aggravating circumstances.[6] These jurisdictions allow special circumstances to fulfill the constitutional narrowing at the guilt phase. In *Jurek v. Texas*, 428 U.S. 262 (1976), the Supreme Court indicated that the Constitution permitted the narrowing process to occur at the guilt phase and did not require more. Notwithstanding *Jurek*, the four jurisdictions utilize at the penalty phase special statutory issues that must be addressed by the factfinder in deciding whether to impose the death penalty. *Jurek* upheld the constitutionality of using special statutory issues instead of statutory aggravators at the penalty phase.

Although special statutory issues and statutory aggravators serve the same function—they are both used to determine whether to impose the death penalty—they differ in one respect. Special statutory issues are constant for all capital felons in that special statutory issues are a series of questions that are asked in all capital prosecutions. Statutory aggravators vary, however, with the circumstances of each capital homicide. The statute set out below illustrates a penalty phase special statutory issue.

Oregon Revised Statutes § 163.150(1)(b):
(A) Whether the conduct of the defendant that caused the death was committed deliberately and with the reasonable expectation that death of the deceased or another would result;
(B) Whether there is a probability that the defendant would commit criminal acts of violence that would constitute a continuing threat to society;
(C) If raised by the evidence, whether the conduct of the defendant in killing the deceased was unreasonable in response to the provocation, if any, by the deceased; and
(D) Whether the defendant should receive a death sentence.

DISTINGUISHING NON-STATUTORY
AND STATUTORY AGGRAVATORS

Statutory aggravators are a limited number of factors that are created by legislators to narrow the class of persons that may be sentenced to death. The Constitution demands this narrowing process. Oftentimes, however, a murder will involve "aggravating" factors that are not codified. These noncodified aggravators are called non-statutory aggravating circumstances.

The most significant difference between non-statutory and statutory aggravators is that the death penalty cannot be imposed solely upon the basis of a non-statutory aggravator, but it can be imposed upon a finding of a single statutory aggravator. In this context non-statutory aggravators serve only

to support imposing the death penalty upon finding the existence of a statutory aggravator.

Criminal Offense Statutory Aggravators

A majority of capital punishment jurisdictions have special circumstance
offenses that involve the commission of separate felony offenses that accom-
pany murder. As special circumstances, all that such death-eligible offenses
do is trigger consideration of a death penalty prosecution. In this section a
review will be given of felony offenses which constitute statutory aggravating circumstances. As statutory aggravators, these offenses permit the
imposition of the death penalty if they are found to exist by the penalty phase
factfinder.

TABLE 10.1

AGGRAVATING CIRCUMSTANCES OF MURDER 1990–1995

Circumstance	Number of Murder Incidents					
	1990	1991	1992	1993	1994	1995
Robbery	1,871	2,226	2,266	2,305	2,076	1,855
Drug law violation	1,367	1,353	1,302	1,295	1,239	1,010
Sexual offenses	229	199	204	161	133	118
Burglary	202	197	212	179	157	123
Larceny	28	32	41	31	30	23
Vehicle Theft	55	53	66	61	53	49
Arson	152	138	148	154	132	109

SOURCE: U.S. Department of Justice, Federal Bureau of Investigation, Uniform Crime
Reports 21, Table 2.14 (1996).

SEXUAL OFFENSES

Sexual offenses include rape, statutory rape, compelled anal and oral
intercourse, sodomy, and deviant sexual behavior with a minor. In and of themselves, sexual offenses are not offenses that are punishable by death. A majority of capital punishment jurisdictions, however, have made sexual offenses
statutory aggravating circumstances.[7] As statutory aggravating circumstances,
sexual offenses are crimes that may constitutionally cause the death penalty
to be imposed when it is shown that the offense occurred during the course of
a murder.

TABLE 10.2

GENDER OF VICTIM OF

AGGRAVATING CIRCUMSTANCES MURDER 1995

Circumstance	*Total Victims*	*Gender*	
		Male	*Female*
Robbery	1,854	1,570	284
Drug law violation	1,010	883	127
Sexual offense	108	23	95
Burglary	123	63	60
Larceny	23	20	3
Vehicle Theft	49	37	12
Arson	109	56	53

SOURCE: U.S. Department of Justice, Federal Bureau of Investigation, Uniform Crime Reports *21, Table 2.15 (1996).*

ROBBERY

The crime of robbery is nothing more than forcible larceny. It is not necessary that force actually be used to constitute the crime of robbery. Mere display of force such as showing a victim a weapon while his or her property is being taken suffices. Robbery standing alone is not a crime punishable with death. A majority of capital punishment jurisdictions, however, make robbery a statutory aggravating circumstance.[8] In such jurisdictions when robbery and murder combine a defendant may be sentenced to death at the penalty phase.

BURGLARY

Under the common law, burglary was defined as breaking and entering the dwelling of another at night with the intent to commit a felony. The common law definition of burglary makes it an inchoate crime in the sense that completion of the intended felony is not necessary. Although most jurisdictions have modified the common law definition of burglary, its essence is still retained by all jurisdictions—intent to commit a felony. Burglary in and of itself is not an offense that permits the punishment of death, but a majority of capital punishment jurisdictions make burglary a statutory aggravating circumstance.[9] In this posture, burglary can cause the imposition of the death penalty.

KIDNAPPING

The criminal prosecution in the last half of the twentieth century that has elicited the most interest from the general public is the unsuccessful criminal prosecution of O. J. Simpson. The most famous criminal prosecution in the first half of the twentieth century, however, was the 1934 prosecution of the man responsible for kidnapping and murdering the child of Charles Lindbergh. The defendant in that case was Bruno Richard Hauptmann. Hauptmann was executed, not because kidnapping was then considered a statutory aggravating circumstance, but because of the murder itself. Today a majority of capital punishment jurisdictions have made kidnapping a statutory aggravating circumstance.[10] When this statutory aggravator accompanies murder, a capital felon may lawfully be executed in a majority of capital punishment jurisdictions.

ARSON

The crime of arson, like burglary, is an offense that has outgrown its common law roots. Under common law, arson meant merely the intentional burning of an occupied dwelling of another. Modern statutes have expanded this narrow definition to include the burning of one's own dwelling, personal property, commercial buildings, boats, trains, and most other things under the sun. There were several catalysts that brought about the expansion of arson, principal among them was the fact that some people began the practice of purposely insuring a possession with the intent of burning it to collect insurance proceeds.

Arson is not an offense that, without more, would permit the imposition of the death penalty, but arson is a statutory aggravating circumstance in the majority of capital punishment jurisdictions.[11] Thus, this offense can cause the imposition of death when it accompanies murder.

ESCAPE

A person who is incarcerated or is in the custody of a law enforcement officer and flees from such confinement or custody commits the offense of escape. A majority of capital punishment jurisdictions have made this offense a statutory aggravating circumstance when it accompanies murder.[12] The death penalty may be imposed when this statutory aggravator is proven to exist.

OTHER CRIMES

In addition to the criminal offenses highlighted above, capital punishment jurisdictions have other offenses which constitute statutory aggravating

TABLE 10.3
WORKPLACES WITH THE
HIGHEST HOMICIDE RATE 1980–1989

Workplace	Number of Homicides	Rate per 100,000
Taxi establishment	287	26.9
Liquor store	115	8.0
Gas station	304	5.6
Detective service	152	5.0
Justice/public order	640	4.4
Grocery store	806	4.2
Jewelry store	56	4.2
Hotel/motel	153	1.5
Eating/drinking place	734	1.5

SOURCE: U.S. Department of Justice, Office of Justice Programs, Questions and Answers in Lethal and Non-Lethal Violence *100, Table 2 (1993).*

circumstances when accompanied by murder. The other offenses, however, do not enjoy majority capital punishment jurisdiction status. They are minority status statutory aggravating circumstances. The following is a representative sample of such statutory aggravating circumstances.

Train wrecking. The offense of train wrecking is a statutory aggravating circumstance when death results therefrom. Two capital punishment jurisdictions have made this offense a statutory aggravating circumstance.[13]

Carjacking. The crime of carjacking involves forcibly taking a vehicle from its owner or possessor. The crime of carjacking has been elevated to a statutory aggravating circumstance when accompanied by murder. Four capital punishment jurisdictions have made this crime a statutory aggravating circumstance.[14]

Plane hijacking. The crime of plane hijacking has taken on the status of a statutory aggravating circumstance when murder results therefrom. This offense has been made a statutory aggravating circumstance in 10 capital punishment jurisdictions.[15]

Train hijacking. The offense of train hijacking has been made a statutory aggravating circumstance when accompanied by murder. Three capital punishment jurisdictions have made this offense a statutory aggravating circumstance.[16]

Aggravated battery. The crime of aggravated battery is not the same as the crime of battery. Aggravated battery occurs when there is serious injury to a victim. The crime of battery can be a mere touching of a victim.

Aggravated battery has been made a statutory aggravating circumstance when murder occurs. Two capital punishment jurisdictions have made this offense a statutory aggravating circumstance.[17]

Ship hijacking. In former days, ship hijacking went under the name of piracy. As an offense, ship hijacking has been made a statutory aggravating circumstance when accompanied by murder. Two capital punishment jurisdictions have made this offense a statutory aggravating circumstance.[18]

Bus hijacking. The offense of bus hijacking has been made a statutory aggravating circumstance when murder accompanies it. Two capital punishment jurisdictions have made this offense a statutory aggravating circumstance.[19]

Drug trafficking. Although the crime of drug trafficking is a monumental problem in the nation, it does not enjoy majority status as a statutory aggravating circumstance. Only eight capital punishment jurisdictions have made this offense a statutory aggravating circumstance.[20]

Identity of Victim
Statutory Aggravators

In the case of *Brecht v. Abrahamson*, 944 F.2d 1363 (7th Cir. 1991), a federal court of appeals ruled that it was permissible for evidence to be introduced which showed that the murder victim disliked homosexuals and, as a result, the defendant (who was a homosexual) killed the victim. The victim in *Brecht* may be classified as a homophobic and, as such, had a unique identity. While no capital punishment jurisdiction currently makes the murder of a homophobic a statutory aggravating circumstance, the *Brecht* decision is instructive of the compassion a victim's unique identity may engender when it is the motive for murder.

Legislators in capital punishment jurisdictions are not oblivious to the compassionate concerns citizens have when a person is murdered solely because of that person's unique identity. Many capital punishment jurisdictions have responded to this concern by enacting various statutory aggravating circumstances that are based upon a victim's unique identity. This section will examine some of those statutory aggravating circumstances.

Correction Officer

A majority of capital punishment jurisdiction legislators have acknowledged the necessary and dangerous work of correction officers. This recognition is evident in that a majority of capital punishment jurisdictions provide that the murder of a correction officer while he or she is on duty is a statutory aggravating circumstance.[21]

TABLE 10.4
OCCUPATIONS WITH THE
HIGHEST RATE OF HOMICIDE 1980–1989

Occupation	Number of Homicides	Rate per 100,000
Taxi driver/chauffeur	289	15.1
Law enforcement officer	520	9.3
Hotel clerk	40	5.1
Gas station attendant	164	3.5
Security guard	253	3.6
Stock handler/bagger	260	3.1
Store owner/manager	1,065	2.8
Bartender	84	2.1

SOURCE: U.S. Department of Justice, Office of Justice Programs, Questions and Answers in Lethal and Non-Lethal Violence *101, Table 3 (1993).*

LAW ENFORCEMENT OFFICER

The vast majority of capital punishment jurisdictions are sensitive to the vital role the police have in society and the dangerous nature of their work. Consequently, the vast majority of capital punishment jurisdictions have made murdering a police officer, while on duty or off duty, because of his or her work, a statutory aggravating circumstance.[22]

FIREFIGHTER

Firefighters perform a critical service in society. The indispensable role of firefighters has caused nearly a majority of capital punishment jurisdictions to provide that the murder of a firefighter while on duty is a statutory aggravating circumstance.[23]

WITNESS

Crime is successfully prosecuted because of witnesses. A large minority of capital punishment jurisdictions have attempted to protect and encourage witnesses to criminal conduct by making the murder of a witness a statutory aggravating circumstance.[24]

PROSECUTOR

During the criminal prosecution of O. J. Simpson, at least one member of the team of prosecutors, Chris Darden, reported that threats on his life had

Table 10.5
Age of Victim That
Constitutes an Aggravating Circumstance

Age	Number of Jurisdictions	Age	Number of Jurisdictions
5 or younger[27]	1	62 or older[32]	1
11 or younger[28]	8	65 or older[33]	1
13 or younger[29]	1	66 or older[34]	1
14 or younger[30]	2	70 or older[35]	1
16 or younger[31]	1		

been made because of his role in the case. The threats Darden received are the potential companion of every prosecutor in the nation. A significant minority of capital punishment jurisdictions have sought to protect prosecutors from personal attacks attributed to their work.[25] This protection is manifested through statutes that make the murder of a prosecutor a statutory aggravating circumstance.

JUDGE

Judges play a critical role in the prosecution of criminals that exposes them to reprisals by criminals. Nearly a majority of capital punishment jurisdictions have sought to protect judges by making the murder of a judge a statutory aggravating circumstance.[26]

OTHER IDENTITIES

The major players in victim-identity statutory aggravating circumstances are correction officials, police officers, firefighters, witnesses, prosecutors, and judges. All enjoy the distinction of having a majority or near majority of capital punishment jurisdictions recognizing their identities as statutory aggravating circumstances. There are, however, other victim-identity statutory aggravating circumstances, most of which do not enjoy significant recognition by capital punishment jurisdictions.

Age of victim. Seventeen capital punishment jurisdictions provide that the age of a victim of murder is a statutory aggravating circumstance that permits the imposition of the death penalty. There is no unity, however, among the jurisdictions regarding the age which constitutes a statutory aggravating circumstance. Table 10.5 sets out the jurisdictional treatment of age as a statutory aggravating circumstance.

Table 10.6
Age and Gender of Murder Victim 1994

Age of Victim	Total Victims	Gender	
		Male	Female
Under 1	257	150	107
1 to 4	470	263	207
5 to 8	103	46	57
9 to 12	120	60	60
13 to 16	944	770	174
17 to 19	2,307	2,052	255
20 to 24	4,088	3,514	574
25 to 29	3,231	2,626	605
30 to 34	2,917	2,209	708
35 to 39	2,249	1,687	562
40 to 44	1,565	1,236	329
45 to 49	1,007	773	234
50 to 54	680	520	160
55 to 59	444	331	113
60 to 64	342	252	90
65 to 69	284	182	102
70 to 74	244	145	99
75 & over	70	65	5

SOURCE: U.S. Department of Justice, Federal Bureau of Investigation, Uniform Crime Reports *16, Table 2.5 (1995).*

Parole/probation officer. The work of parole and probation officers, while essentially the same, is carried out under different circumstances. Parole officers monitor convicted criminals who have been released from confinement prior to the expiration of their sentence. Probation officers monitor convicted criminals who have had their sentence suspended. Parole and probation officers have the authority to cause their respective parolees and probationers to be incarcerated for violating conditions of release. Seven capital punishment jurisdictions have seen the need for making the murder of a parole or proba-tion officer a statutory aggravating circumstance.[36]

Pregnant woman. Only one capital punishment jurisdiction has made the murder of a pregnant woman a statutory aggravating circumstance.[37]

Juror. In routine criminal prosecutions, the identity of jurors is not kept from the public. In high profile criminal prosecutions, like those of former

Mafia kingpin John Gotti or O. J. Simpson, it may be necessary to keep the identity of jurors from the public—at least until after the verdicts are in. Juror intimidation is always a potential impediment to justice. Seven capital punishment jurisdictions have taken this matter seriously and made the murder of a juror a statutory aggravating circumstance.[38]

Informant. Informants are people who provide information to the police that implicates criminal suspects. Two capital punishment jurisdictions have made the murder of an informant a statutory aggravating circumstance.[39]

Elected official. Elected officials cannot please all constituents on all issues. This fact carries with it the potential for violent retaliation by a disgruntled constituent. Nine capital punishment jurisdictions have expressed sensitivity to the ever-present threat elected officials face by making the murder of an elected official a statutory aggravating circumstance.[40]

Handicapped person. In 1985 religious extremists attacked a cruise ship called the *Achille Lauro* off the Egyptian coast and killed a helpless, wheelchair-bound victim.[41] Three capital punishment jurisdictions have sought to curb violence against handicapped persons by making the murder of a handicapped person a statutory aggravating circumstance.[42]

Race, religion, and nationality. In the case of *Barclay v. Florida*, 463 U.S. 939 (1983), the trial judge considered, as a non-statutory aggravating circumstance, the fact that the murder victim was killed for no other reason than his race. The defendant contested consideration of the victim's race during the penalty phase. The Supreme Court found no constitutional impediment to the trial judge's consideration of this non-statutory aggravating circumstance. Two capital punishment jurisdictions have embraced the *Barclay* ruling by making murder motivated by race, religion, or nationality a statutory aggravating circumstance.[43]

Other Statutory Aggravators

Not all murders occur in the commission of another offense, and not all murder victims have statutorily recognized identities that permit imposition of the death penalty. The fact that a murder may not fit either of these situations does not mean, however, that the death penalty is barred as a form of punishment.

Legislators in all capital punishment jurisdictions have carved out a variety of situations that will allow the death penalty to be imposed even though a particular murder did not occur during the commission of another felony or the victim did not have a statutory identity. The necessity of having to create additional types of statutory aggravating circumstances is in keeping with the constitutional requirement of "justify[ing] the imposition of a more severe sentence on the defendant compared to others found guilty of murder."[44] The statutory aggravating circumstances to follow permit the imposition of the death penalty in jurisdictions that recognize them.

TABLE 10.7
OTHER MURDER CIRCUMSTANCES 1990–1995

| | *Number of Murder Incidents* | | | | |
Circumstance	*1990*	*1991*	*1992*	*1993*	*1994*
Gangland killing	104	206	137	142	111
Juvenile gang killing	679	840	813	1,145	1,157
Institutional killing	16	19	18	15	14
Sniper attack	41	12	33	7	2
Drug induced killing	242	254	253	261	211
Alcohol induced killing	533	500	429	383	316

SOURCE:U.S. Department of Justice, Federal Bureau of Investigation, Uniform Crime Reports *21, Table 2.14 (1995).*

HEINOUS, ATROCIOUS, CRUEL, OR DEPRAVED

Jeffrey Dahmer's method of killing his victims illustrates what is contemplated by the terms *heinous, atrocious, cruel,* and *depraved.* Dahmer's victims were cut into pieces, acid was used to remove skin and some were cannibalized. He clearly exhibited the height of heinous, atrocious, cruel, and depraved behavior. Eighteen capital punishment jurisdictions have responded to Dahmer-type homicides by making murder committed in a heinous, atrocious, cruel, or depraved manner a statutory aggravating circumstance.[45]

PECUNIARY GAIN

During the 1996 drug possession prosecution of professional football player Michael Irvin, authorities learned that a Texas police officer attempted to pay someone to kill Irvin. Fortunately, authorities were able to intervene and prevent the murder-for-hire plot from being executed.

The Irvin affair is instructive on the point that human life is like an item in a department store—a price can be attached to it. The stark reality of this point has not gone unnoticed by legislators. The extreme seriousness and frequency of murder taking place for pecuniary gain has caused all capital punishment jurisdictions except Montana to make murder for pecuniary gain a statutory aggravating circumstance.

MULTIPLE HOMICIDES

A single murder is a tragedy. A defendant who murders more than one person in a single episode or incident compounds the tragedy of murder. Legislators have sought to deter the tragedy of multiple homicides by making such conduct a statutory aggravating circumstance. There are currently 23 capital punishment jurisdictions that make multiple homicides a statutory aggravating circumstance.[46]

GREAT RISK TO OTHERS

The statutory aggravator "great risk to others" seeks to punish with death those who, while committing murder, expose unintended persons to death or great bodily harm. There are currently 26 capital punishment jurisdictions that make murder involving a great risk to others a statutory aggravating circumstance.[47]

IN CUSTODY

Custody refers to confinement in prison or jail, or both, depending upon the jurisdiction. There are currently 28 capital punishment jurisdictions that make murder committed while in custody a statutory aggravating circumstance.[48]

PRIOR FELONY OR HOMICIDE

In an attempt to prevent recidivist conduct, legislators have made murder committed by a defendant who was previously convicted of a serious felony involving violence or a prior homicide a statutory aggravator. There are currently 33 capital punishment jurisdictions that make murder committed by a defendant with a prior felony or homicide conviction a statutory aggravating circumstance.[49]

EXPLOSIVES

The term *explosives* refers to any type of device that causes an incendiary-like explosion. There are currently 13 capital punishment jurisdictions that make murder committed with the use of explosives a statutory aggravating circumstance.[50]

TORTURE

Torture refers to the infliction of great pain and suffering. There are currently 14 capital punishment jurisdictions that make murder that involved torture to the victim a statutory aggravating circumstance.[51]

ADDITIONAL FACTORS

In addition to the above statutory aggravators, capital punishment jurisdictions have created a few other statutory aggravating circumstances that have a minority status. A review of these follows.

Disrupting governmental function. The 1995 Oklahoma bombing incident can be viewed from many perspectives. One of those perspectives includes disruption of a governmental function because the deaths that occurred in the bombing resulted from efforts to disrupt the federal governmental operations that took place in the building that was bombed.

Conduct which seeks to disrupt a governmental function does not have to end in tragic deaths. Each day some patriotic libertarian engages in a form of peaceful conduct that seeks to disrupt a governmental function. Peaceful protest has constitutional backing. The Oklahoma incident does not fall under constitutional protection. Currently, seven capital punishment jurisdictions have decided to make disruption of a governmental function a statutory aggravating circumstance when death results therefrom.[52]

TABLE 10.8

GENDER OF VICTIM OF

OTHER MURDER CIRCUMSTANCES 1994

		Gender	
Circumstance	*Total Victims*	*Male*	*Female*
Gangland killing	111	104	7
Juvenile gang killing	1,157	1,105	52
Institutional killing	14	12	2
Sniper attack	2	1	1
Drug induced killing	211	183	28
Alcohol induced killing	316	281	35

SOURCE: U.S. Department of Justice, Federal Bureau of Investigation, Uniform Crime Reports *21, Table 2.15 (1995).*

Parole or probation. As a fundamental matter, parole is the legal status given to someone who has served time in prison and been released before the full sentence has been served. Probation is the legal status given to someone who has not been sentenced to confinement or has had the sentence to confinement suspended and has not been incarcerated.[53] Parole and probation are privileges bestowed by sovereign jurisdictions upon guilty defendants.

As a result of parole and probation being privileges and not rights, society demands nothing short of model behavior by defendants placed on parole or probation. Two capital punishment jurisdictions have elevated the expectations demanded of parolees and probationers by making murder committed by a person on parole or probation a statutory aggravating circumstance.[54]

It will be noted that in the case of *Lindsey v. Smith*, 820 F.2d 1137 (11th Cir. 1987), the Eleventh Circuit pointed out in dicta that being on parole was a weak factor, standing alone, to permit the imposition of the death penalty. The *Lindsey* opinion has waived a yellow flag of caution by indicating that a sentence of death cannot be grounded solely on a parole or probation statutory aggravating circumstance but probably requires an additional statutory aggravating circumstance in order to pass constitutional muster. The Supreme Court has not addressed this issue. Therefore, as of now, parole or probation may constitutionally stand alone as a statutory aggravating circumstance which causes the death penalty to be imposed.

Authorized release from custody. At first blush, parole and probation may seem to be indistinguishable from authorized release from custody. The three legal concepts, however, are different. Authorized release from custody refers to an inmate who has been allowed to leave confinement for a stated period of time and for a specific reason but must return to confinement according to the terms of release.

An example of authorized release from custody would be an inmate who is allowed to leave confinement during the day to work for a private employer. This is a typically practiced form of release that is called work-release. Another example of authorized release from custody is that of furlough programs. Under a furlough program, an inmate is allowed to leave confinement for a day or two as a result of good behavior while incarcerated. The most famous furloughed inmate in Anglo-American jurisprudence is a Massachusetts inmate named Willie Horton (at last count 198 publications referred to him).

During the 1980s, the governor of Massachusetts granted Willie Horton, who was serving a sentence of life imprisonment for murder, a 48-hour furlough pass. While on furlough, Horton is said to have taken a man and woman hostage and tortured them with a knife before raping the woman. Perhaps in response to this case, four capital punishment jurisdictions have made authorized release from custody a statutory aggravating circumstance.[55]

Unlawfully at liberty. The crime of escape may come to mind when looking at the phrase "unlawfully at liberty," but the two matters are different. "Unlawfully at liberty" can be understood by looking at authorized release from custody. An inmate on authorized release from custody has a specific time at which to report back to confinement. If an inmate does not return to confinement as required by the terms of release, the inmate is then unlawfully at liberty. The issue of escape does not come into play because the inmate was lawfully released from custody. Three capital punishment jurisdictions have made murder committed by an inmate unlawfully at liberty a statutory aggravating circumstance.[56]

Use of assault weapon. One capital punishment jurisdiction currently provides that murder committed with the use of an assault weapon is a statutory aggravating circumstance.[57]

Drive-by-shooting. Five capital punishment jurisdictions provide that murder involving drive-by-shooting is a statutory aggravating circumstance.[58]

Ordering killing. Eight capital punishment jurisdictions provide that murder committed upon the order of another is a statutory aggravating circumstance.[59]

Lying-in-wait. Four capital punishment jurisdictions provide that murder committed while lying-in-wait is a statutory aggravating circumstance.[60]

CHAPTER 11

Mitigating Circumstances

In her concurring opinion in *California v. Brown*, 479 U.S. 538 (1987), Justice O'Connor wrote that "evidence about the defendant's background and character is relevant because of the belief, long held by this society, that defendants who commit criminal acts that are attributable to a disadvantaged background, or to emotional and mental problems, may be less culpable than defendants who have no such excuse." Therefore, she continued, "the sentence imposed at the penalty stage should reflect a reasoned moral response to the defendant's background, character, and crime."

The carefully thought-out words of Justice O'Connor appropriately express the narrow scope of this chapter. The focus here is limited to reviewing issues related to the nature and extent of penalty phase-mitigating circumstances. As a general proposition, mitigating circumstances involve any relevant evidence that may justify imposition of a sentence that is less than the maximum possible sentence. Placed in the context of capital punishment, mitigating circumstances involve any relevant evidence that may justify imposition of a less severe penalty than death.[1]

Distinguishing Mitigating and Aggravating Circumstances

The outcome of a penalty phase proceeding will be death or imprisonment for a capital felon. Determining what this outcome will be turns on the factfinder's interpretation of the mitigating and statutory aggravating circumstances presented by the two actors in the proceeding, the capital felon and the prosecutor.

Box 11.0
Penalty Phase Actors, Evidence, and Consequences

Actor	Evidence	Consequence
Prosecutor	aggravating circumstances	death
Capital felon	mitigating circumstances	imprisonment

115

Statutory aggravating circumstances are the tools of the prosecutor,[2] and mitigating circumstances are the tools of the capital felon. Aggravating circumstances which permit the imposition of the death penalty are required to be placed in statutes. Mitigating circumstances are not required to be enacted into law. The function of statutory aggravating circumstances is that of imposing death on the capital felon. Mitigating circumstances serve the function of placing the capital felon in prison for life.

The underlying rationale for utilizing statutory aggravating circumstances is to narrow the class of capital felons who should receive the death penalty. The narrowing process involves utilizing a small number of factors that have been determined to merit the death penalty whenever any of these factors are present in a murder. The underlying rationale for permitting mitigating circumstances to enter the death penalty equation is that of expanding the class of capital felons who should not be put to death. This expansion process involves the utilization of any relevant factor that tends to justify imprisoning, rather than executing, a capital felon.

Significant Supreme Court Decisions

The subject of mitigating circumstances has generated a great deal of issues and litigation. This section examines several Supreme Court cases that have addressed some of those issues.

THE LOCKETT PRINCIPLES

There is no requirement that mitigating circumstances be enacted into law. This issue was squarely addressed by the Supreme Court in *Lockett v. Ohio*, 438 U.S. 586 (1978). In *Lockett* the state of Ohio had provided for three mitigating circumstances in its death penalty statute. The three mitigating circumstances operated in such a manner as to preclude the use of any other mitigating circumstance. In its initial response to this issue, the Supreme Court made the following observations:

> There is no perfect procedure for deciding in which cases governmental authority should be used to impose death. But a statute that prevents the sentencer in all capital cases from giving independent mitigating weight to aspects of the defendant's character and record and to circumstances of the offense proffered in mitigation creates the risk that the death penalty will be imposed in spite of factors which may call for a less severe penalty.

Mitigating circumstances may be statutory. The inference to be made from the language of the passage quoted above is the first of three principles that came out of *Lockett*. The first principle holds that a death penalty statute may create mitigating circumstances. The importance of this principle is that it fostered two categories of mitigating circumstances: (1) statutory mitigating circumstances and (2) non-statutory mitigating circumstances. A majority of capital punishment jurisdictions have created statutory mitigating circumstances, but, because of *Lockett* such statutory mitigating circumstances coexist with non-statutory mitigating circumstances. From a constitutional standpoint, statutory and non-statutory mitigating circumstances stand on equal footing.

Relevant mitigating circumstances cannot be excluded. In addressing the issue of the limitations imposed by the Ohio death penalty statute in *Lockett*, the Supreme Court held that "[t]he limited range of mitigating circumstances which may be considered by the sentencer under the Ohio statute is incompatible with the Eighth and Fourteenth Amendments."

At first glance the above statement by the Supreme Court could be interpreted to mean that all mitigating circumstances are constitutionally required to be admitted into evidence at the penalty phase, but such an interpretation is incorrect. The second principle coming out of *Lockett* states that a death penalty statute must not preclude consideration of any relevant mitigating circumstances.

Irrelevant mitigating circumstances may be excluded. By holding that the Constitution will not tolerate exclusion of any relevant mitigating circumstances, *Lockett* implicitly approved of excluding irrelevant mitigating circumstances.[3] Therefore the third principle coming out of *Lockett* provides that irrelevant mitigating circumstances may be constitutionally precluded from use at penalty phase proceedings.

The third principle from *Lockett* was operationalized in *Robison v. Maynard*, 943 F.2d 1216 (10th Cir. 1991). In *Robison* the court of appeals upheld exclusion of proffered testimony by the murdered victim's sister. The victim's sister wanted to testify that the defendant should not be sentenced to die. The court of appeals held that such testimony was not a relevant mitigating circumstance and could therefore be excluded.[4]

The mere fact that proffered mitigating circumstances are statutory or non-statutory is of no consequence to the issue of relevancy. Both statutory and non-statutory mitigating circumstances may be excluded from the penalty phase if they are irrelevant.[5] There is no magical formula used to determine when mitigating circumstances are relevant or irrelevant. The issue is determined on a case-by-case basis by the presiding judge.[6]

BOX 11.1
THE LOCKETT PRINCIPLES

1. A death penalty statute may create mitigating circumstances.

2. To meet constitutional requirements, a death penalty statute must not preclude consideration of relevant mitigating circumstances.

3. Irrelevant mitigating circumstances may constitutionally be barred from use at capital penalty phase proceedings.

THE DELO RULE

In the case of *Delo v. Lashley*, 113 S.Ct. 1222 (1993), a 17-year-old defendant beat and stabbed to death his cousin, who was physically handicapped, during a robbery attempt. The defendant was convicted of capital murder by a Missouri jury. At the close of the penalty phase, he asked the court to inform the penalty phase jury that they could consider, as a statutory mitigating circumstance, the fact that he did not have a significant prior criminal history. The court refused to give the instruction because no evidence was proffered on the issue of the defendant's prior criminal history. The defendant was subsequently sentenced to die.

During the course of many appeals, the defendant was able to get a federal court of appeals to set aside the death sentence. The court of appeals did so after interpreting the *Lockett* decision as requiring the trial court to give the requested statutory mitigating circumstance instruction. The state of Missouri appealed the case to the Supreme Court.

The issue confronting the Supreme Court in *Delo* was whether *Lockett* required penalty phase factfinders to be instructed to consider any type of relevant mitigating circumstance, even though evidence was not proffered on it. The Supreme Court responded to the issue raised by *Delo* as follows:

> ...[W]e never have suggested that the Constitution requires a state trial court to instruct the jury on mitigating circumstances in the absence of any supporting evidence.... [T]o comply with due process state courts need give jury instructions in capital cases only if the evidence so warrants.... Nothing in the Constitution obligates state courts to give mitigating circumstance instructions when no evidence is offered to support them.

The above quote articulates the *Delo* rule. It should be understood that the *Delo* rule is not inconsistent with *Lockett*. The decision in *Lockett* prohibits exclusion of any relevant mitigating circumstance. The *Delo* rule merely states that if no evidence is presented on a relevant statutory or non-statutory mitigating circumstance, the trial court does not have to instruct the penalty phase jury to consider what was never offered as evidence.[7]

THE AKE RULE

In the case of *Ake v. Oklahoma*, 470 U.S. 68 (1985), the prosecutor relied on expert testimony from a psychiatrist to establish, as a statutory aggravating circumstance, that the defendant would be dangerous in the future. The defendant was indigent, and as a consequence, he was not able to present mitigating circumstance testimony from an independent psychiatrist. The defendant was eventually sentenced to die.

The defendant in *Ake* appealed his sentence to the Supreme Court. The defendant argued that the Due Process Clause required Oklahoma provide him with a psychiatrist to present mitigating circumstance evidence on the issue of his future dangerousness. The Supreme Court agreed with the defendant, using the following language:

> Without a psychiatrist's assistance, the defendant cannot offer a well-informed expert's opposing view, and thereby loses a significant opportunity to raise in the juror's minds questions about the State's proof of an aggravating factor. In such a circumstance, where the consequence of error is so great, the relevance of responsive psychiatric testimony so evident, and the burden on the state so slim, due process requires access to a psychiatric examination on relevant issues, to the testimony of the psychiatrist, and to assistance in preparation at the sentencing phase.

The *Ake* rule provides that when evidence of psychiatric mitigating circumstances is relevant, an indigent capital felon has a constitutional right to be provided with a psychiatrist by the government to prepare and present such evidence.

THE PENRY RULE

The case of *Penry v. Lynaugh*, 492 U.S. 302 (1989), involved a capital felon who was sentenced to death in a jurisdiction that did not have statutory mitigating circumstances. The defendant, however, was allowed to present non-statutory mitigating circumstances to the penalty phase jury. The mitigating circumstances included testimony about the defendant's mental problems and childhood abuse.

One of the issues that the defendant in *Penry* presented to the Supreme Court concerned an omission in the jurisdiction's death penalty statute. The statute did not indicate that the penalty phase jury had to be instructed on the effect of mitigating circumstances on the decision to impose the death penalty. As a result of this omission, the trial court did not instruct the penalty phase jury that it could refuse to impose the death penalty if the mitigating circumstances were found to justify this outcome.

The problem posed by the lack of such an instruction was that the jury could have interpreted the defendant's mental problem and childhood abuse to mean that he would always be dangerous and therefore should be put to death. The defendant believed that he had a right to have the jury instructed that it had to interpret all of his mitigating circumstances as a justification for a sentence of life imprisonment and not as support for imposing the death penalty. The Supreme Court responded to the issue as follows:

... [P]unishment should be directly related to the personal culpability of the defendant [therefore] the jury must be allowed to consider and give effect to mitigating evidence relevant to a defendant's character or record or the circumstances of the offense. Rather than creating the risk of an unguided emotional response, full consideration of evidence that mitigates against the death penalty is essential if the jury is to be given a reasoned moral response to the defendant's background, character, and crime. In order to ensure reliability in the determination that death is the appropriate punishment in a specific case, the jury must be able to consider and give effect to any mitigating evidence relevant to a defendant's background and character or the circumstances of the crime.

In this case, in the absence of instructions informing the jury that it could consider and give effect to the mitigating evidence of Penry's mental [problem] and abused background by declining to impose the death penalty, we conclude that the jury was not provided with a vehicle for expressing its reasoned moral response to that evidence in rendering its sentencing decision.

The initial interpretation of *Penry* was that it created a rule requiring that special instructions be given to penalty phase juries on the effects of each and every tendered mitigating circumstance.[8] The *Penry* rule was restricted, however, by two later Supreme Court cases.[9] The meaning now given to the *Penry* rule is that when a capital felon proffers a mitigating circumstance which has the potential for being interpreted for or against imposition of the death penalty, a special instruction must be given to the jurors that informs them of the effect they must give such evidence.[10]

Statutory Mitigating Circumstances

All capital punishment jurisdictions, except for seven, have created various statutory mitigating circumstances.[11] The mere fact that mitigating circumstances are embodied in statutes does not mean that they are automatically made a part of a penalty phase proceeding. If a statutory mitigating circumstance is not relevant to the proceeding or no evidence is proffered on it, there is no constitutional requirement for its use. This section sets out the majority of statutory mitigating circumstances.

NO SIGNIFICANT PRIOR CRIMINAL HISTORY

A majority of capital punishment jurisdictions have made "no significant prior criminal record" a statutory mitigating circumstance.[12] Note that by using the word *significant*, this mitigating factor leaves room for a capital felon to have some minor prior brushes with the law.[13]

EXTREME MENTAL OR EMOTIONAL DISTURBANCE

A majority of capital punishment jurisdictions provide that "extreme mental or emotional disturbance" at the time of the commission of murder is a statutory mitigating circumstance.[14] This statutory mitigating circumstance does not refer to or include mental retardation or mental impairment resulting from a foreign substance. Its meaning lies somewhere between mental retardation and mental impairment resulting from a foreign substance. It does not extend to insanity because that is a defense to a prosecution.[15]

Some guidance in fashioning an understanding of this statutory mitigating circumstance was provided by the Kentucky Supreme Court in *McClellan v. Commonwealth*, 715 S.W.2d 464 (Ky. 1986). The *McClellan* court held:

> Extreme emotional disturbance is a temporary state of mind so enraged, inflamed, or disturbed as to overcome one's judgment, and to cause one to act uncontrollably from the impelling force of the extreme emotional disturbance rather than from evil or malicious purposes; it is not a mental disease in itself[.]

The definition provided by *McClellan* raises more questions than it answers but does nail home the point that mental or emotional disturbance is not a mental disease.

VICTIM'S CONSENT

Consent is a universally recognized defense to many crimes, but consent as a defense to a murder prosecution has never been accepted in Anglo-American jurisprudence. Although consent is not recognized as a defense to a murder prosecution, it has taken on a mitigating perspective in the context of a penalty phase proceeding. A majority of capital punishment jurisdictions provide that a victim's consent to being killed or participation in the conduct leading to the murder is a statutory mitigating circumstance.[16]

MINOR PARTICIPATION

For the crime of murder, the degree of involvement by a defendant can be significant in determining punishment. A majority of capital punishment jurisdictions have provided by statute that minor participation in a capital offense is a mitigating circumstance.[17]

EXTREME DURESS

A majority of capital punishment jurisdictions have provided that being under extreme duress or substantial domination of another is a statutory mitigating circumstance that may preclude imposition of the death penalty.[18]

CAPACITY SUBSTANTIALLY IMPAIRED

In the case of *State v. Stuard*, 863 P.2d 881 (Ariz. 1993), the Arizona Supreme Court found that the defendant's mental impairment, which included organic brain damage, dementia, and a low I.Q., established that his "capacity to appreciate the wrongfulness of his conduct or to conform his conduct to the requirements of the law was substantially impaired." Therefore the court determined that it was justified in reducing the defendant's three death sentences to consecutive life terms in prison.

The decision in *Stuard* gave recognition to the following statutory mitigating circumstance: The capacity to appreciate the wrongfulness of one's conduct or to conform one's conduct to the requirements of law was substantially impaired at the time of the offense. This statutory mitigating circumstance has been adopted in the statutes of a majority of capital punishment jurisdictions.[19]

The impairment mitigating circumstance is subject to being interpreted differently by courts. It was pointed out in *State v. Cooey*, 544 N.E.2d 895 (Ohio 1989), that some jurisdictions allow impairment to be triggered by alcohol consumption or drug usage. In *State v. Apelt*, 861 P.2d 654 (Ariz. 1993), however, it was said that other jurisdictions require showing that the impairment was initiated by a mental disease or psychological disorder.

AGE OF CAPITAL FELON

A majority of capital punishment jurisdictions have provided by statute that age is a mitigating circumstance.[20] Four jurisdictions specifically require that a capital felon must be under 18 at the time of the murder in order to invoke the statutory age mitigating circumstance.[21] One formal capital punishment jurisdiction required a capital felon be over 75 years of age at the time of the commission of the crime in order for the statutory age mitigating circumstance to be invoked.[22]

A majority of capital punishment jurisdictions that utilize age as a statutory mitigating circumstance do not specify any specific age. As a practical matter, however, the few "under 18" jurisdictions and the "over 75" former capital punishment jurisdiction probably have the right answer. Juries are more likely than not to give significance to age when it concerns a capital felon who committed a murder when he or she was under 18 or over 75 years of age. This point was alluded to in *State v. Ramseur*, 524 A.2d 188 (N.J. 1987), in which the New Jersey Supreme Court suggested that age should be a mitigating circumstance only when the capital felon is relatively young or relatively old.

TABLE 11.0
AGE AND GENDER OF MURDERERS 1994

Age of	Total	Gender	
Murderer	Murderers	Male	Female
Under 1	—	—	—
1 to 4	—	—	—
5 to 8	1	1	—
9 to 12	38	30	8
13 to 16	1,536	1,435	101
17 to 19	3,366	3,222	144
20 to 24	3,897	3,600	297
25 to 29	2,293	1,985	308
30 to 34	1,679	1,434	245
35 to 39	1,225	1,006	219
40 to 44	827	702	125
45 to 49	555	478	77
50 to 54	302	257	45
55 to 59	176	158	18
60 to 64	129	109	20
65 to 69	93	82	11
70 to 74	65	60	5
75 & over	70	65	5

SOURCE: U.S. Department of Justice, Federal Bureau of Investigation, Uniform Crime Reports *16, Table 2.6 (1995).*

OTHER STATUTORY MITIGATING CIRCUMSTANCES

The preceding statutory mitigating circumstances enjoyed majority consensus. The mitigating circumstances to enjoy minority status are the following.

No reasonable foreseeability. The doctrine of foreseeability is a civil law doctrine that occasionally finds application in criminal law. The foreseeability doctrine states that an actor may not be held liable for his or her conduct in harming another if it was not reasonably foreseeable that his or her conduct would bring about such harm. Three capital punishment jurisdictions have taken the foreseeability doctrine and made it a statutory mitigating circumstance.[23]

Moral justification. Murder committed by a capital felon who believed the killing was morally justified is a statutory mitigating circumstance in six capital punishment jurisdictions.[24]

Cooperation with authorities. Four capital punishment jurisdictions provide by statute that cooperation with authorities is a statutory mitigating circumstance.[25] This mitigating circumstance involves two types of cooperation: (1) cooperation by a capital felon with authorities investigating the murder for which the capital felon was charged and (2) cooperation with authorities concerning a felony offense for which the capital felon was not charged with or suspected of committing.

Many defendants have unsuccessfully challenged this statutory mitigating circumstance as being unconstitutional in that it purportedly "allows for imposition of the death penalty based upon the exercise of the right to remain silent."[26] This is to say that the statutory mitigating circumstance indirectly punishes a capital felon who remains silent and does not cooperate in bringing about his or her own conviction. This situation, it is contended, violates a capital felon's constitutional right to remain silent.

On the other hand, capital felons also demand the right to take advantage of this statutory mitigating circumstance. In the case of *State v. Bacon*, 390 S.E.2d 327 (N.C. 1990), the defendant argued that the trial court committed an error by failing to instruct the penalty phase jury that his cooperation in helping authorities apprehend another capital felon was a statutory mitigating circumstance. The North Carolina Supreme Court agreed with the defendant in *Bacon* and reversed his death sentence.

No future threat. If it is determined at the penalty phase proceeding that a capital felon should not be sentenced to death, then he or she will be sentenced to prison for life. What are the chances that a capital felon sentenced to prison for life will not commit murder while in prison? This question, not answered here, forms the heart of the "no future threat" mitigating circumstance. Three capital punishment jurisdictions have made "no future threat" a statutory mitigating circumstance.[27]

Victim-caused post-traumatic stress syndrome. The second prosecution of the Menendez brothers by the state of California ended in 1996. The defendants were found guilty of two counts of first-degree murder in connection with the death of their parents. The penalty phase jury in the case found sufficient mitigating circumstances to spare the defendants from the death penalty. One of the underlying theories offered as an explanation for the defendants' actions in killing their parents was that their parents inflicted extreme physical and emotional abuse on the defendants throughout their upbringing. A clinical consequence of extreme physical and emotional abuse is "post-traumatic stress syndrome." While the defendants may not have used the clinical phrase post-traumatic stress syndrome in arguing to the penalty phase jury, many of their allegations fall under the phrase.

Post-traumatic stress syndrome describes a state of mind that is disoriented because of some extreme emotional experience.[28] Clinical studies have revealed that people who acquire post-traumatic stress syndrome because of conduct by another occasionally strike back at the person who caused the syndrome. One capital punishment jurisdiction has recognized the latter fact and provided by statute that victim-caused post-traumatic stress syndrome is a statutory mitigating circumstance.[29]

Another proximate cause. One capital punishment jurisdiction provides that "another proximate cause" of death is a statutory mitigating circumstance.[30] This mitigating circumstance means that some other factor had a role in causing the victim's death.

War-caused post-traumatic stress syndrome. Every war produces soldiers who are never able to readjust to the society they fought to protect. Mental health professionals have wrestled with trying to understand and treat the psychiatric damage war inflicts on many soldiers. One result of their efforts has been recognizing and diagnosing certain conduct as post-traumatic stress syndrome. As previously mentioned, post-traumatic stress syndrome describes a state of mind that is disoriented because of some extreme emotional experience. In the present context, the agent that triggers the syndrome is war. One former capital punishment jurisdiction had provided that war-caused post-traumatic stress syndrome was a statutory mitigating circumstance.[31]

Codefendant spared death penalty. It is not unusual for equally culpable codefendants to receive different sentences for the same offense. This situation occurs most often when one defendant agrees to testify against the codefendant. This situation can result in a capital felon being sentenced to life in prison, while his or her co-felon is sentenced to death. Two capital punishment jurisdictions have made "codefendant spared death penalty" a statutory mitigating circumstance.[32]

Mentally retarded. Anglo-American jurisprudence distinguishes insanity from mental retardation. It was noted by the Florida Supreme Court in *Campbell v. State*, 571 So.2d 415 (Fla. 1990), that even though a guilt phase jury decides a capital felon is sane, this does not preclude the penalty phase jury from considering mitigating circumstances related to a mental defect that falls short of insanity.[33] Mental retardation falls short of insanity, and as a consequence, three capital punishment jurisdictions provide that mental retardation is a statutory mitigating circumstance.[34]

CHAPTER 12

Penalty Phase
Burden of Proof

Statutory aggravating circumstances permit the death penalty to be imposed. Mitigating circumstances may cause the death penalty not to be imposed. Three extremely critical issues related to the interplay of mitigating and statutory aggravating circumstances are (1) what level of proof is needed to establish that mitigating and statutory aggravating circumstances actually exist, (2) what process is used to compare proven mitigating and statutory aggravating circumstances, and (3) what process is used to determine the result that comes out of comparing proven mitigating and statutory aggravating circumstances. Each of these issues will be discussed in this chapter.

The Meaning of Burden of Proof

The doctrine of burden of proof is concerned with the degree of evidence that the law requires to be produced in order to persuade the factfinder of the truth of an allegation. If proffered evidence does not rise to the level required by the law, then the burden has not been sustained and the allegation is deemed not proven. Burden of proof, as a general proposition, means having the obligation of proffering a specific level of evidence to persuade a factfinder of the truth of an allegation.

The doctrine of burden of proof governs the determination of whether mitigating or statutory aggravating circumstances actually exist. And to a large degree, burden of proof determines the process for comparing mitigating and statutory aggravating circumstances, as well as the process used in reaching a result from such a comparison.

Proving Aggravating Circumstances Exist[1]

In the case of *Woratzeck v. Lewis*, 863 F.Supp. 1079 (D.Ariz. 1994), the federal District Court of Arizona enumerated three key points regarding statutory aggravating circumstances. First, the court pointed out that "[a]n aggravating factor in the penalty phase of a capital proceeding is not an element of the offense." Second, the court pointed out that "the federal constitution does not require that aggravating factors in a capital sentencing proceeding be proven beyond a reasonable doubt." The final point made by *Woratzeck* is that "the Supreme Court ... has [not] determined what burden of proof must be satisfied when proving the existence of aggravating factors."

Whenever the Constitution is deemed silent on an issue, jurisdictions are generally free to address the matter as they deem appropriate. Capital punishment jurisdictions have thus responded to the Constitution's silence on the standard of proof needed to establish the existence of statutory aggravating circumstances. The vast majority of capital punishment jurisdictions demand by statute that the existence of statutory aggravating circumstances be proven beyond a reasonable doubt.[2]

One capital punishment jurisdiction, California, does not require that statutory aggravating circumstances be proven beyond a reasonable doubt. California does, however, require a heightened standard of proof for "other crimes" that are used as statutory aggravating circumstances.[3] Excluding California's heightened standard of proof for other crimes, the state does not statutorily impose any standard of proof on establishing the existence of statutory aggravating circumstances. The factfinder is instructed merely to "consider" evidence submitted to show statutory aggravating circumstances exist.[4]

Proving Mitigating Circumstances Exist

The Supreme Court held in *Walton v. Arizona*, 497 U.S. 639 (1990), that "a defendant's constitutional rights are not violated by placing on him the burden of proving mitigating circumstances sufficiently substantial to call for leniency."

The potential harshness of imposing a burden of persuasion on capital felons was ameliorated by the Supreme Court's rulings in *Mills v. Maryland*, 486 U.S. 367 (1988), and *McKoy v. North Carolina*, 494 U.S. 433 (1990). In both *Mills* and *McKoy*, death penalty statutes required penalty phase juries to agree unanimously that a proffered mitigating circumstance was shown to exist.[5] In both cases the Supreme Court held that requiring unanimity on the existence of mitigating circumstances would result in juries not considering relevant mitigating circumstances if just one juror dissented. This situation would conjure up an indirect violation of the requirement in *Lockett v. Ohio*, 438 U.S. 586 (1978), that all relevant mitigating circumstance evidence be allowed into evidence at the penalty phase. To avoid such a violation, *Mills* and *McKoy* held that requiring unanimity on the determination of whether a mitigating circumstance existed was unconstitutional. Under *Mills* and *McKoy*, if only one penalty phase juror finds that a capital felon carried his or her burden of persuasion on the existence of a mitigating circumstance, then the circumstance is deemed proven.

BEYOND A REASONABLE DOUBT JURISDICTIONS

Although *Walton* approved of placing the burden of persuasion on capital felons to prove the existence of mitigating circumstances, the opinion did not indicate what standard of proof could be imposed and what, if any, standard of proof could not be imposed. This issue looms with some degree of significance in light of *Leland v. Oregon*, 343 U.S. 790 (1952).[6]

In *Leland* the Supreme Court approved of Oregon's requirement that defendants prove the affirmative defense of insanity beyond a reasonable doubt. The *Leland* precedent does not sit well for capital felons in an era of "get tough on crime." At present, however, no capital punishment jurisdiction requires that capital felons prove the existence of mitigating circumstances beyond a reasonable doubt. As a precedent, *Leland* would permit such a standard.

PREPONDERANCE OF EVIDENCE JURISDICTIONS

Nine capital punishment jurisdictions follow *Walton* and require by statute that capital felons prove the existence of mitigating circumstances by a preponderance of evidence.[7]

RAISING THE ISSUE JURISDICTIONS

In the case of *State v. Sivak*, 806 P.2d 413 (Idaho 1990), the Idaho Supreme Court held that "[t]he defendant's burden is merely to raise, in the aggravation-mitigation hearing, any factors which might possibly tend to mitigate his culpability for the offense." The holding in *Sivak* that the capital felon does not bear the burden of persuasion on the existence of mitigating circumstances is in total harmony with the requirement of *Lockett* that all relevant mitigating evidence be allowed into evidence at the penalty phase. *Sivak* recognizes the finality of the execution of the death penalty and bends over backwards to enable a capital felon to plead for mercy.

The statutes of a majority of capital punishment jurisdictions do not provide any standard of proof for establishing the existence of mitigating circumstances.[8] This statutory silence means that capital felons merely have to raise the issue of mitigating circumstances, that is, present some evidence on the issue. Only one jurisdiction, Colorado, explicitly provides by statute that a capital felon merely has to raise the issue of mitigating circumstances.

BURDEN PLACED ON PROSECUTOR

One capital punishment jurisdiction provides by statute that the prosecutor must disprove the existence of mitigating circumstances by a preponderance of evidence.[9] The fact that only one jurisdiction requires that the prosecutor negate the existence of mitigating circumstances indicates the harshness of this requirement.

Weighing Jurisdictions

Determining the existence of mitigating and statutory aggravating circumstances does not end the burden of proof process. Once the existence hurdle is overcome, a second process is triggered: mitigating and statutory aggravating circumstances must be compared with each other. The comparison process is carried out in one of two manners: (1) weighing or (2) nonweighing. This section will look at the weighing process and jurisdictions that utilize it.[10]

THE NATURE OF THE WEIGHING PROCESS

The Utah Supreme Court described the weighing process in *State v. Wood*, 648 P.2d 71 (Utah 1981), as follows:

> [This] standard[] require[s] that the sentencing body compare the totality of the mitigating against the totality of the aggravating factors, not in terms of the relative numbers of the aggravating and the mitigating factors, but in terms of their respective substantiality and persuasiveness. Basically, what the sentencing authority must decide is how ... persuasive the totality of the mitigating factors are when compared against the totality of the aggravating factors. The sentencing body [is] making the judgment that aggravating [or mitigating] factors "outweigh," or are more [persuasive] than, the mitigating [or aggravating] factors[.]

Wood points out that the weighing process does not involve determining if more mitigating circumstances exist than statutory aggravating circumstances. Mere tallying is not the purpose of the weighing process. It matters not, for example, that five statutory aggravating circumstances were proven to exist but only one mitigating circumstance is found to exist. The factfinder could still determine that the mitigating circumstance outweighed the five statutory aggravating circumstances.

The Supreme Court noted in *Harris v. Alabama*, 115 S.Ct. 1031 (1995), that no "specific method for balancing mitigating and aggravating factors in a capital sentencing proceeding is constitutionally required." The "balancing" referred to in *Harris* is the weighing process. The result of the *Harris* pronouncement is that capital punishment jurisdictions may devise weighing processes as they see fit.[11] This discretion has led to the development of two classes of weighing jurisdictions: (1) no standard of proof jurisdictions and (2) standard of proof jurisdictions. A separate discussion of both follows.

NO STANDARD OF PROOF JURISDICTIONS

There are two types of weighing jurisdictions that do not impose a standard of proof on the weighing process. Each type is set out separately below.

Aggravating must outweigh mitigating. Statutes in nine capital punishment jurisdictions require that statutory aggravating circumstances outweigh mitigating circumstances.[12] Two important consequences flow from this particular weighing process.

First, under this process the prosecutor has the burden of showing that statutory aggravating circumstances are more creditable than mitigating circumstances. This situation is favorable to the capital felon.

Second, under this weighing process no standard of proof is imposed on the prosecutor. That is, in weighing mitigating and statutory aggravating circumstances, the factfinder is free to use its own judgment as to why statutory aggravating circumstances appear more creditable than mitigating circumstances.

Mitigating must outweigh aggravating. Twelve capital punishment jurisdictions require that mitigating circumstances outweigh statutory aggravating circumstances.[13] Under this process the capital felon is given the burden of establishing that mitigating circumstances are more creditable than statutory aggravating circumstances. This situation is favorable to the prosecutor.

The burden on the capital felon under this weighing process is lessened by the fact that no specific standard of proof is imposed upon the capital felon. The factfinder uses its own judgment in determining why more credibility should be given to mitigating circumstances.

STANDARD OF PROOF IMPOSED

There are two types of weighing jurisdictions that impose a standard of proof on the weighing process. Each type is reviewed separately.

Aggravating outweighs by a preponderance of evidence. In two capital punishment jurisdictions, statutory aggravating circumstances are required to outweigh mitigating circumstances by a preponderance of evidence.[14] These jurisdictions impose the burden of proof on the prosecutor. More significantly, the prosecutor is required to persuade the factfinder by a preponderance of evidence that the statutory aggravating circumstances outweigh the mitigating circumstances. The standard of proof imposed on the prosecutor makes it more difficult to obtain a sentence of death.

Aggravating outweighs beyond a reasonable doubt. The final weighing process is extremely formidable. This process demands that statutory aggravating circumstances outweigh mitigating circumstances beyond a reasonable doubt. Six capital punishment jurisdictions use this weighing process.[15] Under this process the prosecutor is strapped with the burden of proof. The prosecutor must persuade the factfinder beyond a reasonable doubt that the statutory aggravating circumstances outweigh the mitigating circumstances. This situation is favorable to the capital felon.

Non-Weighing Jurisdictions

The South Carolina Supreme Court held in *State v. Bellamy*, 359 S.E.2d 63 (S.C. 1987), that the penalty phase jury should not be instructed to weigh statutory aggravating circumstances against mitigating circumstances. Instead, the jury had to be instructed to merely consider the mitigating and statutory aggravating circumstances. The holding in *Bellamy* was in accord with a ruling by the Supreme Court in *Zant v. Stephens*, 462 U.S. 862 (1983), that the Constitution does not require weighing mitigating and statutory aggravating circumstances. The decision in *Zant* fostered what are called non-weighing capital punishment jurisdictions.[16] There are currently nine non-weighing capital punishment jurisdictions.[17]

In non-weighing jurisdictions, the factfinder is not instructed or guided on how to compare mitigating and statutory aggravating circumstances. As explained in *Bellamy*, the factfinder in a non-weighing jurisdiction is instructed merely to consider the proffered circumstances for sufficiency. The non-weighing process has developed along three different lines, which will be discussed separately below.

DETERMINE WHETHER MITIGATING IS SUFFICIENT

Seven capital punishment jurisdictions require nothing more than that the penalty phase factfinder determine whether sufficient mitigating circumstances exist to warrant leniency.[18] The method for making this "sufficiency determination" is left up to the factfinder. Moreover, this particular non-weighing process does not have a standard of proof for measuring sufficiency. The factfinder is allowed to determine for itself what constitutes sufficiency. Finally, the burden of proving sufficiency in these jurisdictions is on the capital felon.

Mitigating Not Sufficient Beyond a Reasonable Doubt

Under this non-weighing process, the factfinder must determine whether sufficient mitigating circumstances do not exist beyond a reasonable doubt. One capital punishment jurisdiction utilizes this process.[19]

Two matters distinguish this particular non-weighing process. First, in making its sufficiency determination, the factfinder is provided with a standard of proof for measuring sufficiency. The beyond a reasonable doubt standard of proof is used. Second, the burden of proof is placed on the prosecutor. The prosecutor must persuade the factfinder that mitigating circumstances are not sufficient beyond a reasonable doubt.

Determine If Mitigating Exist

This non-weighing process distinguishes itself from the other non-weighing processes in that it is a "pure" non-weighing process. The unrestricted nature of the previous two non-weighing processes actually allows weighing to occur if the factfinder so chooses. However, under the non-weighing process being considered now, weighing is absolutely impossible. This process requires only that the factfinder determine if at least one mitigating circumstance was proven to exist. Nothing else is required under this process. Not surprisingly, only one capital punishment jurisdiction utilizes this non-weighing process.[20]

Consequences of Weighing and Non-Weighing

The previous sections were concerned with how mitigating and statutory aggravating circumstances are compared to determine which "outweighed" or was more "sufficient" than the other. This section looks at what happens once a weighing or sufficiency determination has been made that is favorable to the prosecutor.[21]

In *Boyde v. California*, 494 U.S. 370 (1990), the Supreme Court held that there was no constitutional requirement that a penalty phase jury must be instructed that it can decline to impose the death penalty, even if it decides that statutory aggravating circumstances outweighs mitigating circumstances. The *Boyde* holding has been interpreted to mean that once a weighing or sufficiency determination has been made that is favorable to the prosecutor, the Constitution permits the death penalty to be imposed. Nothing further is constitutionally required. The *Boyde* decision has promoted two types of jurisdictions: (1) death automatic jurisdictions and (2) death discretionary jurisdictions. Both are presented below.

DEATH AUTOMATIC JURISDICTIONS

A majority of all capital punishment jurisdictions require that death must be imposed once a weighing or sufficiency determination is made that is favorable to the prosecutor. These jurisdictions are broken down into weighing and non-weighing jurisdictions and discussed below.

Weighing jurisdictions that require death. There are 17 weighing capital punishment jurisdictions that require the death penalty be imposed if the weighing process is favorable to the prosecutor.[22] What this means, of course, is that the factfinder is not given any discretion once it plugs in the weighing formula and makes a determination that is favorable to the prosecutor. The capital felon in *Boyde* contended that this lack of factfinder discretion was cruel and unusual punishment. The Supreme Court rejected the argument.

Non-weighing jurisdictions that require death. In three non-weighing jurisdictions, no discretion is given to the factfinder once a pro-prosecutor determination is made.[23] The death penalty must be imposed once a sufficiency determination is made that is favorable to the prosecutor.

DEATH DISCRETIONARY JURISDICTIONS

Notwithstanding a weighing or sufficiency determination that is favorable to the prosecutor, a large minority of capital punishment jurisdictions provide discretion to the factfinder. The factfinder can refuse to impose the death penalty even though the weighing or sufficiency determination was favorable to the prosecutor. The jurisdictions providing such discretion are divided into three types and discussed below.

Weighing jurisdictions that permit discretion. The Supreme Court indicated in *Boyde* that the Constitution does not require giving the factfinder discretion to reject the death penalty, even though the weighing or sufficiency determination was favorable to the prosecutor. This holding by *Boyde* does not mean that the Constitution prohibits giving the factfinder such discretion.

Thirteen weighing capital punishment jurisdictions have taken advantage of *Boyde*'s "window of opportunity" and given discretion to the factfinder.[24] In these jurisdictions the factfinder may reject imposing the death penalty on the capital felon, even though the weighing process called for imposition of the death penalty.

Jurisdictions requiring beyond a reasonable doubt. In the majority of weighing capital punishment jurisdictions that give the factfinder death discretion, no standard of proof is used in determining whether that discretion should be exercised. However, two weighing jurisdictions that afford death discretion to the factfinder impose a standard of proof in determining whether to exercise that discretion.[25] The two jurisdictions in question require that the factfinder determine beyond a reasonable doubt that imposing the death penalty is justified, even though the weighing process was favorable to the prosecutor.

Non-weighing jurisdictions that permit discretion. In four non-weighing capital punishment jurisdictions, the factfinder is given death discretion once it makes a sufficiency determination that is favorable to the prosecutor.[26] In these jurisdictions the capital felon may be spared the death penalty, notwithstanding the fact that the sufficiency determination called for death.

CHAPTER 13

Appellate Review of Death Sentence

Every capital conviction and sentence carries with it the potential for being infected with a prejudicial error. If the final word in a criminal prosecution rested at the trial level, then actual prejudicial errors would go undetected.[1]

BOX 13.0

TYPES OF ERROR

1. **Prejudicial Error**—*an error is deemed prejudicial if it had the potential of causing the outcome that resulted from a criminal prosecution.*
2. **Harmless Error**—*an error is considered harmless if it had no impact on the outcome of a criminal prosecution.*

Anglo-American jurisprudence has long rejected allowing a trial court to have the final word in criminal prosecutions. This rejection is manifested in appellate courts. Part of the function of appellate courts is that of examining criminal convictions and sentences for prejudicial error.[2] All jurisdictions, capital and non-capital, have appellate courts.

Notwithstanding the fact that all jurisdictions have appellate courts, there is no constitutional right to have a conviction or sentence examined by an appellate court. Over 100 years ago, in the case of *McKane v. Durston*, 153 U.S. 684 (1894), the Supreme Court indicated that "a State is not required by the Federal Constitution to provide appellate courts or a right to appellate [examination of errors] at all."[3] While *McKane* is still good law today, its pronouncement is meaningless because all jurisdictions do in fact provide appellate courts.

137

A prejudicial error in the prosecution of a capital felon can take place anywhere along the prosecutorial process: during the initial investigation, postindictment, pretrial, trial, or the penalty phase. This chapter is concerned with only one area in which prejudicial error might occur in the prosecution of a capital felon: the penalty phase. In limiting the scope of this chapter to appellate review of the penalty phase, the issue of a capital felon's innocence is not discussed. The focus is solely upon penalty phase issues.

This chapter outlines the procedures used by appellate courts to review death sentences. The material has been divided into five sections. The first section provides a discussion of the differences that exist between appellate review of a death sentence and the traditional appeal of a conviction and sentence. The second section looks at the issue of procedural-type errors that may occur at the penalty phase. The third section discusses how appellate courts review aggravating and mitigating circumstance issues. The fourth section is concerned with factors appellate courts look at to determine whether a death sentence is appropriate. The fifth and final section examines disposition alternatives available to appellate courts once a sentencing review is completed.

Distinguishing Review from Appeal

Prior to capital punishment being abolished by *Furman v. Georgia*, 408 U.S. 238 (1972), all capital punishment jurisdictions allowed capital felons to bring their conviction and sentence to appellate courts by way of an appeal (or writ of error, as it was sometimes called). When the Supreme Court resurrected the death penalty in *Gregg v. Georgia*, 428 U.S. 152 (1976), by approving of the capital punishment scheme Georgia had created, it noted its approval of one feature of the new procedures in the following terms:

> Finally, the Georgia statute has an additional provision designed to assure that the death penalty will not be imposed on a capriciously selected group of convicted defendants. The new sentencing procedures require that the [Georgia] Supreme Court review every death sentence....
>
> The provision for appellate review in the Georgia capital-sentencing system serves as a check against the random or arbitrary imposition of the death penalty. In particular, the proportionality review substantially eliminates the possibility that a person will be sentenced to die by the action of an aberrant jury. If a time comes when juries generally do not impose the death sentence in a certain kind of murder case, the appellate review procedures assure that no defendant convicted under such circumstances will suffer a sentence of death.

Georgia's appellate review of death sentences is not the traditional appeal. In approving of this new review process, the Supreme Court did not hold that the Constitution required such a process. The Supreme Court indicated merely that the review process was constitutionally acceptable.[4]

Gregg's acceptance of Georgia's appellate review of death sentences quickly motivated other capital punishment jurisdictions to adopt a similar process. As it stands now, Utah is the only jurisdiction that does not utilize a specific appellate review process for death sentences.

It was noted that the traditional appeal involved both guilt phase and penalty phase assignments of error. The appellate review process, on the other hand, involves ostensibly only penalty phase issues. What this means is that the question of whether a capital felon was erroneously found guilty of the offense is not considered during appellate review of a sentence. The only issue at stake in the review process is whether a capital felon was sentenced to die in accordance with the law. Guilt phase issues are brought to the appellate level by way of the traditional appeal.

A minority of capital punishment jurisdictions that utilize appellate review of death sentences provide by statute that if a capital felon institutes a guilt phase appeal, the appeal is to be consolidated with the penalty phase review issues.[5]

Traditional appeals in most instances had to be requested by defendants, but a majority of appellate review jurisdictions provide by statute that the review of a death sentence is automatic.[6] That is, the capital felon does not have to request review of his or her sentence. The review will occur as a matter of law, absent a valid waiver by the capital felon.[7]

A capital felon whose sentence is under review may assign as error any matter he or she believes affected the sentence. In all but seven review jurisdictions, however, statutes set out specific issues that appellate courts must address in making a review.[8]

Procedural Type Errors

The phrase "procedural type errors" is used here to refer to a catch-all category of purported sentencing errors that do not directly involve mitigating or statutory aggravating circumstances. This catch-all category of alleged errors is as expansive as the imagination of appellate defense attorneys. That is, the alleged errors that fall under this category have no limit. While it would not be practical to examine all of the alleged sentencing errors that have heretofore been placed under this category, a representative sample of the issues is warranted.

SELF-REPRESENTATION

The Sixth Amendment guarantees every defendant the right to self-representation (barring mental incompetency). Occasionally capital felons will choose to give up their right to legal counsel and represent themselves. Invariably, self-represented capital felons are found guilty and sentenced to death. It is usually at this point that self-represented capital felons will request and obtain legal counsel to represent them in appellate court.

In the case of *Townes v. Commonwealth*, 362 S.E.2d 650 (Va. 1987), the defendant represented himself and was sentenced to death. One of the issues he raised during appellate review of the sentence was that it was cruel and unusual punishment to impose the death penalty on a defendant who represented himself. The Virginia Supreme Court rejected the argument that a defendant who voluntarily represents himself cannot have the death penalty imposed.

The case of *Bloom v. California*, 774 P.2d 698 (Cal. 1989), also involved a defendant who decided to represent himself. During the penalty phase of his prosecution, the defendant chose not to put on any evidence. He was sentenced to death. During appellate review of the sentence, the defendant contended that his death sentence was not reliable because he had not presented the factfinder with any evidence. The California Supreme Court disagreed with the defendant and held that intentionally failing to put on evidence at the penalty phase does not render a sentencing verdict unreliable.

REQUESTING DEATH

One argument that has been raised in opposition to the death penalty is that life imprisonment has greater retribution potential than the death penalty. Proponents of this argument contend that the death penalty provides a relatively quick and painless end to life for people who should suffer eternally in prison. Occasionally capital felons agree that death is less retributive than life imprisonment and will request at penalty phase proceedings that the factfinder impose death.

Requesting death and actually having the request granted brings astonishingly swift sobriety to capital felons. The case examples that follow illustrate this.

In the case of *People v. Grant*, 755 P.2d 894 (Cal. 1988), the defendant exercised his right of allocution and addressed the penalty phase factfinder. With great bravado the defendant demanded the factfinder return a verdict of death. The factfinder obliged the defendant and returned a verdict of death. When the defendant got his wish, sobriety set in and he sought to retract his request.

A central issue raised by the defendant in *Grant* during appellate review of his sentence was that it was cruel and unusual punishment to sentence a person to death based upon a request to die. The appellate court had little trouble rejecting this argument, after finding that the sentence of death was imposed based upon compliance with statutory criteria. One can only speculate what would happen at penalty phase proceedings if it was unconstitutional to sentence a defendant to death should he or she request death.

The case of *People v. Guzman*, 755 P.2d 917 (Cal. 1988), presented another death-requesting defendant. As in *Grant*, the defendant in *Guzman* realized that asking the factfinder to sentence him to death was not a rational thing to do. Unlike *Grant*, however, the defendant in *Guzman* did not contend during appellate review of his sentence that death could not be imposed on a death-requesting defendant.

The defendant in *Guzman* sought to get out of his predicament by arguing that the trial judge should have instructed the factfinder that it could not base its decision on the imprudent request of the defendant. The appellate court agreed with the defendant that such an instruction should have been given. The appellate court reasoned, however, that the burden was on the defendant to request such an instruction from the trial judge. Since the instructional request was not made, the appellate court concluded that it was not in error in failing to provide the instruction.

The case of *State v. Hightower*, 577 A.2d 99 (N.J. 1990), stretches to the limit attempts to undo death requests. The defendant in that case calmly and voluntarily addressed the factfinder during the penalty phase and implored it to sentence him to death. The factfinder did not disappoint the defendant.

During appellate review of the death sentence in *Hightower*, the defendant postured the novel argument that the trial court had an affirmative duty to prevent him from requesting the death penalty. The defendant contended that failure of the trial court to carry out this purported duty made the imposition of the death penalty cruel and unusual. The appellate court disagreed with the defendant. The appellate court reasoned that the law does not require judges to "gag" defendants who wish to request the death penalty. To do this would infringe upon a defendant's right to allocution, that is, his right to address the factfinder.

REBUTTAL BY THE PROSECUTOR

Capital felons frequently, and usually unsuccessfully, argue during appellate review that improper rebuttal occurred during the penalty phase. In the case of *Pickens v. State*, 783 S.W.2d 341 (Ark. 1990), the appellate court rejected the defendant's contention that it was improper for the prosecutor to rebut his evidence because the prosecutor had the burden of proof. The exact same argument was raised and rejected in *People v. Douglas*, 788 P.2d 640 (Cal. 1990), and *Wood v. State*, 547 N.E.2d 772 (Ind. 1989).

The gist of the argument raised in cases like *Pickens*, *Douglas* and *Wood* is that the prosecutor has the burden of proof (in the jurisdictions where the argument was raised) and therefore should present all his or her evidence during his or her case-in-chief. This argument is sound, but capital felons apply it to situations that are inapplicable, as in the above cited cases. Usually a prosecutor will not be aware of every issue that a capital felon intends to present during the penalty phase. Therefore a prosecutor will frequently fail to address during his or her case-in-chief an issue that a capital felon presents in his or her case-in-chief. When this situation occurs, fairness requires that the prosecutor have an opportunity to rebut the issue.

In both *People v. West*, 560 N.E.2d 594 (Ill. 1990), and *Ex Parte Wilson*, 571 So.2d 1251 (Ala. 1990), the defendants argued that it was improper rebuttal by the prosecutors to call psychiatric expert witnesses who had evaluated them. The thrust of this argument was that self-incriminating statements were given to the psychiatrists by the defendants, and the Fifth Amendment therefore protected the statements from disclosure. The appellate courts rejected the argument, principally because the defendants had been made aware of their Fifth Amendment rights before speaking to the psychiatrists, and secondarily because the issue of guilt had already been determined, making the right against self-incrimination a moot issue.

Reviewing Aggravating
and Mitigating Findings

Appellate review of whether evidence supported the determination made regarding the existence of mitigating and statutory aggravating circumstances does not involve "weighing" or "sufficiency" determinations. (Those issues come at a different stage in the review process.) The focus of review at this point is limited to a determination of whether the factfinder properly found the "existence" of statutory aggravating circumstances and correctly found the "lack of existence" of mitigating circumstances. These two issues are treated separately in the two subsections that follow.

REVIEW OF AGGRAVATING CIRCUMSTANCE FINDING

Appellate courts engage in two types of aggravating circumstance review: (1) determining whether an aggravating circumstance is invalid because of vagueness and (2) determining whether an aggravating circumstance was actually proven to exist. Both matters are presented below.

Determining vagueness. It was pointed out by the South Carolina Supreme Court in *State v. Smith*, 381 S.E.2d 724 (S.C. 1989), that a statutory aggravating circumstance is unconstitutionally vague if it does not properly channel or limit the factfinder's discretion in imposing the death penalty. Capital felons have mounted a legion of arguments challenging statutory aggravating circumstances as being vague. While vagueness challenges for the most part are frivolous, appellate courts must nevertheless make independent evaluations of all arguments. Some of the vagueness arguments made include the examples that follow.

In *People v. Bunyard*, 756 P.2d 795 (Cal. 1988), the defendant argued that the "multiple victims" statutory aggravating circumstance was vague in its application to the murder of a pregnant woman and the fetus she carried. This argument was rejected by the appellate court primarily because the fetus was viable. In *People v. Edelbacher*, 766 P.2d 1 (Cal. 1989), the "pecuniary gain" statutory aggravating circumstance was challenged as being vague in that it did not provide a fair warning of what conduct was prohibited. The appellate court rejected this argument on the grounds that it had previously limited this statutory aggravating circumstance to mean that the victim's death is the consideration for, or an essential prerequisite to, the financial gain sought by the defendant. The statutory aggravating circumstance "under sentence of imprisonment" was challenged in *People v. Davis*, 794 P.2d 159 (Colo. 1990), as being vague in its application to a paroled defendant. The appellate court rebuffed the defendant's argument by holding that the legislature intended for this statutory aggravating circumstance to apply to incarcerated and paroled felons.

The statutory aggravating circumstance that capital felons have been able to successfully challenge as being vague is that of "heinous, atrocious, cruel or depraved." This statutory aggravating circumstance was found unconstitutionally vague in *Wilcher v. Hargett*, 978 F.2d 872 (5th Cir. 1992), and *Moore v. Clarke*, 951 F.2d 895 (8th Cir. 1991), because no definitions for the terms were provided.

Determining if aggravating circumstance proven. Failure of a vagueness challenge does not end appellate review of statutory aggravating circumstances. One of the most critical findings that must be made by an appellate court is whether a statutory aggravating circumstance was properly proven to exist. This determination is made by a thorough and careful review of all evidence in support of and in opposition to the establishment of each proffered statutory aggravating circumstance.

In *State v. Fierro*, 804 P.2d 72 (Ariz 1990), one of the issues confronting the appellate court was determining whether the statutory aggravating circumstance "prior felony using or threatening violence" was properly established. Two prior felony convictions were used by the prosecutor to establish this statutory aggravating circumstance: aggravated assault and robbery. The appellate court examined how each prior felony was statutorily defined. This analysis revealed that both crimes could be committed under their statutory definitions without using or threatening violence. As a result of the broad definition given the offenses, the appellate court found that evidence of the prior offenses did not establish the existence of the statutory aggravating circumstance.

The defendant in *State v. Commer*, 799 P.2d 333 (Ariz. 1990), argued that the statutory aggravating circumstance "pecuniary gain" was not established. The defendant contended that this statutory aggravating circumstance could only be proven by evidence showing that he actually received money or other valuable goods and that the prosecutor failed to prove this. The appellate court rejected this argument and held that merely establishing the defendant's intent to receive, or expectation of receiving, pecuniary gain was adequate. The prosecutor presented evidence to establish such an intent or expectation; therefore the statutory aggravating circumstance was proven to exist.

In the case of *People v. Young*, 538 N.E.2d 461 (Ill. 1989), the defendant contended that the statutory aggravating circumstance "other crimes" was not established because hearsay testimony was used in presenting the issue. The appellate court rejected this argument (noting that the rules of evidence were relaxed in penalty phase proceedings), primarily because the hearsay evidence had strong indicia of reliability. The hearsay was presented by a police officer.

REVIEW OF MITIGATING CIRCUMSTANCE FINDING

All relevant mitigating evidence must be allowed into evidence at the penalty phase. For appellate review purposes, relevant mitigating evidence is divided into two categories: (1) evidence offered to establish the existence of a non-statutory mitigating circumstance and (2) evidence submitted to establish the existence of a statutory mitigating circumstance. Both categories are examined by appellate courts from the perspective that a determination was made that a mitigating circumstance was not established. At this stage, appellate review is not concerned with examining mitigating circumstances that were proven to exist. Analysis of mitigating circumstances proven to exist at the penalty phase, is the subject of "weighing" or "sufficiency" determinations, which are discussed in the next section.

Non-statutory mitigating circumstance review. In the case of *Morrison v. State*, 500 So.2d 36 (Ala. 1985), the defendant contended that evidence presented to show that he was well-behaved during the investigation of his crime and the trial was a non-statutory mitigating circumstance. The appellate court rejected the argument and held that such evidence did not constitute a non-statutory mitigating circumstance.

The case of *Underwood v. State*, 535 N.E.2d 507 (Ind. 1989), presented a novel attempt at creating a non-statutory mitigating circumstance. In *Underwood* the defendant put on evidence concerning the method of execution of the death penalty. The defendant contended that the evidence on this issue established a non-statutory mitigating circumstance. The appellate court rejected this argument, not because the evidence failed to establish how the execution of the death penalty was carried out, but on the grounds that "method of execution" was an improper non-statutory mitigating circumstance.

In *People v. Christiansen*, 506 N.E.2d 1253 (Ill. 1987), the defendant contended that he proffered evidence to establish that he was an alcoholic. The defendant argued that alcoholism was a non-statutory mitigating circumstance. The appellate court agreed with the defendant that alcoholism was a bona fide non-statutory mitigating circumstance but the appellate court found that the defendant failed to establish that he was an alcoholic.

In the case of *State v. Wallace*, 773 P.2d 983 (Ariz. 1989), the defendant argued that "family background" was a non-statutory mitigating circumstance. The defendant presented evidence during the penalty phase to show that he had a very difficult family background. The appellate court agreed that family background was a recognized non-statutory mitigating circumstance in the jurisdiction but disagreed with the defendant's contention that this factor should not have been rejected by the factfinder. The appellate court reasoned that family background was not a mitigating circumstance in this case because the defendant failed to show that his family background contributed to the murders he committed.

Statutory mitigating circumstance review. A majority of capital punishment jurisdictions have statutory mitigating circumstances, but only a small percentage provide by statute that statutory mitigating circumstance rulings must be reviewed by appellate courts.[9] As a practical matter, however, appellate courts address the issue of statutory mitigating circumstances, with or without a statutory mandate.

The statutory mitigating circumstance "extreme mental or emotional disturbance" was the subject in *People v. Crews*, 522 N.E.2d 1167 (Ill. 1988). To support this statutory mitigating circumstance, the defendant proffered evidence at the penalty phase that he was found guilty of the crime charged but was also found mentally ill. The defendant contended that this evidence established the statutory mitigating circumstance of extreme mental or emotional disturbance. The appellate court rejected the argument, holding that mental illness and extreme mental or emotional disturbance were statutorily defined differently. Therefore proof of mental illness did not establish the statutory mitigating circumstance.

The case of *State v. Dickerson*, 543 N.E.2d 1250 (Ohio 1989), presented the duress statutory mitigating circumstance. The defendant presented evidence to show that at the time of the murder he was under stress because of the death of his mother and a breakup with his girlfriend. The defendant argued that this evidence established the duress statutory mitigating circumstance. The appellate court rejected the contention that evidence of stress established the duress statutory mitigating circumstance. In hindsight, the defendant should have argued that stress was an independent non-statutory mitigating circumstance. In *State v. Cummings*, 404 S.E.2d 849 (N.C. 1991), the defendant contended that he established the existence of the impairment statutory mitigating circumstance. The defendant argued that evidence he proffered to show that he was intoxicated at the time of his capital crime established that he lacked the capacity to conform his conduct to the requirements of the law. The appellate court agreed with the defendant and found that the trial court instructed the penalty phase jury in an erroneous manner which precluded consideration of the impairment statutory mitigating circumstance.

Determining Whether
Death Is the Proper Sentence

Once an appellate court determines that at least one statutory aggravating circumstance was validly found by the factfinder and makes its statutory and non-statutory mitigating circumstance analysis, the next stage in the review process is triggered. At this stage the appellate court must determine whether the sentence of death was proper. This determination involves three separate issues: (1) determining whether passion, prejudice, or other arbitrary factor caused death to be imposed, (2) determining whether the sentence was excessive or disproportionate compared to other cases, and (3) making an independent weighing or sufficiency determination.

PASSION, PREJUDICE, OR OTHER ARBITRARY FACTOR

The decision to impose death upon a capital felon must be made without the influence of passion, prejudice, or any other arbitrary factor. If the sentence of death is to be imposed, this result must be the product of evidentiary facts. The decision in *Furman v. Georgia*, 408 U.S. 238 (1972), nullified the death penalty in the nation on the grounds that it was being imposed for arbitrary reasons that had no nexus with evidentiary facts.

In an effort to assure that pre–*Furman* era arbitrariness did not infect a sentence of death, appellate courts review capital sentences to determine whether passion, prejudice, or any other arbitrary factor played a role in the sentencing decision. A majority of capital punishment jurisdictions require by statute that this issue be addressed during appellate review.[10]

Notwithstanding statutory requirements, engaging in a review for arbitrariness (this term is being used to encompass passion and prejudice) is largely dependent upon the capital felon making an allegation that a specific arbitrary factor influenced the decision in the case because an arbitrary factor will rarely stand out on the record in a case. Of course, the mere fact that a capital felon alleges that an arbitrary factor infected the sentencing decision does not mean that the allegation is true. Such an assertion, however, will focus the review to the specific factor alleged.

Commonly asserted arbitrary factors include race, gender, indigence, ethnicity, victim sympathy, adverse publicity, and fear of community response. A truly novel argument was raised in the case of *Baal v. State*, 787 P.2d 391 (Nev. 1990). The defendant in that case argued that the mere use of a three-judge panel at the penalty phase resulted in the arbitrary imposition of the death penalty. The reviewing court rejected this contention and held that the defendant had to present evidence that three-judge panels invariably return death sentences.

While the argument presented in *Baal* was frivolous, the case itself illustrates the necessity for defendants to focus the attention of appellate courts to potential arbitrary factors. If the defendant in *Baal* had not made the allegation, the appellate court would not have been predisposed to making a determination of whether use of a three-judge panel was, in and of itself, an arbitrary factor that influenced the sentencing decision.

EXCESSIVE OR DISPROPORTIONATE SENTENCE

It was pointed out in *People v. Hayes*, 564 N.E.2d 803 (Ill. 1990), that for purposes of imposing the death penalty, the Eighth Amendment demands that a defendant's punishment be proportionate to his or her personal culpability or blameworthiness. *Hayes* correctly stated the law as it presently stands. It was pointed out in *People v. Belmontes*, 755 P.2d 310 (Cal. 1988), however, that appellate court determination of whether imposition of the death penalty on a defendant was disproportionate (or excessive), compared to other cases, is not required by the Eighth Amendment.[11]

Belmontes correctly flushed out the full extent of the law, as partially articulated by *Hayes*. In spite of *Belmontes'* accurate statement of the Eighth Amendment's position, a majority of capital punishment jurisdictions statutorily require that appellate courts review each death sentence to determine whether it is excessive or disproportionate when compared to other cases in the jurisdiction imposing the sentence.[12]

Several matters need to be underscored regarding excessive and disproportionate review. First, *excessive* and *disproportionate* are terms that are used interchangeably by courts, but the terms actually refer to different points of analysis. A review of the extent of a capital felon's role in a crime seeks to determine whether the punishment of death is excessive. A comparison of a capital felon's sentence with similar cases seeks to determine whether the death sentence is disproportionate. In between these two points of analysis, a variety of determinations are made wherein the terms *excessive* and *disproportionate* are used interchangeably.

Second, comparative excessive or disproportionate review is usually confined to cases within an appellate court's jurisdiction. This limitation is necessary for no other reason than the impracticality of comparing a single death sentence with all other similar death penalty cases in other jurisdictions given the great number of capital murder convictions in the annals of Anglo-American jurisprudence.[13]

The final point to be noted is that getting a death sentence vacated as a result of excessive or disproportionate review, while not impossible, comes within a hair of being impossible.

WEIGHING OR SUFFICIENCY DETERMINATION

Provided that an appellate court does not find that a sentence was infected with an arbitrary factor or discern an excessive or disproportionate problem in a case, it may then engage in an independent weighing or sufficiency determination. Currently non-weighing jurisdictions do not statutorily require that appellate courts conduct a sufficiency determination. A minority of weighing jurisdictions do statutorily require that appellate courts engage in an independent weighing process.[14]

Disposition by Appellate Court

Once appellate court review of a death sentence is completed, the case must be disposed of based upon the conclusions reached from the review process. Since the exclusive focus of this chapter has been on the penalty phase, it will be assumed for the purpose of this section that the issue of guilt was not appealed or was upheld by the appellate court after consolidation. In this context, review of a sentencing determination may be disposed of in four ways: (1) affirm, (2) vacate and remand for further proceedings, (3) vacate and remand for imposition of life sentence, or (4) vacate and impose life sentence. Each disposition alternative is examined below.

AFFIRM

All capital punishment jurisdictions allow appellate courts to affirm death sentences. When a death sentence is affirmed, it means that the sentence was validly imposed and may be carried out. The fact that a sentence has been affirmed does not in and of itself mean that no errors were committed during the penalty phase. If a death sentence is affirmed even though errors occurred in the penalty phase proceeding, the errors reflected one of two possibilities.

First, it was previously noted that penalty phase errors may be prejudicial or harmless. If errors occurred during a penalty phase proceeding but the appellate court determined that the errors were harmless, then the sentence will be affirmed, notwithstanding the errors.

Second, not infrequently capital felons receive more than one death sentence when there has been more than one murder victim in a single incident. It is possible for an appellate court to find that one of several death sentences was imposed as a result of prejudicial error. In the latter situation, an appellate court may affirm the sentence that was imposed validly and dispose of the invalidly imposed sentence in one of the disposition alternatives that follow.

VACATE AND REMAND FOR FURTHER PROCEEDINGS

A sentence of death that was reached as a result of prejudicial error is not valid. A capital felon sentenced to death cannot be executed based upon an invalid death sentence. One option available to appellate courts when it is determined that a death sentence is invalid is to vacate the sentence and remand the case for further penalty phase proceedings. A majority of capital punishment jurisdictions provide for this option by statute.[15]

When a death sentence is vacated, it means that the sentence has been set aside or reversed and is no longer legally valid. Remanding means sending the sentencing issue back to the lower court.

A death sentence that has been vacated and remanded for further proceedings involves one of two things. First, the appellate court may remand the case with instructions that a new penalty phase proceeding be held. Second, an appellate court may remand the case with instructions that the lower court "reweigh" the mitigating and statutory aggravating circumstances or make another "sufficiency" determination (depending on the type of jurisdiction). The latter option would mean that the appellate court found that at least one statutory aggravating circumstance was invalid or that a statutory or non-statutory mitigating circumstance existed which had not been previously recognized.

VACATE AND REMAND FOR IMPOSITION OF LIFE SENTENCE

A minority of capital punishment jurisdictions provide by statute that appellate courts may, when appropriate, vacate a death sentence and remand the case with instructions to the trial court to impose a life sentence.[16] One of two factors will usually trigger this type of disposition.

First, the appellate court may determine from its review that the sentence of death is simply improper. Second, an appellate court may find that, as a result of noncorrectable prejudicial error, life imprisonment must be imposed.

VACATE AND IMPOSE LIFE SENTENCE

The final appellate court disposition option is to vacate a death sentence and impose a life sentence. Seven capital punishment jurisdictions provide for this option by statute.[17] This method of disposition involves imposition of a life sentence directly by the appellate court. An appellate court will utilize this option when it finds that the sentence of death was improper or that an egregious error was committed that is not correctable.

PART IV

LAWS RELATED TO EXECUTION

CHAPTER 14

Barriers to Execution

In a practical sense, a death sentence is never final until a capital felon is actually executed. In between imposition of a death sentence and its execution stand a number of factors that may temporarily or permanently delay the execution. The focus of this chapter is limited to reviewing factors that can temporarily or permanently forestall execution of a death sentence.

The issues that are addressed in this chapter are (1) youth of a capital felon, (2) physical condition of a female capital felon, (3) mental condition of a capital felon, (4) judicial stays, and (5) executive clemency.

Youth of a Capital Felon

As of December 31, 1994, there were 41 capital felons on death row waiting to be executed for crimes they committed while under the age of 18.[1] Until recently, youth (age 7–17) did not play a dispositive role in capital punishment. The historical insignificance of youth in capital punishment has its roots embedded in the common law.

THE COMMON LAW EXECUTED MINORS

The Supreme Court made the following observation in the case of *In re Gault*, 387 U.S. 1 (1967):

> At common law, children under seven were considered incapable of possessing criminal intent. Beyond that age, they were subjected to arrest, trial, and in theory to punishment like adult offenders.

In other words, the common law permitted the death penalty to be imposed and executed on youths. One commentator reports that during the period 1801 to 1836, a London court called Old Bailey sentenced to death 103 youths who were under the age of 14.[2]

Prior to the 1900s there were 95 youths executed in the United States, and two of those youths were reportedly 10 years old. From 1900 to 1983, there have been 192 executions of youth in the United States, and the youngest defendant was 13 years old.[3]

THOMPSON REJECTS DEATH PENALTY FOR CERTAIN MINORS

In 1988 the Supreme Court addressed the issue of whether the Eighth Amendment prohibited imposition and execution of the death penalty on youths who were 15 years old or younger at the time of their offense. This issue was presented in the case of *Thompson v. Oklahoma*, 487 U.S. 815 (1988). In its analysis of the issue in *Thompson,* the Supreme Court made the following observations:

> The line between childhood and adulthood is drawn in different ways by various States. There is, however, complete or near unanimity among all 50 States and the District of Columbia in treating a person under 16 as a minor for several important reasons. In no State may a 15-year-old vote or serve on a jury. Further, in all but one State a 15-year-old may not drive without parental consent, and in all but four States a 15-year-old may not marry without parental consent. Additionally, in those States that have legislated on the subject, no one under age 16 may purchase pornographic materials (50 States), and in most States that have some form of legal- ized gambling, minors are not permitted to participate without parental consent (42 States). Most relevant, however, is the fact that all States have enacted legislation designating the maximum age for juvenile court jurisdiction at no less than 16. All of this legislation is consistent with the experience of mankind, as well as the long history of our law, that the normal 15-year-old is not prepared to assume the full responsibilities of an adult....
> ... Inexperience, less education, and less intelligence make the teenager less able to evaluate the consequences of his or her conduct while at the same time he or she is much more apt to be motivated by mere emotion or peer pressure than is an adult. The reasons why juveniles are not trusted with the privileges and responsibilities of an adult also explain why their irresponsible conduct is not as morally reprehensible as that of an adult.

Based upon the above observations, and more, the Supreme Court came to the sober conclusion in *Thompson* that the Eighth Amendment "prohibit[ed] the execution of a person who was under 16 years of age at the time of his or her offense." The *Thompson* decision stands for two propositions. First, if an adult defendant committed a capital offense while he or she was under the age of 16, the death penalty cannot be imposed or executed on him or her.[4] Put another way, if a defendant is 15 or less when he or she commits a capital offense but is not apprehended or prosecuted until he or she is an adult, the death penalty cannot be imposed upon him or her for the offense. Second, if a defendant under 16 is prosecuted and sentenced to death for a capital offense, the execution of the death penalty cannot be carried out.[5]

STANFORD PERMITS DEATH PENALTY FOR CERTAIN MINORS

In *Stanford v. Kentucky*, 492 U.S. 361 (1989), the Supreme Court consolidated two cases from different jurisdictions that concerned youth and the imposition and execution of the death penalty. In one case the defendant was 16 when he committed capital murder, and in the second case the defendant was 17. Both defendants contended that execution of the death penalty on them was cruel and unusual punishment because of their ages when their capital crimes were committed.[6] The Court responded to their argument as follows.

> Neither petitioner asserts that his sentence constitutes one of those modes or acts of punishment that had been considered cruel and unusual at the time that the Bill of Rights was adopted. Nor could they support such a contention. At that time, the common law set the rebuttable presumption of incapacity to commit any felony at the age of 14, and theoretically permitted capital punishment to be imposed on anyone [7 or older]. In accordance with the standards of this common-law tradition, at least 281 offenders under the age of 18 have been executed in this country, and at least 126 under the age of 17....
>
> We discern neither a historical nor a modern societal consensus forbidding the imposition of capital punishment on any person who murders at 16 or 17 years of age. Accordingly, we conclude that such punishment does not offend the Eighth Amendment's prohibition against cruel and unusual punishment.

Physical Condition of a Female Capital Felon

In 1991 a total of 4,745 women were imprisoned in federal facilities.[7] Out of the 2,890 capital felons on death row in 1994, there were 41 females.[8] For female capital felons sentenced to death, gender may temporarily forestall execution of the death penalty.[9]

EXECUTION OF A PREGNANT FEMALE

The Supreme Court has not been given an opportunity to rule upon the following question: May a female capital felon be executed while pregnant?

A majority of capital punishment jurisdictions have addressed this question by enacting statutes that prohibit executing female capital felons while they are pregnant.[10]

Statutes vary in how they address the issue of a female capital felon who alleges she is pregnant. The following two statutes illustrate this point.

Alabama Code § 15-18-86:

(a) If there is reason to believe that a female convict is pregnant, the sheriff must, with the concurrence of a judge of the circuit court, summon a jury of six disinterested persons, as many of whom must be physicians as practicable. The sheriff must also give notice to the district attorney or, in his absence, to any attorney who may be appointed by a circuit judge to represent the state and who has authority to issue subpoenas for witnesses.

(b) The jury, under the direction of the sheriff or officer acting in his place, must proceed to ascertain the fact of pregnancy and must state their conclusion in writing, signed by them and the sheriff. If such jury is of opinion, and so find, that the convict is with child, the sheriff or officer acting in his place must suspend the execution of the sentence and transmit the finding of the jury to the Governor.

(c) Whenever the Governor is satisfied that such convict is no longer with child, he must issue his warrant to the sheriff appointing a day for her to be executed according to her sentence, and the sheriff or other officer must execute the sentence of the law on the day so appointed.

Wyoming Statutes Annotated § 7-13-912 and 913:

(a) If there is good reason to believe that a female sentenced to death is pregnant, the director of the department of corrections shall immediately give written notice to the court in which the judgment of death was rendered and to the district attorney. The execution of the death sentence shall be suspended pending further order of the court.

(b) Upon receiving notice as provided in subsection (a) of this section, the court shall appoint a jury of three (3) physicians to inquire into the supposed pregnancy and to make a written report of their findings to the court.

(a) If the court determines the female is not pregnant, the director of the department of corrections shall execute the death sentence.

(b) If the court determines the female is pregnant, the court shall order the execution of the sentence suspended until it is determined that the female is no longer pregnant at which time the court shall issue a warrant appointing a new date for the execution of the sentence.

Pregnancy is not a permanent barrier to the execution of the death penalty. Once the pregnancy has ended, the death penalty may be carried out. None of the capital punishment jurisdictions that have statutes addressing the issue of a pregnant capital felon indicate what happens to the child that is born to a pregnant capital felon.

Mental Condition of a Capital Felon

The mental condition of a capital felon has legal significance at various stages in a criminal prosecution. If a capital felon is found by proper proof to be insane prior to trial, the trial cannot occur until competent expert testimony indicates his or her sanity has returned. Should a capital felon be competent at the start of his or her trial but become insane during the trial, the proceeding must terminate in a mistrial. A subsequent trial may not occur until the capital felon's sanity is reestablished. If a capital felon is tried but the factfinder determines that he or she was insane at the time of the offense, it must render a verdict of not guilty by reason of insanity. Should a capital felon be tried and convicted of the offense charged but become insane before the sentence is imposed, the penalty phase proceeding must be continued until the capital felon's sanity returns. Two issues not mentioned, insanity and mental retardation at the time of execution, are addressed in the subsections that follow.

INSANITY AND CAPITAL PUNISHMENT UNDER THE COMMON LAW

Many of the most painful forms of capital punishment were approved of by the common law. The common law did not twinge at the sight of a defendant being quartered or beheaded. Ice flowed, in a manner of speaking, through the veins of the common law when it came to methods of carrying out capital punishment.

In view of the common law's tolerance of cruel forms of capital punishment, it would not be surprising if the common law had condoned executing insane capital felons, but the common law prohibited executing an insane capital felon. It may appear, in the first instance, that it was not logical for the common law to revel in gruesome forms of capital punishment but show compassion for a condemned insane capital felon. This dichotomous position by the common law was, however, perfectly logical.

Well-developed principles form the foundation of criminal punishments. One such principle is embodied in the term *deterrence*. The logic behind the common law's ghoulish methods of capital punishment was centered on the deterrent aspect of publicly executing a criminal in a hideous manner. The common law reasoned, however, that executing an insane capital felon would not deter rational or irrational people from committing crimes. The lack of deterrence value in executing insane capital felons was the primary reason for the common law's prohibition of such punishment on the insane.

STATUTORY BAR TO EXECUTING
AN INSANE CAPITAL FELON

The common law gave birth to Anglo-American jurisprudence. While many common law principles have been repudiated by various jurisdictions, one common law principle that has stood the test of time in all jurisdictions is that an insane capital felon cannot be executed.[11]

A majority of capital punishment jurisdictions have codified the common law rule that insane capital felons should not be executed.[12] The two statutes that follow illustrate how this issue is addressed.

Mississippi Code § 99-19-57(2):

(a) If it is believed that a convict under sentence of death has become insane since the judgment of the court, the following shall be the exclusive procedural and substantive procedure. The convict, or a person acting as his next friend, or the commissioner of corrections may file an appropriate application seeking post conviction relief with the Mississippi Supreme Court. If it is found that the convict is insane, as defined in this subsection, the court shall suspend the execution of the sentence. The convict shall then be committed to the forensic unit of the Mississippi State Hospital at Whitfield. The order of commitment shall require that the convict be examined and a written report be furnished to the court at that time and every month thereafter stating whether there is substantial probability that the convict will become sane under this subsection within the foreseeable future and whether progress is being made toward that goal. If at any time during such commitment the appropriate official at the state hospital shall consider the convict is sane under this subsection, such official shall promptly notify the court to that effect in writing, and place the convict in the custody of the commissioner of corrections. The court shall thereupon conduct a hearing on the sanity of the convict. The finding of the circuit court is a final order [that is] appealable[.]

(b) For the purposes of this subsection, a person shall be deemed insane if the court finds the convict does not have sufficient intelligence to understand the nature of the proceedings against him, what he was tried for, the purpose of his punishment, the impending fate which awaits him, and a sufficient understanding to know any fact which might exist which would make his punishment unjust or unlawful and the intelligence requisite to convey such information to his attorneys or the court.

Maryland Code Annotated Art. 27 § 75A:

(a) In this section, the following words have the meanings indicated:

(1) "Inmate" means an individual who has been convicted of murder and sentenced to death; and

(2)(i) "Incompetent" means the state of mind of an inmate who, as a result of a mental disorder or mental retardation, lacks awareness:

1. Of the fact of his or her impending execution; and

2. He or she is to be executed for the crime of murder.

(ii) An inmate is not incompetent merely because his or her competence is dependent upon continuing treatment, including the use of medication.

(b) The State may not execute the death sentence against an inmate who has become incompetent.

(c)(1) The following individuals may file a petition alleging that an inmate is incompetent and seeking to revoke the warrant to execute the death sentence against the inmate:

(i) The inmate;

(ii) If the inmate is represented by counsel, counsel for the inmate; or

(iii) If the inmate is not represented by counsel, any other person on the inmate's behalf.

(2)(i) The petition shall be filed in the circuit court of the county in which the inmate is confined.

(ii) Upon the filing of such a petition, the court may in its discretion stay any warrant of execution that was previously issued and has not yet expired.

(3) The petition must be accompanied by an affidavit of at least one psychiatrist, based, at least in part, on personal examination, attesting:

(i) That, in the psychiatrist's medical opinion, the inmate is incompetent;

(ii) The pertinent facts on which the opinion is based.

(4) A copy of the petition shall be served on the Attorney General and the Office of the State's Attorney who prosecuted the inmate[.]

(5) Unless the inmate is already represented by counsel, the court shall promptly appoint the public defender, or, if the public defender for good cause declines representation, other counsel to represent the inmate in the proceeding.

(6) Unless the State stipulates to the inmate's incompetence, it shall cause the inmate to be examined and evaluated by one or more psychiatrists of its choosing.

(7) The inmate is entitled to be independently examined by a psychiatrist of the inmate's choosing, provided the request is reasonable and timely made.

(8) Unless, with the court's approval, the parties waive a hearing, the administrative judge of the court shall designate a time for an evidentiary hearing to determine the inmate's competence. The hearing shall be held without a jury in court, at the place where the inmate is confined, or at any other convenient place.

(9) At the hearing, the inmate:

(i) Subject to the reasonable restrictions related to the inmate's condition, has the right to be present;

(ii) Has the right through counsel to offer evidence, cross-examine witnesses against the inmate, and make argument; and

(iii) Has the burden of establishing incompetence by a preponderance of the evidence.

(d)(1) The court shall enter an order declaring the inmate to be competent or incompetent and stating the findings on which the conclusion is based.

(2) If the court finds the inmate to be competent, it shall immediately:

(i) Lift any stay of a warrant of execution that was previously issued and has not yet expired; or

(ii) If all previously issued warrants of execution have expired, notify the court in which the sentence of death was imposed and request that the court issue a new warrant of execution.

(3) If the court finds the inmate to be incompetent it shall stay any warrant of execution that was previously entered and has not yet expired and remand the case to the court in which the sentence of death was imposed, which shall strike the sentence of death and enter in its place a sentence of life imprisonment without the possibility of parole. The sentence shall be mandatory and may not be suspended, in whole or in part[.]

Three points of note will be mentioned regarding the insanity statutes of Mississippi and Maryland. First, Maryland requires that a defendant establish incompetency by a preponderance of evidence, but Mississippi does not. Second, Maryland provides that if a defendant is found incompetent, his or her capital sentence must be reduced to life imprisonment. Mississippi has settled on waiting for the defendant to return to sanity. Third, Maryland's statute encompasses both insanity and mental retardation. Mississippi's statute concerns only insanity.

FORD BARS EXECUTING AN INSANE FELON

In *Ford v. Wainwright*, 477 U.S. 399 (1986), the Supreme Court was asked for the first time to determine whether it is cruel and unusual punishment to execute an insane defendant. The Supreme Court responded as follows:

> ... Today, no State in the Union permits the execution of the insane. It is clear that the ancient and human limitation upon the State's ability to execute its sentences has as firm a hold upon the jurisprudence of today as it had centuries ago in England. The various reasons put forth in support of the common-law restriction have no less logical, moral, and practical force than they did when first voiced. For today, no less than before, we may seriously question the retributive value of executing a person who has no comprehension of why he has been singled out and stripped of his fundamental right to life. Similarly, the natural abhorrence civilized societies feel at killing one who has no capacity to come to grips with his own conscience or deity is still vivid today. And the intuition that such an execution simply offends humanity is evidently shared across this

Nation. Faced with such widespread evidence of a restriction upon sovereign power, this Court is compelled to conclude that the Eighth Amendment prohibits a State from carrying out a sentence of death upon a prisoner who is insane. Whether its aim be to protect the condemned from fear and pain without comfort of understanding, or to protect the dignity of society itself from the barbarity of exacting mindless vengeance, the restriction finds enforcement in the Eighth Amendment.

EXECUTION OF MENTALLY RETARDED FELONS

In *Penry v. Lynaugh*, 492 U.S. 302 (1989), the Supreme Court was asked to decide whether it is cruel and unusual punishment to execute mentally retarded capital felons.[13] The Supreme Court responded as follows:[14]

> ... [M]ental retardation is a factor that may well lessen a defendant's culpability for a capital offense. But we cannot conclude today that the Eighth Amendment precludes the execution of any mentally retarded person.... While a national consensus against execution of the mentally retarded may someday emerge reflecting the evolving standards of decency that mark the progress of a maturing society, there is insufficient evidence of such a consensus today[.]

Judicial Stays

There were 257 capital felons executed during the period 1977–1994. It is estimated that these executed capital felons spent an average of eight years on death row.[15] The ability of a capital felon to remain on death row for an average of eight years is due to the Anglo-American appellate process. To shed some light on how the appellate process impacts on the period between sentence and execution, this section will review the path taken by the average "state" capital felon upon receiving a sentence of death.[16]

Before embarking upon the review that follows, a word must be said here regarding judicial stay and the structure of the court systems in the nation. A judicial stay involves entry of an order by a court which stops an event from occurring until the court examines an allegation that concerns the event. A judicial stay is temporary. In the context of capital punishment, a judicial stay is a court order halting the scheduled execution of a capital felon pending the court's examination of allegations that the death penalty should not be executed.

The judicial systems in the nation may be broken down into two categories: (1) three-tier systems and (2) two-tier systems. Jurisdictions that utilize a three-tier system have a (1) court of general jurisdiction, (2) intermediate appellate court, and (3) final appellate court. Two-tier system jurisdictions have a (1) court of general jurisdiction and (2) appellate court. The majority of capital punishment jurisdictions utilize a three-tier system.[17]

BOX 14.0
COURT SYSTEMS

Type of System	Court of General Jurisdiction	Intermediate Appellate Court	Final Appellate Court
two-tier	yes	no	yes
three-tier	yes	yes	yes

STAY DURING STATE APPELLATE REVIEW AND APPEAL

The first judicial stay that surfaces when a capital felon is sentenced to death occurs immediately after the sentence is imposed. This stay is necessary to allow the capital felon to have his or her sentence and conviction examined by the state appellate court. The length of time involved at this stage depends upon several factors.

If the state has a two-tier judicial system, then the initial stay should be less than eight months. Also, if the state has a three-tier system, but the appeal and review go directly from the trial court to the final appellate court, then the initial stay in this system should also be less than eight months. However, if the state is a three-tier system and the intermediate appellate court is permitted to hear the review and appeal before the matter is brought to the final appellate court, then there will be two stays. There will be an approximate eight-month stay imposed for intermediate appellate court examination and a stay of about five months imposed for final appellate court examination.

STAY DURING SUPREME COURT APPEAL

Assuming that a capital felon did not obtain relief at the state appellate court level, the next step will usually be that of entering the federal system.[18] This initial journey in the federal system will usually be directly to the Supreme Court.[19] Provided that the Supreme Court grants a writ of certiorari, a stay will be imposed by it pending its review. This stay can remain in place up to a year.

STAY DURING STATE HABEAS CORPUS PROCEEDINGS

Provided that the capital felon is denied relief by the Supreme Court, the capital felon usually will begin an attack on his or her conviction and sentence indirectly by filing a petition for a writ of habeas corpus. A habeas corpus proceeding involves allegations by a capital felon that his or her conviction and sentence were imposed in violation of his or her constitutional rights.[20]

During this first round of habeas corpus proceedings, the capital felon usually will start out at the state level, though this process can begin in the federal system. Depending upon the requirements of the particular state, the habeas corpus petition will be filed in the trial court where the capital felon was convicted and sentenced, or in the state's highest court.

If the capital felon is permitted to file the habeas corpus petition in the trial court, a stay will be entered pending review by the trial court. The case could linger in the trial court for six months to a year.

Provided that the trial court did not grant the capital felon relief, he or she will appeal the denial of his or her requested relief. If the state has a three-tier judicial system, this appeal will usually go initially to the intermediate appellate court. A stay will be entered pending disposition by the intermediate appellate court. This stay will last up to eight months.

If the intermediate appellate court does not grant relief (or if the state has a two-tier judicial system), the capital felon will appeal to the highest court in the state. While the state high court reviews the habeas corpus appeal, a stay will be imposed that can last eight months.

STAY DURING FEDERAL HABEAS CORPUS PROCEEDINGS

If the highest court in the state denies the capital felon habeas corpus relief, he or she will enter the federal system again. This time, however, the capital felon will start out in a federal district court.[21] During this initial round of habeas corpus proceedings in the federal system, the district court will stay execution of the death penalty. This stay can last a year.

Should the capital felon not obtain relief in the federal district court, he or she will appeal to a federal court of appeals. A stay will be granted by the court of appeals which can last eight months. If the court of appeals denies relief, the capital felon will seek an appeal to the Supreme Court. If the Supreme Court grants certiorari, a stay will be in place for up to a year.[22]

THE GREAT WRIT WAR

If the capital felon fails to obtain habeas corpus relief from the Supreme Court on an initial attempt, then the great writ war begins. At this stage a capital felon has argued all possible rational reasons for vacating his or her sentence and conviction but has been denied relief. In order to continue to cling to life, the capital felon will begin filing endless petitions for writs of mandamus, coram nobis, prohibition, and habeas corpus. Statistics indicate that in the past, capital felons were able to squeeze out an additional five or so years through judicial stays because of this great writ war. Recent changes in state and federal laws are expected to cut the great writ war time in half.[23]

Executive Clemency

During the period 1977–1994, a total of 21 death row inmates had their death sentences commuted to life imprisonment as a result of executive clemency.[24] It was said in *People v. Arellano*, 524 P.2d 305 (Colo. 1974), that once a defendant has exhausted all appellate remedies in seeking relief from a conviction and sentence, any further attempt at relief must be made, not to the judiciary, but to the executive department of government. *Arellano*, while correct, stated matters in part, not whole. Executive clemency may be obtained before or after exhausting all judicial appellate avenues.

As a general matter, executive clemency refers to granting a specific form of leniency from a conviction and sentence. Executive clemency is a matter of grace, not of right. No defendant has a right to obtain executive clemency.[25]

All capital punishment jurisdictions provide by statute or constitution for executive clemency. As pointed out by *Arellano*, executive clemency resides in the executive branch of government; governors and the president control executive clemency. Jurisdictions vary as to the autonomy granted chief executive officers in making executive clemency decisions. A few jurisdictions attach no strings to the chief executive officer's authority in this area, while others require involvement of a council, board, or commission. The following statutes are provided to illustrate how capital punishment jurisdictions address the matter.

Texas Code Annotated-C.C.P. Art. 48.01:
In all criminal cases, except treason and impeachment, the Governor shall have power, after conviction, on the written signed recommendation and advice of the Board of Pardons and Paroles, or a majority thereof, to grant reprieves and commutations of punishments and pardons.... The Governor shall have the power to grant one reprieve in any capital case for a period not to exceed 30 days; and shall have power to revoke conditional pardons[.]

Washington Code Annotated § 8.01.120:
Whenever a prisoner has been sentenced to death, the governor shall have power to commute such sentence to imprisonment for life at hard

labor; and in all cases in which the governor is authorized to grant pardons or commute sentence of death, he may, upon the petition of the person convicted, commute a sentence or grant a pardon, upon such conditions, and with such restrictions, and under such limitations as he may think proper.... The governor may also, on good cause shown, grant respites or reprieves from time to time as he may think proper.

730 Illinois Comp. Stat. Ann. § 5/3-3-13:

(a) Petitions seeking pardon, commutation or reprieve shall be addressed to the Governor and filed with the Prisoner Review Board. The petition shall be in writing and signed by the person under conviction or by a person on his behalf. It shall contain a brief history of the case and the reasons for executive clemency.

(b) Notice of the proposed application shall be given by the Board to the committing court and the state's attorney of the county where the conviction was had.

(c) The Board shall, if requested and upon due notice, give a hearing to each application, allowing representation by counsel, if desired, after which it shall confidentially advise the Governor by a written report of its recommendations which shall be determined by majority vote. The Board shall meet to consider such petitions no less than 4 times each year.

(d) The Governor shall decide each application and communicate his decision to the Board which shall notify the petitioner.

Executive clemency may manifest itself in three ways: (1) reprieve (sometimes called "respite"), (2) commutation, or (3) pardon. Each type of executive clemency has its own unique consequence for a capital felon. The review of these forms of executive clemency that follows will explain the consequences of each.

EXECUTIVE REPRIEVE

A reprieve serves the same function as that of a judicial stay. It merely postpones an execution temporarily. Capital felon reprieves usually occur in one of two contexts.

First, if a capital felon has filed a habeas corpus or other type of petition with a court but the court refuses to grant a stay while the matter is before it, then the capital felon can request a reprieve while the court evaluates the matter. Second, if a capital felon requests a pardon or commutation, a reprieve may be granted while the application for pardon or commutation is under review.

EXECUTIVE COMMUTATION

The court in *State ex rel. Maurer v. Steward*, 644 N.E.2d 369 (Ohio 1994), defined commutation as "the change of a punishment to which a person has been condemned into a less severe one." Most capital punishment jurisdictions limit commutation of a death sentence to the imposition of life imprisonment.[26] In theory, when this limitation is not imposed, a capital felon can have his or her death sentence commuted to time served, which would mean immediate release.

As a practical matter, however, commutations are always confined to life imprisonment. Usually commutations are made with a condition that the capital felon will not seek parole. Commutations may also take on any other conditions deemed appropriate and in compliance with general laws. A violation of a condition of commutation can in theory result in the death penalty being reinstated and carried out.

EXECUTIVE PARDON

It was pointed out in *Ex Parte May*, 717 S.W.2d 84 (Tex.Cr.App. 1986), that unlike commutation and reprieve, "a pardon may be granted by proper authority at any time—even before a criminal charge has been lodged against the offender." The court in *State ex rel. Maurer v. Steward*, 644 N.E.2d 369 (Ohio 1994), made the following observations regarding a pardon:

> A pardon discharges the individual designated from all or some specified penal consequences of his crime. It may be full or partial, absolute or conditional.
> A full and absolute pardon releases the offender from the entire punishment prescribed for his offense, and from all the disabilities consequent on his conviction.

Pardons for capital felons waiting to be executed have been rare. This is because of the nature of a pardon—it allows the immediate release of the capital felon. The beneficiaries of pardons are usually defendants who have received sentences less than death.

CHAPTER 15

Witnessing An Execution

The primary focus of this chapter is to provide a review of statutes that control public access to executions. Prior to examining these laws, some discussion is devoted to the origin of public executions, the movement away from them, and efforts to make executions public again.

Origin of Public Executions

The common law tolerated, for reasons that are forthcoming, having capital felons executed in full view of the public. Attending an execution was a routine part of life in England under the common law. People gathered, much as they gather today at sporting events, with joy and enthusiasm to watch the condemned be put to death.[1]

Anglo-American jurisprudence embraced England's practice of inviting the public to watch capital felons die. Public executions were an integral part of the early development of America. Prior to 1835 all capital punishments in the United States were open to the public.

Neither England nor the United States permitted public executions for the sake of entertaining citizens. Two fundamental reasons guided the decision to allow the public to observe capital felons being put to death. One reason was aimed at the capital felon and the other was centered on the public.

The first justification for holding public executions involved the dehumanization of the capital felon. Capital crimes were offenses that society deemed unforgivable. Because of the perceived reprehensible nature of capital crimes, it was believed necessary to humiliate and degrade a capital offender by parading him or her in front of the public before, during, and after execution. Whether a capital felon felt humiliated and degraded, as opposed to feeling scared to death, is an issue for psychologists to digest. Penologists believed capital felons felt dehumanized by being brought before the public for execution.

The second justification for holding public executions was grounded in the deterrent principle underpinning criminal punishment in general. It was thought that exposing the public to executions would deter others from committing capital crimes.

Movement Away from Public Executions

New York is credited with being the first jurisdiction to permit nonpublic executions. It did so by enacting a statute in 1835 which allowed the sheriff to hold executions out of public view.[2] Without realizing it, New York set in motion a penological reform movement that would eventually engulf the nation.

The New York statute was heralded as representing the evolving decency of society. Public executions were symbolic of a crude and unsophisticated society. Such a spectacle dehumanized not only the capital felon, it took away the humanity of those observing. In slow but steady fashion, the notion of evolving decency moved across the nation, and jurisdictions began enacting statutes which took away the public's ability to view executions. The force of this movement influenced England, which in 1868 abolished the practice of holding public executions.

The theme of evolving decency came full circle in 1936. It was in 1936 that the last public execution occurred in the United States. This execution took place in Owensboro, Kentucky. It was said that between 10 and 20 thousand people came out to see the state of Kentucky hang 22-year-old Ramsey Bethea.

Judicial Challenges
to Nonpublic Executions

Removal of executions from the public's eye has not gone unchallenged. Numerous attacks cloaked in diverse motives have been made to remove secrecy from executions. Some of the legal battles waged to reopen executions to the public follow.

THE RIGHT OF THE CAPITAL FELON AND THE PUBLIC

Penologists formerly believed that public executions humiliated and degraded capital felons. This belief is difficult to reconcile with the demand by some capital felons to have public executions. The first challenge to nonpublic executions came in 1890 and was made by a capital felon.

The Supreme Court picked up this challenge in the case of *Holden v. Minnesota*, 137 U.S. 483 (1890). The defendant in *Holden* had been sentenced to death for committing capital murder. At the time of his offense, Minnesota permitted public executions. (Minnesota currently does not allow capital punishment.) Shortly before his scheduled execution, however, the state changed the law so that executions could no longer be held in public. The defendant argued that the change in law should not affect him because at the time of his offense executions were public. It was contended by the defendant that the Constitution's ban on ex post facto laws prohibited the new law from applying to him.

The Supreme Court rejected the defendant's position and held the following:

> Whether a convicted, sentenced to death, shall be executed ... within or without the walls of the jail, or within or outside of some other enclosure, and whether the enclosure within which he is executed shall be higher than the gallows, thus excluding the view of persons outside, are regulations that do not affect [the defendant's] substantial rights. The same observation may be made touching the restriction ... as to the number and character of those who may witness the execution, and the exclusion altogether of reporters or representatives of newspapers. These are regulations which the legislature, in its wisdom, and for the public good, could legally prescribe in respect to executions occurring after the passage of the [law], and cannot, even when applied to offenses previously committed, be regarded as ex post facto within the meaning of the Constitution.

Holden has stood the test of time in championing the proposition that a capital felon does not have a right to a public execution. The case has also stood for the proposition that the general public does not have a right to attend an execution.

THE MEDIA'S RIGHT TO FILM EXECUTIONS

The First Amendment is a powerful constitutional provision. In crystal clear words, this amendment heralds the independence of the press (media) by proclaiming that "governments" cannot abridge the freedom of the press. Upon first impression it would seem that governments cannot bar the media from filming or photographing executions, but this first impression has not been upheld in judicial decisions.

In 1990, California was preparing to execute its first capital felon in 23 years. The recipient of this dubious distinction was named Robert Alton Harris. A local San Francisco television station, KQED, wanted to film the execution for posterity. The station approached California officials with a request to record the execution but was turned down. Unperturbed, the station filed an equity proceeding, styled *KQED v. Vasquez*, No. C-90-1383 (N.D.Cal. August 6, 1991), in a federal district court seeking to force California to allow it to film Harris's execution. The district court rebuffed the station, and held that the state of California could constitutionally exclude cameras from its execution chamber.

In the case of *Halquist v. Dept. of Corrections*, 783 P.2d 1065 (Wash. 1989), a producer of radio and television documentaries asked officials in the state of Washington to allow him to videotape the execution of Charles Campbell. When the producer was turned down, he filed an equity proceeding before the Washington Supreme Court, contending that he had a right under the constitution of Washington to film the execution.

The state constitutional provision relied upon by the producer in *Halquist* provided that "Every person may freely speak, write and publish on all subjects, being responsible for the abuse of that right." The producer argued that the latter state constitutional provision guaranteed him the right to film the execution. The court rebuffed this argument by noting that "the right to publish applies only to those who have previously and lawfully obtained information." The court also added that there was "a substantial difference between the right to publish already acquired information and the right to attend a proceeding for the purpose of news gathering." Finally, the court observed that the United States Supreme Court took the position that "the First Amendment does not guarantee the press a constitutional right of special access to information not available to the public generally."

In *Garrett v. Estelle*, 556 F.2d 1274 (5th Cir. 1977), the state of Texas sought reversal of a federal district court's decision ordering it to permit a television news cameraman to film executions. In reversing the decision of the federal district court, the court of appeals held the following:

> Garrett asserts a first amendment right to gather news, which he contends can be limited only on account of a compelling state interest. He further argues that preventing him from using a motion picture camera to gather news denies him use of the tool of his trade and therefore denies him equal protection of the laws....
>
> News gathering is protected by the first amendment, for without some protection for seeking out the news, freedom of the press could be eviscerated. This protection is not absolute, however. As the late Chief Justice Warren wrote for the Supreme Court, "The right to speak and publish does not carry with it the unrestrained right to gather information[.]"
>
> ... [T]he press has no greater right of access to information than does the public at large and ... the first amendment does not require government to make available to the press information not available to the public. This principle marks a limit to the first amendment protection of the press' right to gather news. Applying this principle to the present case,

we hold that the first amendment does not invalidate nondiscriminatory prison access regulations.

... While we agree that the death penalty is a matter of wide public interest, we disagree that the protections of the first amendment depend upon the notoriety of an issue. The Supreme Court has held that the first amendment does not protect means of gathering news in prisons not available to the public generally, and this holding is not predicated upon the importance or degree of interest in the matter reported....

Garrett next argues that to prevent his filming executions denies him equal protection of the law, since other members of the press are allowed free use of their usual reporting tools. This argument is also without merit. The Texas media regulation denies Garrett use of his camera, and it also denies the print reporter use of his camera, and the radio reporter use of his tape recorder. Garrett is free to make his report by means of anchor desk or stand-up delivery on the TV screen, or even by simulation. There is no denial of equal protection.

THE RIGHT OF A FELON TO VIDEOTAPE AN EXECUTION

Capital felons have argued that the methods used to execute the death penalty are cruel and unusual. Several capital felons have sought to prove this argument by offering into evidence videotapes of capital felons being put to death. To obtain such evidence, capital felons have to establish that they have a right to videotape executions.

In the case of *Campbell v. Blodgett*, 1993 U.S. App. LEXIS 1036 (9th Cir., 1/25/93), a capital felon, Charles Campbell, filed an action in a federal district court seeking to force officials to allow him to videotape the hanging execution of Westley Allan Dodd.[3] Campbell wanted to use the videotape in another proceeding in which he had alleged that hanging was a cruel and unusual form of punishment, but the federal district court denied the request. Campbell then appealed to a federal court of appeals. The court of appeals stated that a videotape of Dodd's hanging would be insufficient proof that hanging was cruel and unusual because it could not establish what degree of pain and suffering was endured. Therefore the court of appeals affirmed the denial.

The case of *Fierro v. Gomez*, 1993 U.S. Dist. LEXIS 14445 (N.D.Cal., 10/13/93), presented a ray of hope for capital felons seeking to prove death penalty methods were cruel and unusual.[4] Three capital felons brought this case into federal court: David Fierro, Alejandro Gilbert Ruiz, and Robert Alton Harris. In an effort to support their claim that California's use of lethal gas to execute felons was cruel and unusual punishment, the capital felons asked a federal district court to issue an order permitting them to videotape the execution of Harris. The capital felons argued that the videotape would conclusively establish that death by lethal gas was cruel and unusual punishment.

The district court held that such a videotape would have some relevancy on the defendants' claim and issued an order allowing the capital felons to videotape the execution of Harris. The court explicitly required that only Harris be videotaped and not anyone else attending the execution.

In the case of *Petition of Thomas*, 155 F.R.D. 124 (D.Md. 1994), a capital felon challenged the state of Maryland's method of execution as being cruel and unusual punishment. In an effort to prove his claim, the defendant asked a federal district court to allow him to conduct discovery on the state. Part of the discovery that the defendant wanted to engage in was that of videotaping the execution of another capital felon. The court in that case ultimately ruled that the defendant could conduct discovery to support his challenge to the state's method of execution and, as part of that discovery, he could videotape the execution of a consenting death-row inmate.

Statutory Limitations
on Access to Executions

Methodically detailed rules and regulations have been promulgated by correctional agencies which set out what the environment will consist of when an execution occurs. The overwhelming majority of capital punishment jurisdictions have provided by statute a few restrictions that help make up the rules and regulations for conducting an execution.[5]

This section will review most of the statutory guidelines for carrying out the death penalty. It should be kept in mind that the bulk of the procedures for carrying out the death penalty are contained in administrative rules and regulations.

ATTENDANCE BY FAMILY MEMBERS OF THE VICTIM

Only four capital punishment jurisdictions allow by statute family members of a victim to attend the execution. Two of the jurisdictions allow only one family member of the victim to attend the execution.[6] Another jurisdiction sets the limit at three family members.[7] The fourth jurisdiction imposes no statutory limit on the number of family members that can attend the execution.[8]

FAMILY AND FRIENDS OF CAPITAL FELON

Although the majority of capital punishment jurisdictions do not allow members of a victim's family to attend the execution, the situation is different for the capital felon. A majority of jurisdictions provide by statute that a capital felon's family and friends may attend the execution. Restrictions are placed on the number of family members and friends of the capital felon who may attend the execution. The numerical restrictions are found in Table 15.0.

TABLE 15.0
FAMILY/FRIENDS THAT MAY VIEW EXECUTION

Number of Jurisdictions	Number of Family/Friends
Two[9]	10
Ten[10]	5
One[11]	4
Five[12]	3
One[13]	2
Five[14]	no statutory limit

MEDIA REPRESENTATION

The majority of capital punishment jurisdictions do not provide by statute for media attendance at executions. The jurisdictions that do provide for media attendance by statute are divided into two types: (1) newspaper reporters only and (2) media (which includes newspaper, television, and radio reporters).

Newspaper reporters only. Three capital punishment jurisdictions restrict by statute media presence at executions to that of newspaper reporters. Two of the jurisdictions do not set a numerical limitation on the number of newspaper reporters,[15] while the third jurisdiction limits the number to eight.[16]

Media in general. The statutes in 11 capital punishment jurisdictions provide for media representation at executions. The numerical limitations imposed on media representation are contained in Table 15.1.

TABLE 15.1
MEDIA REPRESENTATION AT EXECUTIONS

Jurisdiction	Total Media Representation
Kentucky	9
Utah	9
New Jersey	8
Tennessee	7
Pennsylvania	6
South Carolina	5
Ohio	3
South Dakota	1
Florida	no statutory limit
Oklahoma	no statutory limit
Washington	no statutory limit

Audio-visual restrictions. Although no capital punishment jurisdiction currently allows executions to be televised, the unanimous bar is not found in statutes. Only four jurisdictions set out in statutes that audio-visual recorders are prohibited from being used at executions.[17]

PUBLIC REPRESENTATION

The majority of capital punishment jurisdictions provide by statute for limited "respectable citizen" representation at executions.[18] All of these jurisdictions, except for Delaware, authorize correctional officials to select the public representation.[19] Table 15.2 sets out the numerical representation of the jurisdictions.

TABLE 15.2
PUBLIC REPRESENTATION AT EXECUTIONS

Number of Jurisdictions	Public Representation
1	15
7	12
1	10
1	9
1	8
1	7
8	6
1	3
2	2
2	no statutory limit

Citizen representation at an execution is voluntary. Persons selected by appropriate authority do not have to attend the execution. It should also be noted that the statutes use the phrases "respectable citizens" or "reputable citizens" to describe those who are selected as public representatives to attend executions.

INMATE REPRESENTATION

Statutes that use the phrases "respectable citizens" or "reputable citizens" do not define the terms. Doubtless, any definition given to the terms would exclude inmates. Does this mean that inmates are excluded per se from attending executions? Not necessarily.

Only four capital punishment jurisdictions specifically exclude, by statute, inmates from attending a capital felon's execution.[20] What this means, in theory, is that inmates in a majority of capital punishment jurisdictions may be able to attend executions as "friends" requested by capital felons. North Carolina by statute explicitly allows a capital felon to invite inmate friends to view the execution.

SPIRITUAL ADVISER

Hollywood popularized the notion of a capital felon going to the execution chamber with a priest close at hand. The classic depiction of this scenario involved Pat O'Brien playing a priest who attended James Cagney as he was ushered to the death chamber. Reality is not far behind Hollywood's fictional accounts of executions. A majority of capital punishment jurisdictions allow, by statute, spiritual advisers to be present at executions. Two types of spiritual advisers are provided for in statutes: (1) prison chaplains and (2) personal spiritual advisers.

Prison chaplain. All long-term correctional institutions have prison chaplains on staff. Prison chaplains play a crucial role in fulfilling the "rehabilitation" goal of the criminal justice system and may even provide some hope of spiritual rehabilitation for capital felons. This slim possibility has prompted five capital punishment jurisdictions to permit, by statute, prison chaplains to attend executions. Three of those jurisdictions limit prison chaplain representation to one.[21] The remaining two jurisdictions do not limit the number of prison chaplains who may attend executions.[22]

Personal spiritual adviser. Thirty capital punishment jurisdictions allow capital felons to invite their own personal spiritual advisers to be present at executions. These jurisdictions vary on the number of personal spiritual advisers who may be in attendance. Twelve jurisdictions limit personal spiritual adviser representation to one.[23] Ten jurisdictions set the number at two.[24] Eight jurisdictions do not have a statutory limit.[25]

PHYSICIAN REPRESENTATION

The question of whether an execution is successful, that is, is the capital felon dead, is important. For the majority of capital punishment jurisdictions, the question is answered by a physician.[26]

Physician representation at executions varies.[27] Some jurisdictions limit that representation to one,[28] a few jurisdictions set the limit at two,[29] and others allow three physicians to be in attendance.[30] Finally, a few jurisdictions do not have a statutory limit.[31]

Age Restrictions

A minority of capital punishment jurisdictions provide statutory restrictions on the age of persons allowed to be in attendance at executions. Seven jurisdictions provide that no minors are to be in attendance,[32] while two jurisdictions restrict attendance to persons 21 or over.[33]

Other Witnesses

All executions are attended by correctional commissioners or wardens (or their respective designated representatives), executioners, limited security personnel, and, of course, the capital felon scheduled for execution. Statutes round out execution witnesses with a limited number of other individuals.

Capital felon's counsel. A minority of capital punishment jurisdictions allow legal counsel for a capital felon to attend the execution.[34]

Attorney general. The statutes in eight capital punishment jurisdictions allow the jurisdiction's attorney general to attend executions.[35]

Prosecutor. Five capital punishment jurisdictions allow the prosecutor responsible for bringing about the capital felon's conviction and sentence to attend the execution.[36]

Judge. It is provided in the statutes of four capital punishment jurisdictions that the judge who presided over the capital felon's case may attend the execution.[37]

Court clerk. New Hampshire is the only jurisdiction that allows the clerk of the court wherein the capital felon was convicted and sentenced to attend the execution.

CHAPTER 16

Execution Methods
and Corpse Disposal

Under the common law a sentence of death was permitted to be carried out in a variety of painful and tortuous ways such as decapitation, quartering, and burning. The Eighth Amendment of the Constitution has been used to bar methods of execution that involve torture or great pain and suffering.

This chapter offers a review of the five methods of execution utilized by capital punishment jurisdictions: (1) firing squad, (2) hanging, (3) lethal injection, (4) electrocution, and (5) lethal gas. The chapter will conclude with a review of how death penalty statutes provide for disposal of the corpses of executed felons.

Execution Option Jurisdictions

As a preliminary to the individual treatment of death penalty methods, some discussion is in order regarding execution option jurisdictions. The phrase "execution option jurisdiction" refers to capital punishment jurisdictions that have statutes which provide for alternative methods of execution. There are three types of execution option jurisdictions: (1) capital felon option, (2) federal option, and (3) fallback option. A review of each follows.

CAPITAL FELON OPTION JURISDICTIONS

Capital felon option jurisdictions allow condemned felons to choose the method of execution. There are currently nine capital felon option jurisdictions.[1] All capital felon option jurisdictions provide two methods of execution. These jurisdictions also provide by statute that if a capital felon refuses to select a method of execution or fails to select a method within the statutory time frame given, then a statutory default method will be used. Capital felons have an average of about ten days, prior to the week of the scheduled execution, to select an execution method.

There are four categories of capital felon option jurisdictions. Each category is presented separately below.

Lethal injection–lethal gas jurisdictions. Missouri, North Carolina, and California permit capital felons to select between lethal injection and lethal gas as the method of execution. North Carolina's statute provides that lethal gas is a default method of execution, that is, a capital felon's failure to select or timely select a method would result in execution by lethal gas. California provides in its statute that lethal injection is the default method of execution.[2] Missouri's statute does not provide for a default method of execution.

Electrocution–lethal injection jurisdictions. Three jurisdictions, Ohio, South Carolina, and Virginia, allow capital felons to select as a method of death electrocution or lethal injection. The default method of execution in Ohio is electrocution. Lethal injection is the default method of execution in South Carolina and Virginia.

Hanging–lethal injection jurisdictions. The states of Montana and Washington provide by statute that capital felons may choose, as a method of execution, between hanging and lethal injection. Both jurisdictions utilize hanging as the default method of execution.[3]

Firing squad–lethal injection jurisdictions. Only one jurisdiction, Utah, provides the execution option of firing squad or lethal injection. The default method of execution in this jurisdiction is lethal injection.

FEDERAL OPTION JURISDICTION

The federal system has the most unique execution option statute. The federal option is set out in the following statute.

> **Federal System 18 U.S.C. A. § 3597(a):**
> A person who has been sentenced to death ... shall be committed to the custody of the Attorney General until exhaustion of the procedures for appeal of the judgment of conviction and for review of the sentence. When the sentence is to be implemented, the Attorney General shall release the person sentenced to death to the custody of a United States marshal, who shall supervise implementation of the sentence in the manner prescribed by the law of the State in which the sentence is imposed. If the law of the State does not provide for implementation of a sentence of death, the court shall designate another State, the law of which does provide for the implementation of a sentence of death, and the sentence shall be implemented in the latter State in the manner prescribed by such law.

As the above statute shows, execution in the federal system may take one of two paths. If the state in which the capital sentence was obtained is a capital punishment jurisdiction, then whatever method of execution is provided by that state will be imposed upon the capital felon. However, if the capital sentence was obtained in a non–capital punishment jurisdiction, the capital felon will be transported to a judicially determined capital punishment jurisdiction and executed according to the laws of that state.

FALLBACK OPTION JURISDICTIONS

Subsequent sections in this chapter will address the constitutionality of each method of execution currently being used. A matter related to this issue concerns alternative methods of execution should a particular method of execution be invalidated for any reason.

A minority of capital punishment jurisdictions have hedged their execution statutes by providing fallback option methods of execution.[4] Should the designated method of execution be found invalid, an alternative method of execution is provided for. There are two types of fallback option jurisdictions: (1) single fallback option and (2) dual fallback option.

Single fallback option jurisdictions. A single fallback option jurisdiction is one that has provided only a single alternative method of execution should the primary method be found invalid. Table 16.0 sets out single fallback option jurisdictions and the option provided by each.

TABLE 16.0
SINGLE FALLBACK OPTION JURISDICTIONS

	Fallback Options				
Jurisdiction	*Lethal injection*	*Lethal gas*	*Firing squad*	*Hanging*	*Electrocution*
Arkansas					X
California	X	X			
Delaware				X	
Idaho			X		
Illinois					X
Mississippi		X			
New Hampshire				X	
Ohio					X
South Carolina					X
Wyoming		X			

It will be noted that California's single fallback option, lethal injection or lethal gas, is not pure. This is because its options are its primary methods of execution. What California has done is provided that if either of its two primary methods is invalidated, then the remaining method of execution becomes the fallback option.

Dual fallback option jurisdictions. A dual fallback option jurisdiction is one that has provided a fallback option for its fallback option. Currently Oklahoma is the only dual fallback option jurisdiction. Oklahoma provides that electrocution is its initial fallback option, but should this option be invalidated, its second fallback option, hanging, is the method of execution.

Execution by Firing Squad

Death by firing squad is rooted in military tradition. Mutiny and desertion were among the offenses that militaries punished with death by firing squad. The common law did not accept or reject execution by firing squad. Common law judges simply never resorted to this method of execution.

The exact date that execution by firing squad was adopted by civilian law in the United States is not known. Records do show, however, that by the 1850s death by firing squad was a part of civilian law in the nation.

Several arguments are advanced against using firing squads for the imposition of the death penalty. First, it has been argued that death by firing squad is not a clean method of execution. One commentator noted that blood flows everywhere when a firing squad finishes its task.[5] The flow of blood is not something that anyone attempts to stop because that would defeat the purpose of the wounds. Splattered and flowing blood have been an anchor, for some, to support the contention that executions should not be carried out by using firing squads.

Second, it is argued that a firing squad is lucky if it brings death instantaneously to a capital felon. Death usually will not come swiftly. The capital felon is allowed to languish in pain and blood as the wounds slowly bring on death. Any cry for help must go unheard, for this would defeat the reason for the pain.

The final criticism of death by firing squad involves the use of a hood and circular target that are draped over the capital felon. It is said that placing a hood over the head of a capital felon depersonalizes him, so that the firing squad may carry out its duty. The circular target placed over the torso of a capital felon, while used for the purpose of directing the aim of the firing squad, reinforces the depersonalization of the capital felon.[6]

TABLE 16.1
NUMBER OF EXECUTIONS 1977–1994

	Number Executed		
Year of execution	*All races*	*White*	*Black*
1977–83	11	9	2
1984	21	13	8
1985	18	11	7
1986	18	11	7
1987	25	13	12
1988	11	6	5
1989	16	8	8
1990	23	16	7
1991	14	7	7
1992	31	19	11
1993	38	23	14
1994	31	20	11
Total	257	156	99

SOURCE: Capital Punishment 1994, Bureau of Justice Statistics Bulletin, *U.S. Department of Justice, p.10 (February 1996).*

FIRING SQUAD JURISDICTIONS

Only three capital punishment jurisdictions, Utah, Oklahoma, and Idaho, allow execution by firing squad. In Utah the firing squad is one of two methods of execution from which a capital felon may select. Idaho utilizes the firing squad as its single fallback option in the event its primary option is invalidated. Oklahoma provides for the use of a firing squad as a dual fallback option. Death by firing squad was deemed constitutional in *Wilkerson v. Utah,* 99 U.S. 130 (1878).[7]

Execution by Hanging

The common law accepted death by hanging as a legitimate method of execution.[8] Hanging has also been a traditional part of Anglo-American jurisprudence as a result of its common law lineage. Two principal arguments are waged in opposition to hanging as a method of execution. First, there is a risk that death will occur as a result of asphyxiation. This will happen if the execution is not properly done. Death by asphyxiation is slow and painful. As a result of the risk of asphyxiation and its attendant slow and agonizing pain, it is argued by some commentators that hanging should be prohibited as a method of execution.

The second, and most profound, argument against hanging is that there is a risk of decapitation. If the hanging is done improperly, the head of a capital felon could be torn from its trunk during the process. While decapitation was accepted and practiced under the common law as a method of execution, it has not been accepted by Anglo-American jurisprudence. Antihanging proponents contend that because of the risk of decapitation, hanging should not be used as a method of execution.[9]

HANGING JURISDICTIONS

In the early history of the nation, hanging was a method of execution used by all capital punishment jurisdictions, but industrial and medical technological advances have reduced reliance upon hanging as a method of execution. Currently only five capital punishment jurisdictions recognize hanging as a method of execution. Two of those jurisdictions utilize hanging as a capital felon option.[10] In both jurisdictions hanging is the default method of execution. Two jurisdictions utilize hanging as a single fallback option.[11] That is, if the primary method of execution is invalidated, hanging will be used. The fifth jurisdiction utilizes hanging as a dual fallback option, that is, should its initial fallback option be invalidated, hanging becomes the method of execution.[12]

In dicta the Supreme Court indicated in *Wilkerson v. Utah*, 99 U.S. 130 (1878), that death by hanging did not violate the Constitution. In the relatively recent decision of *Campbell v. Wood*, 18 F.3d 662 (1994), it was indicated on the merits that hanging did not violate the Constitution. In *Rupe v. Wood*, 863 F.Supp. 1307 (W.D.Wash. 1994), however, it was held that hanging was unconstitutional as a method of execution for the defendant in that case because there was a substantial likelihood that he would be decapitated if hung because of his weight (in excess of 400 pounds).

Execution by Lethal Injection

Lethal injection as a method of execution was not known to the common law. In the decision of *Ex parte Granviel*, 561 S.W.2d 503 (Tex.Cr.App. 1978), the court noted that "[t]he intravenous injection of a lethal substance as a means of execution has not been heretofore utilized in this nation[.]"

Injection of a barbiturate and a paralytic agent into the bloodstream of a capital felon represents a new method of execution. Lethal injection, as this new method is called, is a child of the 1970s. (Oklahoma was the first jurisdiction to provide by statute for execution by lethal injection, doing so on

TABLE 16.2
METHODS OF EXECUTION
USED DURING THE PERIOD 1977–1994

Method of execution	Number of times used
Firing squad	1
Hanging	2
Lethal gas	9
Electrocution	114
Lethal injection	131

SOURCE: Capital Punishment 1994, Bureau of Justice Statistics Bulletin, *U.S. Department of Justice, p.11 (February 1996).*

May 10, 1977.) As shown by Table 16.2, lethal injection has rapidly become the leading method of execution in the nation.

The swiftness with which lethal injection has become the executioner's choice reflects the majority view that it is the most humane method devised to inflict death legally. Of course there is another side to the coin.

Lethal injection has been criticized on various fronts as being an unacceptable method of execution. One commentator reported that utilizing a needle to produce death can be painful and necessitate surgery to impart the needle. It was reported that in a 1985 execution in Texas, it took a total of 23 attempts, covering a span of 40 minutes, to inject the needle in a capital felon.

Next, it is argued that the drugs used do not always induce a quick and painless death. When death comes slowly, it is contended that capital felons endure psychological trauma and in some instances physical pain.

The most thorny issue raised by proponents against lethal injection is that the drugs used have not been approved by the federal Food and Drug Administration (FDA) for the purpose in which they are being used. This issue was litigated in the Supreme Court in the case of *Heckler v. Chaney*, 470 U.S. 821 (1985).

The plaintiffs in *Heckler* had requested that the FDA investigate and prosecute governmental officials who used drugs for the purpose of inflicting death without getting FDA approval to use the drugs for such a purpose. FDA refused the request. The matter entered the federal judicial system for the purpose of compelling the FDA to enforce federal laws.

The federal district court dismissed the litigation on the grounds that "decisions of executive departments and agencies to refrain from instituting investigative and enforcement proceedings are essentially unreviewable by the courts." The plaintiffs appealed the dismissal of their case to a federal court of appeals.

The federal court of appeals disagreed with the district court and held that courts could review decisions by executive administrative agencies not to investigate potential violations of law. The court of appeals noted that because "the FDA assumed jurisdiction over drugs used to put animals to sleep," it was irrational not to investigate the plaintiffs' claim "that use of the drugs could lead to a cruel and protracted death[.]"

FDA took the case to the Supreme Court. The position taken by FDA was that courts could not review its decision to refuse to investigate a matter. The Supreme Court agreed with the FDA. In doing so the Supreme Court made the following observations:

> ... First, an agency decision not to enforce [statutes] often involves a complicated balancing of a number of factors which are peculiarly within its expertise. Thus, the agency must not only assess whether a violation has occurred, but whether agency resources are best spent on this violation or another, whether the agency is likely to succeed if it acts, whether the particular enforcement action requested best fits the agency's over-all policies, and, indeed, whether the agency has enough resources to undertake the action at all. An agency generally cannot act against each technical violation of the statute it is charged with enforcing. The agency is far better equipped than the courts to deal with the many variables involved in the proper ordering of its priorities....
>
> In addition to these administrative concerns, we note that when an agency refuses to act it generally does not exercise its coercive power over an individual's liberty or property rights, and thus does not infringe upon areas that courts often are called upon to protect. Similarly, when an agency does act to enforce, that action itself provides a focus for judicial review, inasmuch as the agency must have exercised its power in some manner. The action at least can be reviewed to determine whether the agency exceeded its statutory powers.

The Supreme Court went on to reverse the decision of the court of appeals.

The decision in *Heckler* has kept alive the debate as to whether drugs may be used to execute capital felons when the FDA has not given its stamp of approval to such usage.

LETHAL INJECTION JURISDICTIONS

As the executioner's choice of inflicting death, 31 capital punishment jurisdictions currently utilize lethal injection as a method of carrying out the death penalty. Nine jurisdictions provide lethal injectio as a capital felon option.[13] Four of the latter jurisdictions provide that lethal injection is the default method of execution.[14] The remaining 22 lethal injection jurisdictions utilize this method exclusively.[15] The statutes below illustrate the variation in how capital punishment jurisdictions provide for lethal injection.

Colorado Revised Statutes § 16-11-401 and 402:

The manner of inflicting the punishment of death shall be by the administration of a lethal injection.... For the purposes of this part ... "lethal injection" means a continuous intravenous injection of a lethal quantity of sodium thiopental or other equally or more effective substance sufficient to cause death....

... The execution shall be performed in the room or place by a person selected by the executive director and trained to administer intravenous injections. Death shall be pronounced by a licensed physician or a coroner according to accepted medical standards.

Oregon Revised Statutes § 137.473:

(1) The punishment of death shall be inflicted by the intravenous administration of a lethal quantity of an ultra-short-acting barbiturate in combination with a chemical paralytic agent and potassium chloride or other equally effective substances sufficient to cause death....

(2) The person who administers the lethal injection ... shall not thereby be considered to be engaged in the practice of medicine.

South Dakota Codified Laws § 23A-27A-32:

The punishment of death shall be inflicted by the intravenous administration of a lethal quantity of an ultra-short-acting barbiturate in combination with a chemical paralytic agent and continuing the application thereof until the convict is pronounced dead by a licensed physician according to accepted standards of medical practice. An execution carried out by lethal injection shall be performed by a person selected by the warden and trained to administer the injection. The person administering the injection need not be a physician, registered nurse or licensed practical nurse.... Any infliction of the punishment of death by administration of the required lethal substance or substances in the manner required by this section may not be construed to be the practice of medicine and any pharmacist or pharmaceutical supplier is authorized to dispense the drugs to the warden without prescription, for carrying out the provisions of this section[.]

Two issues need to be highlighted regarding the above statutes. First, none of the statutes require that a medical professional administer the lethal drug. This issue has been a source of litigation by capital felons, who contend that the use of nonmedical professionals increases the risk that death will be slow and agonizing. This argument has been rejected as a basis for holding that lethal injection is cruel and unusual punishment.[16]

A second matter involves the absence of a named ultra-short-acting barbiturate in the Oregon and South Dakota statutes. The Colorado statute designates (as an option) sodium thiopental as the lethal drug of choice. The majority of lethal injection jurisdictions follow Oregon and South Dakota in failing to name a specific lethal drug. This issue was litigated in *Ex parte Granviel*, supra, in which the defendant contended that failure to name a specific lethal drug made the death penalty statute vague and therefore constitutionally void. The defendant's position and the state's responses were set out in *Granviel* as follows:

> [The defendant] argues it cannot be ascertained from the statute what substance or substances can be used in the injection and that the statute fails to offer any hint as to which substance or substances would be permissible. The State points out that the ... electrocution statutes throughout the United States have not prescribed the use of a chair, the amount of voltage, the volume of amperage, the place of attachment of electrodes, or whether or not AC or DC current shall be used. The earlier hanging statutes did not, the State argues, prescribe the type of gallows, the height of the fall, the type of rope or type of knot used, etc. Likewise, the State says, the laws relating to execution by firing squads did not specify the number of executioners, the muzzle velocity of the rifles, the type of bullets, or the distance of the guns to the condemned. The State urges the earlier execution statutes were never in any greater detail than the statute under attack and that none of them had been declared unconstitutional on the basis of being vague.

The *Granviel* court rejected the defendant's vagueness challenge and held:

> While neither the exact substance to be injected nor the procedure surrounding the execution is expressly set forth in [the statute] we cannot conclude that failure to specify the exact substances and the procedure to be used render the statute unconstitutionally vague. The statute here, unlike penal statutes, was not intended to give fair notice of what specific behavior ... constitutes a criminal offense.... The context of the statute is a public statement of the general manner of execution. In this sense the statute is sufficiently definite....
>
> ... So long as the statute is sufficiently complete to accomplish the regulation of the particular matters falling within the Legislature's jurisdiction, the matters of detail that are reasonably necessary for the ultimate application, operation and enforcement of the law may be expressly delegated to the authority charged with the administration of the statute.

The position of the *Granviel* court was not that the issue of the type of lethal drug used was irrelevant. The opinion acknowledged that the issue of the drug of choice was highly relevant and important, but the court believed that the drug of choice was a matter that could be delegated to administrative officials to determine.

Execution by Electrocution

Use of electricity to execute the death penalty dates back to the late nineteenth century. Two primary arguments have persisted for over 100 years as to why electrocution should not be used as a method of execution.

First, death by electrocution is not always immediate. For example, it was reported that in executing the defendant in *In re Kemmler*, 136 U.S. 436 (1890), electricity jolted through his body for five minutes. Throughout the ordeal the defendant had to endure great pain. It was said that his blood turned black and purple foam drooled from his mouth.

The second major argument against electrocution is that it grotesquely disfigures and mutilates the capital felon's body. It has been reported that the eyes of capital felons burst out or hideously melt, brains bake rock solid, flames burst through skin and bodies are burned to charcoal.

When done correctly, death by electrocution is immediate and arguably painless, but electrocution is not always carried out correctly. It is because of inadequately trained electrocutionists and their painfully long executions that this method of death is constantly the source of litigation. Most capital felons put to death by electrocution have died slow, agonizing deaths.[17]

ELECTROCUTION JURISDICTIONS

At present 13 capital punishment jurisdictions utilize electrocution as a method of execution. Three of these jurisdictions provide electrocution as a capital felon option;[18] only one such jurisdiction, Ohio, provides that electrocution is the default method. Two jurisdictions utilize electrocution solely as a single fallback option.[19] One jurisdiction utilizes electrocution as part of its dual fallback option.[20] The remaining seven jurisdictions utilize electrocution exclusively.[21]

The constitutionality of this method of execution was challenged in *Kemmler*. The Supreme Court held in that case that electrocution was not a cruel and unusual method of execution.

In another case, *Francis v. Resweber*, 329 U.S. 459 (1947), the defendant was electrocuted but did not die. The state of Louisiana sought to electrocute him a second time. The defendant presented three constitutional arguments as to why Louisiana should be prohibited from carrying out a second execution of him. The Supreme Court responded to the arguments as follows:

> First. Our minds rebel against permitting the same sovereignty to punish an accused twice for the same offense. But where the accused successfully seeks review of a conviction, there is no double jeopardy upon a new trial.... When an accident, with no suggestion of malevolence, prevents the consummation of a sentence, the state's subsequent course in

the administration of its criminal law is not affected on that account by any requirement of due process under the Fourteenth Amendment. We find no double jeopardy here which can be said to amount to a denial of federal due process in the proposed execution.

Second. We find nothing in what took place here which amounts to cruel and unusual punishment in the constitutional sense.... The traditional humanity of modern Anglo-American law forbids the infliction of unnecessary pain in the execution of the death sentence....

Petitioner's suggestion is that because he once underwent the psychological strain of preparation for electrocution, now to require him to undergo this preparation again subjects him to a lingering or cruel and unusual punishment. Even the fact that petitioner has already been subjected to a current of electricity does not make his subsequent execution any more cruel in the constitutional sense than any other execution. The cruelty against which the Constitution protects a convicted man is cruelty inherent in the method of punishment, not the necessary suffering involved in any method employed to extinguish life humanely. The fact that an unforeseeable accident prevented the prompt consummation of the sentence cannot, it seems to us, add an element of cruelty to a subsequent execution. There is no purpose to inflict unnecessary pain nor any unnecessary pain involved in the proposed execution.... We cannot agree that the hardship imposed upon the petitioner rises to that level of hardship denounced as denial of due process because of cruelty.

Third. The Supreme Court of Louisiana also rejected petitioner's contention that death inflicted after his prior sufferings would deny him the equal protection of the laws, guaranteed by the Fourteenth Amendment. This suggestion ... is based on the idea that execution, after an attempt at execution has failed, would be a more severe punishment than is imposed upon others guilty for a like offense. That is, since others do not go through the strain of preparation for execution a second time or have not experienced a non-lethal current in a prior attempt at execution, as petitioner did, to compel petitioner to submit to execution after these prior experiences denies to him equal protection. Equal protection does not protect a prisoner ... against accidents during his detention for execution. Laws cannot prevent accidents nor can a law equally protect all against them. So long as the law applies to all alike, the requirements of equal protection are met. We have no right to assume that Louisiana singled out Francis for a treatment other than that which has been or would generally be applied.

Execution by Lethal Gas

The use of lethal gas as a method of execution is an early twentieth-century Anglo-American jurisprudential phenomenon. The chemical agent used to carry out this method of execution is cyanide gas.

Two arguments are offered against the use of lethal gas as a method of execution. First, it is asserted that cyanide gas induces excruciating pain. Capital felons have been known to urinate, defecate, vomit, and drool while undergoing death by lethal gas. Second, and the primary threat to continued use of lethal gas, death by this method can take over ten minutes. It is argued that such a span of time amounts to pure torture.

LETHAL GAS JURISDICTIONS

Currently five capital punishment jurisdictions provide by statute for the use of lethal gas to execute the death penalty. Three jurisdictions utilize lethal gas as a capital felon option,[22] while two other jurisdictions utilize lethal gas as a single fallback option.[23]

Prior to 1983 no federal court had ever rendered an opinion on the constitutionality of execution by lethal gas. Several state appellate courts had prior to 1983 addressed the issue of whether execution by lethal gas was a cruel and unusual method of punishment. The first such court to do so was the Nevada Supreme Court in the case of *State v. Gee Jon*, 211 P. 676 (Nev. 1923). The *Gee Jon* court found the method constitutional.[24]

Since 1983 several federal appellate courts have addressed the issue of whether lethal gas is a cruel and unusual punishment. The federal appellate courts are split on this issue. Two courts, concluded in *Gray v. Lucas*, 710 F.2d 1048 (5th Cir. 1983), and *Hunt v. Nuth*, 57 F.3d 1327 (4th Cir. 1995), that lethal gas was not cruel and unusual punishment, while the third court came to the opposite conclusion, in *Fierro v. Gomez*, 77 F.3d 301 (9th Cir. 1996), *reversed*, 117 S.Ct. 285 (1996). Although the Supreme Court eventually vacated the court of appeals decision in *Fierro*, it did so without any guidance on the issue it reversed. In a terse one-paragraph memorandum opinion, the Court vacated the judgment and merely remanded the case with instructions that the appellate court reconsider its judgment in light of the fact that the jurisdiction in controversy (California) amended its death penalty statute so that lethal gas would be used only if requested by a capital felon.

Disposal of Executed Corpse

The present state of the law protects the corpse of a capital felon. There are five statutorily recognized dispositions for the bodies of executed capital felons.[25] Each disposition follows.

PERMIT RELATIVES TO TAKE THE CORPSE

Sixteen capital punishment jurisdictions provide by statute that the corpse of an executed felon is to be turned over to a requesting relative.[26] Six of those jurisdictions go so far as to pay the cost of shipping the corpse to a requesting relative at the last residence of the capital felon.[27]

PERMIT A FRIEND TO TAKE THE CORPSE

The statutes in 11 capital punishment jurisdictions provide that the corpse of an executed felon may be turned over to a requesting friend.[28] In this situation the corpse would only be given to a friend of the capital felon if no relative made a request for the corpse.

A PERSON DESIGNATED BY THE FELON

Currently only two capital punishment jurisdictions provide by statute that the corpse of an executed felon may be turned over to a person designated by the capital felon prior to execution.[29] This type of disposal contemplates having the corpse sent to a medical facility for research.

UNCLAIMED CORPSE
DONATED TO MEDICAL CENTER

The statutes in five capital punishment jurisdictions provide that the corpse of a capital felon may be turned over to a medical center for research.[30] This type of disposal is only triggered if neither relatives nor friends of the capital felon request the corpse.

UNCLAIMED CORPSE BURIED BY THE JURISDICTION

If no claim is made for the corpse of an executed felon, the statutes in 15 capital punishment jurisdictions provide for burial by the jurisdiction.[31] These statutes also provide that the cost of burial is borne by the jurisdiction.

Tables of Selected
Death Penalty Provisions

A few prefatory remarks are in order to assist the reader in understanding the tables that comprise Appendix I. Table A-1 sets out examples of statutory criteria that allow a murder suspect to be prosecuted under death penalty laws, as opposed to being prosecuted for murder under nondeath penalty laws. Table A-2 is fairly straightforward in showing the method of execution allowed in each capital punishment jurisdiction. Table A-3 provides information regarding the disposition of the bodies of executed felons. It should be kept in mind that many capital punishment jurisdictions do not indicate in their death penalty statutes in what manner the bodies of executed felons are to be disposed. Table A-4 provides information regarding who may be present during an execution. Table A-5 sets out the first illustration of factors that permit the death penalty to be actually imposed upon a felon. These factors are all underlyng crimes that occur at the time a murder is committed. Table A-6 is the second illustration of factors that permit the death penalty to be imposed. These factors involve the identity of the victim of murder. Table A-7 is the final illustration of factors that permit the imposition of the death penalty. Table A-8 sets out examples of factors that mitigate against imposing the death penalty. In reviewing all of the tables the reader should keep in mind that the text of the book explains and qualifies much of the raw information contained in the tables. Therefore, the reader should consult (using the index or table of contents) the pertinent text material for a complete grasp of what the tables convey.

Death-Eligible Offense

Jurisdiction	Murder Without More	Felony Murder	Victim Specific Murder	Murder for Hire	Drive-by Shooting Murder	Specific Device Murder	Multiple Victim Murder	Murder on the Run	Perpetrator Status Murder
Alabama		*	*	*	*	*	*		*
Arizona	*	*						*	
Arkansas	*	*	*	*	*			*	*
California	*	*	*	*	*	*	*	*	*
Colorado	*	*						*	
Connecticut		*	*	*			*		*
Delaware	*	*	*			*		*	
Florida	*	*				*		*	
Georgia	*	*							
Idaho	*	*	*			*		*	*
Illinois	*	*	*	*	*				*
Indiana	*	*							
Kansas		*	*	*			*		*
Kentucky	*	*							
Louisiana	*	*	*	*	*		*		
Maryland	*	*				*		*	

State								
Mississippi			*		*			*
Missouri	*							
Montana	*							
Nebraska	*						*	
Nevada	*						*	*
New Hampshire	*				*		*	*
New Jersey	*				*			
New Mexico	*							
New York	*			*	*		*	*
North Carolina	*			*				
Ohio	*						*	
Oklahoma	*				*		*	
Oregon		*			*		*	*
Pennsylvania	*							
South Carolina	*	*		*				
South Dakota	*	*		*				
Tennessee	*	*		*				
Texas	*				*	*	*	*
Utah	*				*	*	*	*
Virginia	*			*	*	*		
Washington	*			*	*	*	*	*
Wyoming	*			*				
Federal System	*			*	*	*	*	*

TABLE A-2
METHOD OF EXECUTION BY JURISDICTION

Method of Execution

Jurisdiction	Firing Squad	Hanging	Lethal Injection	Electrocution	Lethal Gas
Alabama				*	
Arizona			*		
Arkansas			*	*	
California			*		*
Colorado			*		
Connecticut				*	
Delaware		*	*		
Florida				*	
Georgia				*	
Idaho	*		*		
Illinois			*	*	
Indiana			*		
Kansas			*		
Kentucky				*	
Louisiana			*		
Maryland			*		
Mississippi			*		*

State					
Missouri			*		*
Montana		*	*		
Nebraska				*	
Nevada		*	*		
New Hampshire		*	*		
New Jersey			*		
New Mexico			*		
New York			*		
North Carolina			*		*
Ohio			*	*	
Oklahoma		*	*	*	
Oregon			*		
Pennsylvania			*		
South Carolina			*	*	
South Dakota			*		
Tennessee			*	*	
Texas			*		
Utah	*		*		
Virginia			*	*	
Washington		*	*		
Wyoming			*		*
Federal System					

* Uses the method of the state wherein the crime occurred.

TABLE A-3
DISPOSITION OF EXECUTED CORPSE BY JURISDICTION**

Jurisdiction	Disposition				
	Relative Takes	Friend Takes	Designated Person Takes	Medical Center	Jurisdiction Buries
Alabama	*	*	*		*
Arizona					
Arkansas					
California					
Colorado					
Connecticut	*	*			*
Delaware					
Florida	*	*			*
Georgia	*	*			*
Idaho					
Illinois					
Indiana					
Kansas		*			
Kentucky	*	*			*
Louisiana					
Maryland				*	
Mississippi	*	*			*

State				
Missouri				
Montana				
Nebraska				
Nevada				
New Hampshire				
New Jersey	*	*	*	*
New Mexico				
New York	*	*	*	*
North Carolina	*	*		*
Ohio	*	*		*
Oklahoma				
Oregon				
Pennsylvania	*		*	*
South Carolina	*			*
South Dakota	*			*
Tennessee				
Texas	*	*	*	*
Utah				
Virginia	*			
Washington		*		
Wyoming	*			*
Federal System				

**These data reflect what is contained in the death penalty statutes of each jurisdiction.

Table A-4
Execution Witnesses by Jurisdiction**

Jurisdiction	Witness								
	Victim Family	Felon Family	Limited Public	Other Inmates	Minister	Doctor	Felon Counsel	Prosecutor	Judge
Alabama		*			*	*			
Arizona		*	*		*	*			
Arkansas		*							
California			*		*	*			
Colorado			*			*			
Connecticut			*	*	*				
Delaware	*		*						
Florida			*		*	*	*		
Georgia		*	*		*	*	*		
Idaho									
Illinois			*						
Indiana		*			*	*			
Kansas		*	*		*	*			
Kentucky		*			*	*			
Louisiana	*		*		*	*			
Maryland					*		*		
Mississippi		*			*	*			

State	1	2	3	4	5	6	7	8	9	10	11
Missouri	*							*			
Montana											
Nebraska		*						*			
Nevada							*		*		
New Hampshire			*			*			*		*
New Jersey			*			*			*		
New Mexico			*			*			*		
New York			*			*	*		*		*
North Carolina			*		*	*	*		*		
Ohio	*		*			*			*		
Oklahoma			*			*			*	*	
Oregon			*			*			*		
Pennsylvania				*		*			*		
South Carolina				*		*	*		*		
South Dakota			*			*	*		*		*
Tennessee			*			*			*		
Texas			*			*			*		*
Utah			*			*	*		*		
Virginia				*		*			*		
Washington		*				*	*		*		*
Wyoming			*			*			*		
Federal System											

*These data reflect what is contained in the death penalty statutes of each jurisdiction.

TABLE A-5
OFFENSE STATUTORY
AGGRAVATING CIRCUMSTANCES BY JURISDICTION

Criminal Offense Aggravator

Jurisdiction	Sexual Offense	Robbery	Burglary	Kidnap	Arson	Escape	Plane Hijack	Drug Offense	Carjack
Alabama	*	*	*	*		*			
Arizona									
Arkansas						*			
California	*	*	*	*	*	*			*
Colorado	*	*	*	*	*	*			
Connecticut									
Delaware	*	*	*	*	*	*			
Florida	*	*	*	*	*	*	*	*	
Georgia			*	*	*	*			
Idaho	*	*	*	*	*				
Illinois	*	*	*	*	*		*	*	*
Indiana	*	*	*	*	*			*	*
Kansas									
Kentucky	*	*	*		*				
Louisiana	*	*	*	*	*	*		*	
Maryland	*	*		*	*	*			*

State							
Mississippi		*	*	*	*	*	*
Missouri		*		*		*	*
Montana			*	*	*	*	
Nebraska							
Nevada			*	*	*	*	*
New Hampshire					*	*	
New Jersey			*	*	*	*	*
New Mexico				*	*	*	
New York			*	*	*	*	*
North Carolina		*		*	*	*	*
Ohio				*	*	*	*
Oklahoma					*	*	
Oregon					*	*	
Pennsylvania	*	*	*	*	*	*	*
South Carolina	*		*	*	*	*	
South Dakota	*				*	*	
Tennessee		*	*	*	*	*	*
Texas			*	*	*	*	*
Utah		*	*	*	*	*	*
Virginia				*	*	*	
Washington			*		*	*	*
Wyoming		*	*	*	*	*	
Federal System	*	*	*	*	*		

Table A-6
Identity of Victim Statutory Aggravating Circumstances by Jurisdiction

Identity of Victim Aggravator

Jurisdiction	Prison Guard	Police	Fire-fighter	Witness	Prose-cutor	Judge	Juror	Elected Official	Pregnant Woman
Alabama									
Arizona		*							
Arkansas									
California		*	*	*	*	*	*	*	*
Colorado		*	*	*	*	*			
Connecticut									
Delaware	*	*	*	*	*	*			
Florida		*						*	
Georgia	*	*			*	*			
Idaho		*	*	*	*	*			
Illinois	*	*	*	*	*	*			
Indiana	*	*	*	*		*			
Kansas									
Kentucky	*	*						*	
Louisiana	*	*	*	*	*	*	*		*
Maryland		*							
Mississippi									

State										
Missouri	*			*		*	*	*	*	*
Montana		*								
Nebraska	*	*								
Nevada		*	*							
New Hampshire										
New Jersey										
New Mexico	*	*				*				
New York		*				*	*			
North Carolina	*	*	*		*	*	*		*	*
Ohio		*				*	*		*	
Oklahoma	*	*								
Oregon	*	*			*	*	*	*	*	
Pennsylvania	*	*				*	*			*
South Carolina	*	*	*				*			
South Dakota	*	*	*				*			
Tennessee	*	*	*				*			
Texas	*	*	*							
Utah	*	*	*		*	*	*		*	*
Virginia		*								
Washington	*	*	*		*	*	*		*	*
Wyoming		*			*	*	*		*	*
Federal System										*

TABLE A-7
OTHER STATUTORY AGGRAVATING
CIRCUMSTANCES BY JURISDICTION

				Other Aggravator					
Jurisdiction	Heinous, Cruel	Obtain Money	Multiple Victims	Risk to Others	In Custody	Prior Felony	Explosives	Torture	Order Killing
Alabama	*	*		*	*	*			
Arizona	*	*	*	*	*	*			
Arkansas	*	*	*	*	*	*	*		
California	*	*	*			*	*	*	
Colorado	*	*	*	*	*	*	*		
Connecticut	*	*		*		*			
Delaware		*	*		*	*	*	*	*
Florida	*	*		*	*	*	*		
Georgia		*		*	*	*		*	*
Idaho	*	*	*	*		*			
Illinois		*			*	*		*	*
Indiana		*			*	*	*		
Kansas	*	*		*	*	*			*
Kentucky		*	*	*	*	*			
Louisiana	*	*		*	*	*			
Maryland		*	*		*				

Mississippi	*	*				*		*		*	*
Missouri		*	*		*	*	*	*		*	*
Montana		*			*		*	*		*	
Nebraska	*	*		*	*	*		*		*	
Nevada		*	*		*	*	*	*		*	
New Hampshire		*		*		*		*		*	
New Jersey		*	*	*		*		*		*	*
New Mexico		*					*				
New York		*	*		*		*	*		*	
North Carolina	*	*	*	*		*		*	*	*	
Ohio		*	*				*	*		*	
Oklahoma	*	*	*	*		*	*	*		*	
Oregon		*	*	*			*	*	*	*	
Pennsylvania		*		*		*		*		*	
South Carolina		*	*	*	*	*		*		*	*
South Dakota		*	*		*	*		*		*	*
Tennessee	*	*		*	*	*	*	*	*	*	
Texas		*	*	*			*	*		*	
Utah	*	*	*	*		*	*	*	*	*	
Virginia		*	*	*		*		*		*	*
Washington		*	*	*		*		*			
Wyoming	*	*	*	*		*	*	*	*	*	
Federal System	*	*	*	*		*	*	*	*	*	*

TABLE A-8
STATUTORY MITIGATING CIRCUMSTANCES BY JURISDICTION

Statutory Mitigator

Jurisdiction	No Prior Record	Mental Problem	Victim Consent	Minor Role	Extreme Duress	Impaired	Age	No Threat	Cooperation
Alabama	*	*	*	*	*	*			
Arizona				*	*	*	*		
Arkansas	*	*		*	*	*	*		
California	*	*	*	*	*	*	*		
Colorado	*	*		*	*	*	*	*	*
Connecticut				*	*	*			
Delaware									
Florida	*	*	*	*	*	*	*		
Georgia									
Idaho									
Illinois	*	*	*	*	*				
Indiana	*	*	*	*	*	*			
Kansas	*	*	*	*	*	*	*		
Kentucky	*	*	*	*	*	*	*		
Louisiana	*	*		*		*	*		
Maryland	*		*			*	*	*	
Mississippi	*	*	*	*		*	*		

State									
Missouri	*	*	*	*	*	*	*	*	
Montana	*	*	*	*	*	*	*	*	
Nebraska	*	*	*	*	*	*	*	*	
Nevada	*	*	*	*	*	*		*	
New Hampshire	*	*	*	*	*	*	*	*	*
New Jersey	*	*	*	*		*	*	*	
New Mexico	*	*	*		*	*	*	*	*
New York	*	*		*	*	*	*		*
North Carolina	*	*	*		*	*	*	*	*
Ohio	*		*	*	*	*	*		
Oklahoma	*								
Oregon	*	*	*			*	*		
Pennsylvania	*	*	*	*	*	*	*	*	
South Carolina	*	*	*	*	*	*	*	*	
South Dakota									
Tennessee	*	*	*	*	*	*	*	*	
Texas									
Utah	*	*	*	*	*	*	*	*	
Virginia	*	*	*	*		*	*	*	
Washington									
Wyoming	*	*	*	*	*	*	*	*	
Federal System	*	*	*	*	*	*	*		

Federal Death Penalty Laws

18 U.S.C.A 3591. Sentence of Death.

(a) A defendant who has been found guilty of—
    (1) an offense described in section 794 or section 2381; or
    (2) any other offense for which a sentence of death is provided, if the defendant, as determined beyond a reasonable doubt at the hearing under section 3593—
        (A) intentionally killed the victim;
        (B) intentionally inflicted serious bodily injury that resulted in the death of the victim;
        (C) intentionally participated in an act, contemplating that the life of a person would be taken or intending that lethal force would be used in connection with a person, other than one of the participants in the offense, and the victim died as a direct result of the act; or
        (D) intentionally and specifically engaged in an act of violence, knowing that the act created a grave risk of death to a person, other than one of the participants in the offense, such that participation in the act constituted a reckless disregard for human life and the victim died as a direct result of the act,

shall be sentenced to death if, after consideration of the factors set forth in section 3592 in the course of a hearing held pursuant to section 3593, it is determined that imposition of a sentence of death is justified, except that no person may be sentenced to death who was less than 18 years of age at the time of the offense.

(b) A defendant who has been found guilty of—
    (1) an offense referred to in section 408(c)(1) of the Controlled Substances Act (21 U.S.C. 848(c)(1)), committed as part of a continuing criminal enterprise offense under the conditions described in subsection (b) of that section which involved not less than twice the quantity

of controlled substance described in subsection (b)(2)(A) or twice the gross receipts described in subsection (b)(2)(B);
or
(2) an offense referred to in section 408(c)(1) of the Controlled Substances Act (21 U.S.C. 848(c)(1)), committed as part of a continuing criminal enterprise offense under that section, where the defendant is a principal administrator, organizer, or leader of such an enterprise, and the defendant, in order to obstruct the investigation or prosecution of the enterprise or an offense involved in the enterprise, attempts to kill or knowingly directs, advises, authorizes, or assists another to attempt to kill any public officer, juror, witness, or members of the family or household of such a person,

shall be sentenced to death if, after consideration of the factors set forth in section 3592 in the course of a hearing held pursuant to section 3593, it is determined that imposition of a sentence of death is justified, except that no person may be sentenced to death who was less than 18 years of age at the time of the offense.

18 U.S.C.A. 3592. Mitigating and Aggravating Factors to Be Considered in Determining Whether a Sentence of Death Is Justified

(a) Mitigating factors. — In determining whether a sentence of death is to be imposed on a defendant, the finder of fact shall consider any mitigating factor, including the following:

(1) Impaired capacity. — The defendant's capacity to appreciate the wrongfulness of the defendant's conduct or to conform conduct to the requirements of law was significantly impaired, regardless of whether the capacity was so impaired as to constitute a defense to the charge.

(2) Duress. — The defendant was under unusual and substantial duress, regardless of whether the duress was of such a degree as to constitute a defense to the charge.

(3) Minor participation. — The defendant is punishable as a principal in the offense, which was committed by another, but the defendant's participation was relatively minor, regardless of whether the participation was so minor as to constitute a defense to the charge.

(4) Equally culpable defendants. — Another defendant or defendants, equally culpable in the crime, will not be punished by death.

(5) No prior criminal record. — The defendant did not have a significant prior history of other criminal conduct.

(6) Disturbance. — The defendant committed the offense under severe mental or emotional disturbance.

(7) Victim's consent. — The victim consented to the criminal conduct that resulted in the victim's death.

(8) Other factors. — Other factors in the defendant's background, record, or character or any other circumstance of the offense that mitigate against imposition of the death sentence.

(b) Aggravating factors for espionage and treason. — In determining whether a sentence of death is justified for an offense described in section 3591(a)(1), the jury, or if there is no jury, the court, shall consider each of the following aggravating factors for which notice has been given and determine which, if any, exist:

(1) Prior espionage or treason offense. — The defendant has previously been convicted of another offense involving espionage or treason for which a sentence of either life imprisonment or death was authorized by law.

(2) Grave risk to national security. — In the commission of the offense the defendant knowingly created a grave risk of substantial danger to the national security.

(3) Grave risk of death. — In the commission of the offense the defendant knowingly created a grave risk of death to another person.

The jury, or if there is no jury, the court, may consider whether any other aggravating factor for which notice has been given exists.

(c) Aggravating factors for homicide. — In determining whether a sentence of death is justified for an offense described in section 3591(a)(2), the jury, or if there is no jury, the court, shall consider each of the following aggravating factors for which notice has been given and determine which, if any, exist:

(1) Death during commission of another crime. — The death, or injury resulting in death, occurred during the commission or attempted commission of, or during the immediate flight from the commission of, an offense under section 32 (destruction of aircraft or aircraft facilities), section 33 (destruction of motor vehicles or motor vehicle facilities), section 36 (violence at international airports), section 351 (violence against Members of Congress, Cabinet officers, or Supreme Court Justices), an offense under section 751 (prisoners in custody of institution or officer), section 794 (gathering or delivering defense information to aid foreign government), section 844(d) (transportation of explosives in interstate commerce for certain purposes), section 844(f) (destruction of Government property by explosives), section 1118 (prisoners serving life term), section 1201 (kidnapping), section 844(i) (destruction of property affecting interstate commerce by explosives), section 1116 (killing or attempted killing of diplomats), section 1203 (hostage taking), section 1992 (wrecking trains), section 2280 (maritime violence), section

2281 (maritime platform violence), section 2332 (terrorist acts abroad against United States nationals), section 2332a (use of weapons of mass destruction), or section 2381 (treason) of this title, or section 46502 of title 49, United States Code (aircraft piracy).

(2) Previous conviction of violent felony involving firearm.—For any offense, other than an offense for which a sentence of death is sought on the basis of section 924(c), the defendant has previously been convicted of a Federal or State offense punishable by a term of imprisonment of more than 1 year, involving the use or attempted or threatened use of a firearm (as defined in section 921) against another person.

(3) Previous conviction of offense for which a sentence of death or life imprisonment was authorized.—The defendant has previously been convicted of another Federal or State offense resulting in the death of a person, for which a sentence of life imprisonment or a sentence of death was authorized by statute.

(4) Previous conviction of other serious offenses.—The defendant has previously been convicted of 2 or more Federal or State offenses, punishable by a term of imprisonment of more than 1 year, committed on different occasions, involving the infliction of, or attempted infliction of, serious bodily injury or death upon another person.

(5) Grave risk of death to additional persons.—The defendant, in the commission of the offense, or in escaping apprehension for the violation of the offense, knowingly created a grave risk of death to 1 or more persons in addition to the victim of the offense.

(6) Heinous, cruel, or depraved manner of committing offense.—The defendant committed the offense in an especially heinous, cruel, or depraved manner in that it involved torture or serious physical abuse to the victim.

(7) Procurement of offense by payment.—The defendant procured the commission of the offense by payment, or promise of payment, of anything of pecuniary value.

(8) Pecuniary gain.—The defendant committed the offense as consideration for the receipt, or in the expectation of the receipt, of anything of pecuniary value.

(9) Substantial planning and premeditation.—The defendant committed the offense after substantial planning and premeditation to cause the death of a person or commit an act of terrorism.

(10) Conviction for two felony drug offenses.—The defendant has previously been convicted of 2 or more State or Federal offenses punishable by a term of imprisonment of more than one year, committed on different occasions, involving the distribution of a controlled substance.

(11) Vulnerability of victim.—The victim was particularly vulnerable due to old age, youth, or infirmity.

(12) Conviction for serious Federal drug offenses.—The defendant had previously been convicted of violating title II or III of the Comprehensive Drug Abuse Prevention and Control Act of 1970 for which a sentence of 5 or more years may be imposed or had previously been convicted of engaging in a continuing criminal enterprise.

(13) Continuing criminal enterprise involving drug sales to minors.— The defendant committed the offense in the course of engaging in a continuing criminal enterprise in violation of section 408(c) of the Controlled Substances Act (21 U.S.C. 848(c)), and that violation involved the distribution of drugs to persons under the age of 21 in violation of section 418 of that Act (21 U.S.C. 859).

(14) High public officials.—The defendant committed the offense against—

(A) the President of the United States, the President-elect, the Vice President, the Vice President-elect, the Vice President-designate, or, if there is no Vice President, the officer next in order of succession to the office of the President of the United States, or any person who is acting as President under the Constitution and laws of the United States;

(B) a chief of state, head of government, or the political equivalent, of a foreign nation;

(C) a foreign official listed in section 1116(b)(3)(A), if the official is in the United States on official business; or

(D) a Federal public servant who is a judge, a law enforcement officer, or an employee of a United States penal or correctional institution—

(i) while he or she is engaged in the performance of his or her official duties;

(ii) because of the performance of his or her official duties; or

(iii) because of his or her status as a public servant.

For purposes of this subparagraph, a "law enforcement officer" is a public servant authorized by law or by a Government agency or Congress to conduct or engage in the prevention, investigation, or prosecution or adjudication of an offense, and includes those engaged in corrections, parole, or probation functions.

(15) Prior conviction of sexual assault or child molestation.—In the case of an offense under chapter 109A (sexual abuse) or chapter 110 (sexual abuse of children), the defendant has previously been convicted of a crime of sexual assault or crime of child molestation.

(16) Multiple killings or attempted killings.—The defendant intentionally killed or attempted to kill more than one person in a single criminal episode.

The jury, or if there is no jury, the court, may consider whether any other aggravating factor for which notice has been given exists.

(d) Aggravating factors for drug offense death penalty.—In determining whether a sentence of death is justified for an offense described in section 3591(b), the jury, or if there is no jury, the court, shall consider each of the following aggravating factors for which notice has been given and determine which, if any, exist:

(1) Previous conviction of offense for which a sentence of death or life imprisonment was authorized.—The defendant has previously been convicted of another Federal or State offense resulting in the death of a person, for which a sentence of life imprisonment or death was authorized by statute.

(2) Previous conviction of other serious offenses.—The defendant has previously been convicted of two or more Federal or State offenses, each punishable by a term of imprisonment of more than one year, committed on different occasions, involving the importation, manufacture, or distribution of a controlled substance (as defined in section 102 of the Controlled Substances Act (21 U.S.C. 802)) or the infliction of, or attempted infliction of, serious bodily injury or death upon another person.

(3) Previous serious drug felony conviction.—The defendant has previously been convicted of another Federal or State offense involving the manufacture, distribution, importation, or possession of a controlled substance (as defined in section 102 of the Controlled Substances Act (21 U.S.C. 802)) for which a sentence of five or more years of imprisonment was authorized by statute.

(4) Use of firearm.—In committing the offense, or in furtherance of a continuing criminal enterprise of which the offense was a part, the defendant used a firearm or knowingly directed, advised, authorized, or assisted another to use a firearm to threaten, intimidate, assault, or injure a person.

(5) Distribution to persons under 21.—The offense, or a continuing criminal enterprise of which the offense was a part, involved conduct proscribed by section 418 of the Controlled Substances Act (21 U.S.C. 859) which was committed directly by the defendant.

(6) Distribution near schools.—The offense, or a continuing criminal enterprise of which the offense was a part, involved conduct proscribed by section 419 of the Controlled Substances Act (21 U.S.C. 860) which was committed directly by the defendant.

(7) Using minors in trafficking.—The offense, or a continuing criminal enterprise of which the offense was a part, involved conduct proscribed by section 420 of the Controlled Substances Act (21 U.S.C. 861) which was committed directly by the defendant.

(8) Lethal adulterant.—The offense involved the importation, manufacture, or distribution of a controlled substance (as defined in section 102 of the Controlled Substances Act (21 U.S.C. 802)), mixed with a

with respect to any aggravating factor must be unanimous. If no aggravating factor set forth in section 3592 is found to exist, the court shall impose a sentence other than death authorized by law.

(e) Return of a finding concerning a sentence of death.—If, in the case of—

(1) an offense described in section 3591(a)(1), an aggravating factor required to be considered under section 3592(b) is found to exist;

(2) an offense described in section 3591(a)(2), an aggravating factor required to be considered under section 3592(c) is found to exist; or

(3) an offense described in section 3591(b), an aggravating factor required to be considered under section 3592(d) is found to exist,

the jury, or if there is no jury, the court, shall consider whether all the aggravating factor or factors found to exist sufficiently outweigh all the mitigating factor or factors found to exist to justify a sentence of death, or, in the absence of a mitigating factor, whether the aggravating factor or factors alone are sufficient to justify a sentence of death. Based upon this consideration, the jury by unanimous vote, or if there is no jury, the court, shall recommend whether the defendant should be sentenced to death, to life imprisonment without possibility of release or some other lesser sentence.

(f) Special precaution to ensure against discrimination.—In a hearing held before a jury, the court, prior to the return of a finding under subsection (e), shall instruct the jury that, in considering whether a sentence of death is justified, it shall not consider the race, color, religious beliefs, national origin, or sex of the defendant or of any victim and that the jury is not to recommend a sentence of death unless it has concluded that it would recommend a sentence of death for the crime in question no matter what the race, color, religious beliefs, national origin, or sex of the defendant or of any victim may be. The jury, upon return of a finding under subsection (e), shall also return to the court a certificate, signed by each juror, that consideration of the race, color, religious beliefs, national origin, or sex of the defendant or any victim was not involved in reaching his or her individual decision and that the individual juror would have made the same recommendation regarding a sentence for the crime in question no matter what the race, color, religious beliefs, national origin, or sex of the defendant or any victim may be.

18 U.S.C.A. 3594. Imposition of a Sentence of Death

Upon a recommendation under section 3593(e) that the defendant should be sentenced to death or life imprisonment without possibility of release, the court shall sentence the defendant accordingly. Otherwise, the court shall impose any lesser sentence that is authorized by law. Notwithstanding any other law, if the maximum term of imprisonment for the offense is life imprisonment, the court may impose a sentence of life imprisonment without possibility of release.

18 U.S.C.A. 3595. Review of a Sentence of Death

(a) Appeal.—In a case in which a sentence of death is imposed, the sentence shall be subject to review by the court of appeals upon appeal by the defendant. Notice of appeal must be filed within the time specified for the filing of a notice of appeal. An appeal under this section may be consolidated with an appeal of the judgment of conviction and shall have priority over all other cases.

(b) Review.—The court of appeals shall review the entire record in the case, including—
   (1) the evidence submitted during the trial;
   (2) the information submitted during the sentencing hearing;
   (3) the procedures employed in the sentencing hearing; and
   (4) the special findings returned under section 3593(d).

(c) Decision and disposition.—
   (1) The court of appeals shall address all substantive and procedural issues raised on the appeal of a sentence of death, and shall consider whether the sentence of death was imposed under the influence of passion, prejudice, or any other arbitrary factor and whether the evidence supports the special finding of the existence of an aggravating factor required to be considered under section 3592.
   (2) Whenever the court of appeals finds that—
      (A) the sentence of death was imposed under the influence of passion, prejudice, or any other arbitrary factor;
      (B) the admissible evidence and information adduced does not support the special finding of the existence of the required aggravating factor; or
      (C) the proceedings involved any other legal error requiring reversal of the sentence that was properly preserved for appeal under the rules of criminal procedure,
the court shall remand the case for reconsideration under section 3593 or imposition of a sentence other than death. The court of appeals shall not reverse or vacate a sentence of death on account of any error which can be harmless, including any erroneous special finding of an aggravating factor, where the

Government establishes beyond a reasonable doubt that the error was harmless.

(3) The court of appeals shall state in writing the reasons for its disposition of an appeal of a sentence of death under this section.

18 U.S.C.A. 3596. Implementation of a Sentence of Death

(a) In general.—A person who has been sentenced to death pursuant to this chapter shall be committed to the custody of the Attorney General until exhaustion of the procedures for appeal of the judgment of conviction and for review of the sentence. When the sentence is to be implemented, the Attorney General shall release the person sentenced to death to the custody of a United States marshal, who shall supervise implementation of the sentence in the manner prescribed by the law of the State in which the sentence is imposed. If the law of the State does not provide for implementation of a sentence of death, the court shall designate another State, the law of which does provide for the implementation of a sentence of death, and the sentence shall be implemented in the latter State in the manner prescribed by such law.

(b) Pregnant woman.—A sentence of death shall not be carried out upon a woman while she is pregnant.

(c) Mental capacity.—A sentence of death shall not be carried out upon a person who is mentally retarded. A sentence of death shall not be carried out upon a person who, as a result of mental disability, lacks the mental capacity to understand the death penalty and why it was imposed on that person.

18 U.S.C.A. 3597. Use of State Facilities

(a) In general.—A United States marshal charged with supervising the implementation of a sentence of death may use appropriate State or local facilities for the purpose, may use the services of an appropriate State or local official or of a person such an official employs for the purpose, and shall pay the costs thereof in an amount approved by the Attorney General.

(b) Excuse of an employee on moral or religious grounds.—No employee of any State department of corrections, the United States Department of Justice, the Federal Bureau of Prisons, or the United States Marshals Service, and no employee providing services to that department, bureau, or service under contract shall be required, as a condition of that employment or contractual obligation, to be in attendance at or to participate in any prosecution or execution under this section if such participation is contrary to the moral or religious convictions of the employee. In this subsection, "participation in executions" includes personal preparation of the condemned individual and the apparatus used for execution and supervision of the activities of other personnel in carrying out such activities.

18 U.S.C.A. 3598. Special Provisions for [Native American] Country

Notwithstanding sections 1152 and 1153, no person subject to the criminal jurisdiction of [Native American] tribal government shall be subject to a capital sentence under this chapter for any offense the Federal jurisdiction for which is predicated solely on [Native American] country (as defined in section 1151 of this title) and which has occurred within the boundaries of [Native American] country, unless the governing body of the tribe has elected that this chapter have effect over land and persons subject to its criminal jurisdiction.

Glossary of Legal Terms

acquittal a verdict made by a judge or jury that a defendant is not guilty of a charged offense.

advisory jury a jury whose verdict recommendation is not binding on a court.

affirm to agree that a conviction and/or sentence is correct.

affirmative defense refers to a justification or excuse offered by a defendant for which the defendant has the burden of proof.

aggravating circumstance a factor which, if created by statute, will permit the death penalty to be imposed in a capital prosecution.

allocution personal statement by a defendant to a judge or jury during the sentencing proceeding.

appeal the process of having an appellate court examine possible errors in a criminal judgment.

appellant the person who brings a case to an appellate court for examination of alleged errors committed in the proceeding.

appellate court a court whose jurisdiction is limited to examining the record of a case for possible errors.

appellate review examination of a sentence by an appellate court.

appellee the person in a case who has not taken the case to an appellate court, but must defend against an adverse action to the case by the appellate court.

arbitrary refers to a decision reached without a legally recognized rationalization.

arraignment a stage in a criminal prosecution where a defendant is formally charged with an offense and enters a plea of not guilty or guilty.

assignment of error refers to specifically alleged mistakes during a criminal prosecution.

bench trial a criminal trial that is presided over by the court as the factfinder.

burden see *burden of proof.*

burden of proof the obligation of persuading a factfinder of the truth of an issue.

capital crime a criminal offense that is punishable with death.

capital felon a defendant charged with, convicted of or sentenced for a capital crime.

capital felony see *capital crime.*

capital murder see *capital crime.*

capital offense see *capital crime.*

capital punishment jurisdiction refers to the federal government and states that impose the death penalty for capital crimes.

capital sentence see *death sentence.*

certiorari see *writ of certiorari.*

charge an allegation that a person has committed a specific offense; also refers to instructions given by a court to a jury.

clemency an act by an executive branch of government (governor or President) that permits permanent or temporary relief from punishment.

co-defendant an accomplice to a crime.

co-felon see *co-defendant.*

commutation reducing a punishment to a lesser sanction.

concurring opinion a written decision by an appellate court judge who agrees with the outcome of a case decided by the appellate court, but disagrees with the reason given by other members of the appellate court for the outcome.

consolidation refers to combining an appeal of a conviction and review of a sentence by an appellate court.

constitutional refers to any conduct or decision that is permitted by the constitution.

constitutionally valid see *constitutional.*

conviction a determination that a defendant is guilty of a charged offense.

coram nobis see *writ of coram nobis.*

corpse a dead body.

court of general jurisdiction a judicial forum that has authority to preside over most criminal and civil cases.

crime an act or conduct that is prohibited by a statute or regulation.

cruel and unusual punishment refers to the guarantee by the Eighth Amendment that a criminal sanction must be reasonable in the manner in which it is imposed or executed.

death-eligible offense see *capital crime*.

death penalty a criminal sanction that calls for the life of a defendant to be taken.

death-qualified jury persons selected as jurors in a capital prosecution who are not predisposed to or against the death penalty.

death sentence a determination that a defendant will be legally killed for an offense he was convicted of committing.

defendant a person who has been formally accused of committing an offense.

dicta language in a judicial opinion that is not necessary for the decision reached in a case and is not binding authority that must be followed.

direct appeal appellate court examination of possible nonconstitutional errors in a criminal judgment.

dismissal the rejection of a charge against a defendant by a court that prohibits the prosecutor from proceeding further on the matter.

due process a right, guaranteed by the Fifth and Fourteenth amendments, to have fair legal proceedings before an adverse action can be imposed upon a person.

element a factor that is part of an offense or principle of law.

equal protection a right, expressly guaranteed by the Fourteenth Amendment and inferred in the Fifth Amendment, not to be arbitrarily or capriciously treated differently from those similarly situated.

error a mistake or alleged mistake in a criminal prosecution.

evidence anything that is accepted by a court as tending to prove or disprove a matter in dispute.

exclude to keep out.

execute to carry out a punishment.

execution see *execute*.

factfinder a jury or judge who hears evidence and must make a determination of what the evidence means.

felon a person prosecuted for committing a felony offense.

felony a crime that is generally punishable by more than a year incarceration.

final appellate court the highest court in a judicial system.

finding a determination made by a court or jury.

freedom of association a guarantee by the First Amendment that a person may, without governmental interference, associate with whomever he desires.

frivolous having no merit.

furlough the temporary release of an inmate from confinement due to good conduct while confined.

grand jury a group of persons (usually 16) selected according to law to investigate criminal allegations brought against a person and to determine whether the person should be prosecuted.

guilt phase the trial stage of a criminal prosecution.

habeas corpus see *writ of habeas corpus*.

harmless error a mistake made during a criminal prosecution that did not affect the outcome of the case.

hearsay any statement made outside of a criminal proceeding that is being offered as substantively truthful in a criminal proceeding.

homicide causing the death of another person without legal justification or excuse.

hung jury a jury that cannot decide an issue unanimously or under a lesser legally permitted vote.

incarceration confinement in a jail or prison.

inchoate crime refers to conduct that is an offense, but which falls short of completion of the intended offense.

indictment an instrument used by a grand jury to formally accuse a person of a crime.

information an instrument drawn up by a prosecutor to formally accuse a person of a crime.

instruction refers to statements by a court to a jury.

intermediate appellate court refers to the second tier court in a three-tier system.

introduce see *proffer*.

irrelevant having no bearing on the truth or nontruth of an issue in dispute.

issue a matter that is in dispute.

judgment a final determination by a court.

judicial stay see *stay*.

jurisdiction the territory over which a court has authority, or the subject matter or person over which a court has authority.

jury deadlock see *hung jury*.

jury instruction see *instruction*.

jury override a decision by a court to impose a penalty different from that recommended by a jury.

mandamus see *writ of mandamus*.

misdemeanor a crime that is generally punishable by not more than one year incarceration.

mitigating circumstance a factor which may cause less than the maximum penalty to be imposed.

nolle prosequi a determination by a prosecutor that he will not pursue a charge against a defendant.

nolo contendere refers to a defendant not admitting guilt to a crime, but accepting the punishment.

non-weighing process refers to examining aggravating and mitigating circumstances to determine which are sufficient to affect the type of punishment a defendant will receive.

not true bill a determination by a grand jury that an allegation against a person is false.

notice informing a party in a criminal proceeding of the intent to do, or refrain from doing something prior to when it should be done.

nullify to render meaningless or unenforceable.

offense see *crime*.

outweigh see *weighing process*.

override see *jury override*.

panel of judges a group of three or more judicial officers who are chosen to hear and decide an issue in a case.

pardon absolves a defendant of all consequences of an offense or a conviction and sentence.

pass constitutional muster see *constitutional*.

penalty phase refers to the sentencing stage of a criminal prosecution.

per curiam opinion a written decision of an appellate court that does not reveal the name of the appellate judge who wrote the decision.

petit jury the jury presiding over a criminal trial.

petition a request made to a court asking it to do something or prohibit an occurrence.

petitioner a person who institutes a proceeding in court.

plea bargaining the process wherein the prosecutor and defendant (through counsel) attempt to negotiate an adverse plea by the defendant, in exchange for some benefit from the prosecutor.

preclude see *exclude.*

prejudicial error a mistake made during a criminal prosecution that influenced the outcome of the case.

preliminary hearing a stage in a prosecution wherein a court (usually magistrate) determines whether a case should be turned over to a grand jury.

privilege the ability to do something because the law permits it, though the law can prohibit it.

proffer something that is offered as proof on an issue.

prohibition see *writ of prohibition.*

prosecute to formally bring charges against a person and seek to convict and . sentence the person so charged.

prosecutor an attorney legally authorized to bring criminal charges against a person and to pursue a judicial conviction and sentence of the person.

prosecutorial discretion a prosecutor's ability to determine such things as whether to charge a person with a crime, the type of charges to bring or whether—in a capital crime—the death penalty should be sought.

relevant having the tendency to establish the truth or nontruth of an issue in dispute.

remand to send a case back to a lower court for further action.

reprieve temporary halt to enforcement of a sentence until some requested matter is examined.

respondent a person who is named in a judicial proceeding and must answer allegations made in the proceeding.

reverse to set aside a judgment.

reversible error a mistake caused during a criminal prosecution that requires a conviction and/or sentence to be vacated.

review see *appellate review.*

right against self-incrimination involves the guarantee by the Fifth Amendment that a person may not be compelled by a government entity to say anything that he may be later criminally prosecuted over.

right to allocution see *allocution.*

sentence the punishment imposed on a defendant.

special circumstances factors which cause murder to become a death-eligible offense.

standard of proof the level of evidence that must be presented in order to prevail on an issue.

stay a temporary postponement of execution of a sentence or other matter.

sua sponte action by a court without prompting by the parties in the litigation.

sufficiency determination see *non-weighing process*.

three-tier system a judicial structure that has a court of general jurisdiction, intermediate appellate court and final appellate court.

trial court the court which determines in the first instance a defendant's guilt or innocence.

true bill a determination by a grand jury that an allegation against a person is valid for prosecution.

two-tier system a judicial structure that has a court of general jurisdiction and appellate court.

unconstitutional prohibited by the constitution.

vacate see *reverse*.

vagueness challenge an allegation that a law or element in a law has no clear meaning.

verdict the decision of a jury or judge in a nonjury proceeding.

victim a person against whom a crime has been perpetrated.

victim identity refers to a specific characteristic of a person that is legally recognized as a basis for imposing the death penalty when such person is murdered because of the characteristic.

victim impact evidence information given to a factfinder that involves a murder victim's identity, personal characteristics and the hardship of the victim's death on his family.

waive to give up some right through silence, inaction or voluntarily.

weighing process refers to comparing aggravating and mitigating circumstances to determine which is more persuasive in affecting the type of punishment a defendant will receive.

work-release refers to allowing an inmate to leave confinement for the purpose of engaging in private employment, but returning to confinement at the end of the work day.

writ of certiorari a document issued by an appellate court ordering a lower court to produce the record of its proceeding in a case.

writ of coram nobis a document issued by a court to correct a judgment based upon an error that did not appear on the record of a case.

writ of habeas corpus a document directing a person holding a defendant to produce the defendant to the court, so the court may determine the lawfulness of the defendant's confinement.

writ of mandamus a document directing a government entity to perform some act it has a legal duty to perform.

writ of prohibition a document forbidding a government entity from performing some act.

Notes

Chapter 1

1. This point was noted in *Gilman v. Choi*, 406 S.E.2d 200 (W.Va. 1990), in which the court said that "[t]he term 'common law' came into use in England during the reign of Edward I (1272-1307)[.]"

2. Id.

3. See, William Holdsworth, *A History of English Law*, vol. XI, pp. 556–557 (1966). Use of the pillory could be dangerous and even fatal. Holdsworth describes how several prisoners were killed because people in the community hurled stones at them while they were confined to the pillory.

4. W. F. Finalason, *Reeves' History of the English Law*, vol. I, p. 235 (1880).

5. Id., at 192 n.(a).

6. See Marshall D. Ewell, *Ewell's Essentials of the Law—Blackstone*, vol. 1, p. 785 (1915).

7. See William Holdsworth, *A History of English Law*, vol. XIII, pp. 283–285 (1971).

8. Holdsworth, supra note 3, at 560.

9. W. F. Finalason, *Reeves' History of the English Law*, vol. III, p. 69 (1879).

10. Holdsworth, supra note 3, at 561.

11. Id., at 556.

Chapter 2

1. For a discussion of the historical development of the first ten amendments to the Constitution see R. Rutland, *The Birth of the Bill of Rights 1776–1791* (1955).

2. For a general discussion of this clause, see Anthony F. Granucci, "Nor Cruel and Unusual Punishments Inflicted: The Original Meaning," 57 *Cal. L. Rev.* 839 (1969).

3. *Furman v. Georgia*, 408 U.S. 238 (1972).

4. Id. Other instances in which members of the original 13 colonies adopted similar clauses include: Delaware's Declaration of Rights (1776), Maryland's Declaration of Rights (1776), Massachusetts' Declaration of Rights (1780), and New Hampshire's Bill of Rights (1783).

5. See Granucci, supra note 2.

6. This principle seeks to determine if the punishment involves the infliction of physical or mental suffering.

7. This principle seeks to determine if the punishment is uniformly imposed on everyone subject to the punishment.

8. This principle seeks to determine if society finds a particular punishment acceptable.

9. This principle seeks to determine whether a punishment is proportionately consistent with the crime. A proportionality test was developed in *Solem v. Helm*, 463 U.S. 277 (1983), which examines (1) the gravity of the offense and the harshness of the penalty, (2) the sentences imposed on other criminals in the same jurisdiction, and (3) the sentences imposed for commission of the crime in other jurisdictions. The continued validity of the *Solem* test has, however, been put in doubt. See *Harmelin v. Michigan*, 501 U.S. 957 (1991).

10. See also *Proffitt v. Florida*, 428 U.S. 242 (1976); *Jurek v. Texas*, 428 U.S. 262 (1976).

11. The defendant was also charged with and convicted of armed robbery.

12. For a general discussion of mandatory sentencing, see Orrin G. Hatch, "The Role of Congress in Sentencing: The United States Sentencing Commission, Mandatory Minimum Sentences and the Search for a Certain and Effective Sentencing System," 28 *Wake Forest L. Rev.* 185 (1993).

13. Both defendants were also convicted of armed robbery. One of the defendants was also convicted of assault with a deadly weapon.

14. On the same day that *Woodson* was decided, the Supreme Court also found Louisiana's mandatory death penalty statute unconstitutional in the case of *Roberts v. Louisiana*, 428 U.S. 325 (1976). Nevada's mandatory capital punishment statute for inmates convicted of murder while serving life imprisonment without parole was found unconstitutional in *Sumner v. Shuman*, 483 U.S. 66 (1987).

15. *Tison v. Arizona*, 481 U.S. 137 (1987). For a discussion of the felony-murder doctrine in the context of death-eligible offenses, see Richard A. Rosen, "Felony Murder and the Eighth Amendment Jurisprudence of Death," 31 *B.C. L. Rev.* 1103 (1990); Norman J. Finkel, "Capital Felony-Murder, Objective Indicia, and Community Sentiment," 32 *Ariz. L. Rev.* 819 (1990).

16. There was a third confederate in the crime, but she was tried separately.

17. For a discussion of this case and its impact, see Andrew H. Friedman, "Tison v. Arizona: The Death Penalty and the Non-triggerman: The Scales

of Justice Are Broken," 75 *Cornell L. Rev.* 123 (1989); Lynn D. Wittenbrink, "Overstepping Precedent? Tison v. Arizona Imposes the Death Penalty on Felony Murder Accomplices," 66 *N.C. L. Rev.* 817 (1988); James J. Holman, "Redefining a Culpable Mental State for a Non-triggerman—Tison v. Arizona," 33 *Vill. L. Rev.* 367 (1988); Stephen Taylor, "Cruel and Unusual Punishment—Imposition of the Death Penalty on a Non-triggerman—Tison v. Arizona," 13 *T. Marshall L. Rev.* 211 (1987); Karen M. Quinn, "A Reckless Indifference to Human Life Is Sufficient Evidence to Prove Culpability in a Felony-Murder Case and Therefore Imposition of the Death Penalty Is Not a Violation of the Eighth Amendment—Tison v. Arizona," 37 *Drake L. Rev.* 767 (1988).

18. See *Furman v. Georgia*, 408 U.S. 238 (1972).

20. Id. For an exhaustive treatment, see Hugo Bedau, *The Death Penalty in America* (1967).

CHAPTER 3

1. *Jurek v. Texas*, 428 U.S. 262 (1976).

2. For a discussion along these lines, see Franklin E. Zimring and Gordon Hawkins, "A Punishment in Search of a Crime: Standards for Capital Punishment in the Law of Criminal Homicide," 46 *Md. L. Rev.* 115 (1986).

3. For a general discussion, see John W. Poulos, "The Lucas Court and Capital Punishment: The Original Understanding of the Special Circumstances," 30 *Santa Clara L. Rev.* 333 (1990).

4. Arizona, California, Colorado, Delaware, Florida, Georgia, Idaho, Illinois, Indiana, Kentucky, Maryland, Missouri, Montana, Nebraska, Nevada, New Jersey, New Mexico, North Carolina, Ohio, Oklahoma, Pennsylvania, South Carolina, South Dakota, Tennessee, Texas, Wyoming, and the federal system.

5. Arizona, California, Colorado, Delaware, Florida, Illinois, Maryland, Missouri, Nebraska, Nevada, New Mexico, North Carolina, Oklahoma, Pennsylvania, South Dakota, Tennessee, Wyoming, and the federal system.

6. Georgia, Idaho, Indiana, Kentucky, New Jersey, South Carolina, and Texas.

7. Montana.

8. Ohio.

9. *State v. Keel*, 423 S.E.2d 458 (N.C. 1992).

10. *People v. Oaks*, 662 N.E.2d 1328 (Ill. 1996).

11. *Epperly v. Booker*, 997 F.2d 1 (4th Cir. 1993).

12. *People v. Mitchell*, 183 Cal.Rptr. 166 (1982).

13. *Clay v. State*, 440 N.E.2d 466 (Ind. 1982).

14. *State v. Cook*, 509 N.W.2d 200 (Neb. 1993).

15. *State v. Dixon*, 655 S.W.2d 547 (Mo.App. 1983). See also *State v. Privett*, 717 P.2d 55 (N.M. 1986).

16. *People v. Phillips*, 711 P.2d 423 (Cal. 1985).

17. *Hernandez v. State*, 819 S.W.2d 806 (Tex.Cr.App. 1991).

18. *Hounshell v. State*, 486 A.2d 789 (Md.App. 1985).

19. *State v. Raines*, 606 A.2d 265 (Md. 1992).

20. *State v. Marks*, 537 N.W.2d 339 (Neb. 1995).

21. *State v. Gallden*, 340 S.E.2d 673 (N.C. 1986).

22. *State v. West*, 844 S.W.2d 144 (Tenn. 1992).

23. *People v. Van Ronk*, 217 Cal.Rptr. 581 (1985).

24. *People v. Cisneros*, 720 P.2d 982 (Colo.App. 1986).

25. *State v. Craig*, 642 S.W.2d 98 (Mo. 1982). See also *Commonwealth v. Almon*, 441 N.E.2d 758 (Mass. 1982); *State v. Prevette*, 345 S.E.2d 159 (N.C. 1986).

26. *State v. Abeyta*, 901 P.2d 164 (N.M. 1995).

27. *State v. Solomon*, 456 S.E.2d 778 (N.C. 1995).

28. *Hounshell v. State*, 486 A.2d 789 (Md. App. 1985). See *Holt v. State*, 365 N.E.2d 1209 (Ind. 1977), holding that premeditation may occur instantaneously. In accord, *Cigainero v. State*, 838 S.W.2d 361 (Ark. 1992); *Boyd v. State*, 839 P.2d 1363 (Okl. Cr. 1992); *State v. Spears*, 908 P.2d 1062 (Ariz. 1996); *State v. Clark*, 913 S.W.2d 399 (Mo. App. 1996).

29. See also *State v. Bolder*, 635 S.W.2d 673 (Mo. 1982); *State v. Olin*, 648 P.2d 203 (Idaho 1982); *Johnson v. State*, 486 So.2d 657 (Fla.App. 4 Dist. 1986); *State v. Hunter*, 664 P.2d 195 (Ariz. 1983). But see *State v. Brown*, 836 S.W.2d 530 (Tenn. 1992), holding that premeditation by its very nature is not instantaneous and requires some time interval for formation—more than a split second is required to form a premeditated intent to kill.

30. In accord, *State v. Drinkwalter*, 493 N.W.2d 319 (Neb. 1992).

31. *Dino v. State*, 405 So.2d 213 (Fla.App. 1981).

32. *Archie v. Commonwealth*, 420 S.E.2d 718 (Va.App. 1992).

33. *State v. Helmer*, 545 N.W.2d (S.D. 1996). See *State v. Pirtle*, 904 P.2d 245 (Wash. 1995), holding that factors which are relevant in determining premeditation include motive, procurement of weapon, stealth, and method of killing.

34. *Hardnett v. State*, 564 S.W.2d 852 (Mo. 1978). But see *State v. Enno*, 807 P.2d 610 (Idaho 1991), holding that there is no legal distinction between malice and malice aforethought.

35. *State v. Proctor*, 564 S.E.2d 544 (Mo.App. 1977).

36. *State v. Love*, 250 S.E.2d 220 (N.C. 1978).

37. *State v. Marshall*, 264 N.W.2d 911 (S.D. 1978). But see *Commonwealth v. Weinstein*, 451 A.2d 1344 (Pa. 1982), holding that malice aforethought was a general prerequisite to finding murder-without-more and that it distinguishes this offense from any other type of homicide and includes cruelty and recklessness of consequences and social duty.

38. *State v. Chaney*, 497 A.2d 152 (Md. 1985).

39. *People v. Evans*, 416 N.E.2d 377 (Ill.App. 1981).

40. *Keys v. State*, 766 P.2d 270 (Nev. 1988).

41. *People v. Brown*, 42 Cal.Rptr.2d 155 (1995). See also *United States v. Sheffey*, 57 F.3d 1419 (6th Cir. 1995).

42. *State v. Lacquey*, 571 P.2d 1027 (Ariz. 1977). See also *Tucker v. State*, 263 S.E.2d 109 (Ga. 1980).

43. *Rivers v. Commonwealth*, 464 S.E.2d 549 (Va.App. 1995).

44. *People v. Nieto-Benitez*, 840 P.2d 969 (Cal. 1992).

45. *State v. Irby*, 439 S.E.2d 226 (N.C. App. 1994).

46. *Commonwealth v. Seguin*, 656 N.E.2d 1229 (Mass. 1995).

47. *Dixon v. State*, 252 S.E.2d 431 (Ga. 1979).

48. *Wright v. State*, 335 S.E.2d 857 (Ga. 1985).

49. *State v. McBride*, 425 S.E.2d 731 (N.C.App. 1993).

50. *Commonwealth v. Johnson*, 663 N.E.2d 559 (Mass. 1996).

51. *State v. Pierce*, 414 N.E.2d 1038 (Ohio 1980).

52. *State v. Jenkins*, 355 N.E.2d 825 (Ohio App. 1976).

53. *State v. Richardson*, 658 N.E.2d 321 (Ohio App. 1 Dist. 1995).

54. Alabama, Arizona, Arkansas, California, Colorado, Connecticut, Delaware, Florida, Georgia, Idaho, Illinois, Indiana, Kansas, Kentucky, Louisiana, Maryland, Mississippi, Montana, Nebraska, Nevada, New Hampshire, New Mexico, New York, North Carolina, Ohio, Oklahoma, South Dakota, Tennessee, Texas, Utah, Virginia, Washington, Wyoming, and the federal system.

55. *Watkins v. Callahan*, 724 F.2d 1038 (1st Cir. 1984).

56. Alabama, Arkansas, California, Connecticut, Delaware, Idaho, Illinois, Kansas, Louisiana, Mississippi, New Hampshire, New York, Oregon, Texas, Utah, Virginia, Washington, and the federal system.

57. See 18 U.S.C. § 1751.

58. See 18 U.S.C. § 351.

59. Alabama, Arkansas, California, Connecticut, Illinois, Kansas, Louisiana, Mississippi, New Hampshire, New Jersey, New York, Oklahoma, Oregon, Texas, Utah, Virginia, Washington, and the federal system.

60. See Michael R. Pahl, "Wanted: Criminal Justice—Colombia's Adoption of a Prosecutorial System of Criminal Procedure," 16 *Fordham Int. L. J.* 608 (1993).

61. See *U.S. v. Locasio*, 6 F.3d 924 (2nd Cir. 1993); Jason Sabot, "Expert Testimony on Organized Crime under the Federal Rules of Evidence: United States v. Frank Locasio and John Gotti," 22 *Hofstra L. Rev.* 177 (1993).

62. For a discussion of drugs and athletes, see Kerrie S. Covell and Annette Gibbs, "Drug Testing and the College Athlete," 23 *Creighton L. Rev.* 1 (1990).

63. See Michael D. Paley, "Prosecuting Failed Attempts to Fix Prices as

Violations of the Mail and Wire Fraud Statutes: Elliot Ness Is Back," 78 *Wash. U. L.Q.* 333 (1995).

64. See Paul J. Arougheti, "Imposing Homicide Liability on Gun Battle Participants for the Deaths of Innocent Bystanders," 27 *Colum. J. L. & Soc. Probs.* 467 (1994).

65. Alabama, Arkansas, California, Illinois, Louisiana, Washington, and the federal system.

66. Alabama, California, Delaware, Florida, Idaho, Maryland, Mississippi, Nebraska, Nevada, North Carolina, Oregon, South Carolina, South Dakota, Tennessee, Utah, and the federal system.

67. *Vincent v. State*, 418 S.E.2d 138 (Ga. 1992).

68. For further discussion see P. K. Menon, "The International Personality of Individuals in International Law: A Broadening of the Traditional Doctrine," 1 *J. Transnat. L. & Pol.* 151 (1992).

69. Alabama, California, Connecticut, Kansas, Louisiana, New York, Oregon, Texas, Utah, Virginia, and Washington.

70. A total of 6,556 drug-related murders occurred during this period. See U.S. Department of Justice, Federal Bureau of Investigation, *Uniform Crime Reports* 21 (1994).

71. For a discussion of death-eligible offenses for drug-related murder, see Peggy M. Tobolowsky, "Drugs and Death: Congress Authorizes the Death Penalty for Certain Drug-Related Murders," 18 *J. Contemp. L.* 47 (1992); Sandra R. Acosta, "Imposing the Death Penalty Upon Drug Kingpins," 27 *Harv. J. on Legis.* 596 (1990).

72. Arizona, Arkansas, Florida, Illinois, Indiana, Louisiana, New Hampshire, New Jersey, and Oklahoma.

73. See Cythia F. Zebrowitz, "Offenses Against Public Administration: Increase the Possible Sentences for Prison Escape," 11 *Ga. St. U. L. Rev.* 122 (1994); Padraic P. Lyndon, "Escape: A Deadly Proposition? Prisoners and Pretrial Detainees," 21 *New Eng. J. on Crim. & Civ. Conf.* 203 (1995).

74. Arizona, Arkansas, California, Colorado, Delaware, Florida, Idaho, Maryland, Nevada, New York, Ohio, Oklahoma, Oregon, Texas, and Utah.

75. California, Colorado, Illinois, New Mexico, and Utah.

76. In some jurisdictions no distinction is made in the nature of the proceeding, that is, felony or misdemeanor. Jurisdictions that require that the false testimony affect a felony utilize the offense of false swearing if the false testimony affects a misdemeanor.

77. *People v. Sesi*, 300 N.W. 2d 535 (Mich. 1981).

78. Colorado and Nebraska.

79. Alabama, Arkansas, California, Connecticut, Idaho, Illinois, Kansas, Mississippi, New Hampshire, New York, Oregon, Texas, Utah, Washington, and the federal system.

80. See *State v. Hines*, 919 S.W.2d 573 (Tenn. 1996).

81. See *State v. Cook*, 913 P.2d 97 (Kan. 1996).

82. California, Idaho, Illinois, Nevada, New York, North Carolina, Oregon, Utah, and the federal system.

83. California, Idaho, Maryland, Nevada, North Carolina, and the federal system.

84. Illinois, Louisiana, Oklahoma, Texas, Virginia, and Wyoming.

CHAPTER 4

1. The nonecclesiastic courts were the Crown's courts, and judges were appointed by the Crown. All monies paid to the court belonged to the Crown. Frederick Pollock and Frederic Maitland, *The History of English Law*, vol. I, pp. 153–162 (1968).

2. The ordinary citizen was required to assist in the arrest of felons and misdemeanants. During the thirteenth century, communities were fined if they failed to apprehend a homicide suspect. William Holdsworth, *A History of English Law*, vol. III, pp. 598–607 (1973).

3. William Holdsworth, *A History of English Law*, vol. VII, p. 4 (1973).

4. William Holdsworth, *A History of English Law*, vol. VI, pp. 466–481 (1971).

5. *Skinner v. Dostert*, 278 S.E.2d 624 (W.Va. 1981).

6. Id.

7. Id.

8. William Holdsworth, *A History of English Law*, vol. IX, pp. 236–244 (1966).

9. William Holdsworth, *A History of English Law*, vol. II, pp. 357–369 (1971).

10. England did not utilize a public prosecutor until 1879, when it created the Director of Public Prosecutions office. See W. Scott Van Alstyne, Jr., "The District Attorney—A Historical Puzzle," 1952 *Wis. L. Rev.* 125 (1952).

11. Sanford H. Kadish, *Encyclopedia of Crime and Justice*, vol. 3, p. 1286 (1983).

12. Id.

13. Id.

14. Alstyne, supra note 10.

15. Id.

16. Id.

17. Id. England conquered New Netherland in 1664.

18. Connecticut (criminal justice commission appoints prosecutors); Delaware (attorney general appoints prosecutors); Florida (attorney general appoints prosecutors); New Jersey (governor appoints prosecutors); Rhode Island (attorney general appoints prosecutors); federal system (president appoints prosecutors).

19. See Wayne Logan, "A Proposed Check on the Charging Discretion of Wisconsin Prosecutors," 1990 *Wis. L. Rev.* 1695 (1990); Russell Leblang, "Controlling Prosecutorial Discretion Under State Rico," 24 *Suffolk U.L. Rev.* 79 (1990); Gregory Zafiris, "Limiting Prosecutorial Discretion Under the Oregon Environmental Crimes Act: A New Solution to an Old Problem," 24 *Envtl. L.* 1673 (1994); Douglas Noll, "Controlling a Prosecutor's Screening Discretion Through Fuller Enforcement," 29 *Syracuse L. Rev.* 697 (1978); Charles Bubany and Frank Skillern, "Taming the Dragon: An Administrative Law for Prosecutorial Decisionmaking," 13 *Am. Cr. L. Rev.* 473 (1976); James Vorenberg, "Narrowing the Discretion of Criminal Justice Officials," 1976 *Duke L. J.* 651 (1976); Kenneth Melilli, "Prosecutorial Discretion in an Adversary System," 1992 *B.Y.U.L. Rev.* 669 (1992).

20. Some jurisdictions provide for binding punishment recommendations that judges must follow, if accepted by the court, for example, Rule 11(1)(e)(C) of the Federal Rules of Criminal Procedure. "Type C" agreements, as they are called, are rare because they do in fact invade the province of the judiciary in determining the sentence.

21. *People ex rel. Carey v. Cousins*, 397 N.E.2d 809 (Ill. 1979).

22. *State v. Koedatich*, 548 A.2d 939 (N.J. 1988).

23. *Gregg v. Georgia*, 428 U.S. 153 (1976). See *United States v. Walker*, 910 F.Supp. 837 (N.D.N.Y. 1995), holding that mere assertion, without more, by a defendant that he or she was arbitrarily singled out by the prosecutor for death penalty prosecution will not suffice to dismiss the death penalty charging instrument, so long as there is probable cause to believe the defendant committed the charged capital offense.

24. For a general discussion of concurrent jurisdiction prosecution, see Michael A. Dawson, "Popular Sovereignty, Double Jeopardy, and the Dual Sovereignty Doctrine," 102 *Yale L.J.* 281 (1992).

CHAPTER 5

1. Frederick Pollock and Frederic Maitland, *The History of English Law*, vol. I, pp. 137–153 (1968).

2. Id.

3. There are currently only 19 jurisdictions that require that felony prosecutions be initiated by grand jury indictment, in absence of a valid waiver by the defendant.

4. *Sanghetti v. State*, 618 S.W.2d 383 (Tex.Cr.App. 1981).

5. *State v. Height*, 649 N.E.2d 294 (Ohio App. 10 Dist. 1994). See also *Morris v. State*, 892 S.W.2d 205 (Tex.App.-Texarkana 1994).

6. *Pachecano v. State*, 881 S.W.2d 537 (Tex.App.-Fort Worth 1994).

7. *People v. Diaz*, 834 P.2d 1171 (Cal. 1992). See also *Ross v. State*, 519 A.2d 735 (Md. 1987).

8. *People v. Nitz,* 610 N.E.2d 1289 (Ill.App. 5 Dist. 1993).

9. *Johnson v. State,* 584 So.2d 881 (Ala.Cr.App. 1991).

10. *People v. Weber,* 636 N.E.2d 902 (Ill.App. 1 Dist. 1994). See also *State v. Just,* 675 P.2d 1353 (Ariz.App. 1983).

11. *People v. Jackson,* 599 S.E.2d 1192 (Ill.App. 1 Dist. 1992).

12. *Frazier v. State,* 362 S.E.2d 351 (Ga. 1987).

13. *Huff v. State,* 596 So.2d 16 (Ala.Cr.App. 1991).

14. *Moreno v. State,* 721 S.W.2d 295 (Tex.Cr.App. 1986). In accord, *Nethery v. State,* 692 S.W.2d 686 (Tex.Cr.App. 1985); *Aranda v. State,* 640 S.W.2d 766 (Tex.App. 4 Dist. 1982).

15. *Yokey v. State,* 801 S.W.2d 232 (Tex.App.-San Antonio 1990).

16. *Phillips v. State,* 367 S.E.2d 805 (Ga. 1988).

17. *Ramirez v. State,* 815 S.W.2d 636 (Tex.Cr.App. 1991).

18. *Rivera v. State,* 808 S.W.2d 80 (Tex.Cr.App. 1991).

19. *Willie v. State,* 585 So.2d 660 (Miss. 1991).

20. *Acres v. State,* 548 So.2d 459 (Ala.Cr.App. 1987).

21. *State v. King,* 733 P.2d 472 (Or.App. 1987). See also *Lundy v. State,* 539 So.2d 324 (Ala.Cr.App. 1988).

22. *Beck v. State,* 485 So.2d 1203 (Ala.Cr.App. 1984).

23. *Livingston v. State,* 542 S.W.2d 655 (Tex.Cr.App. 1976). In accord, *Ex Parte Davis,* 542 S.W.2d 192 (Tex.Cr.App. 1976).

24. *Garrison v. State,* 521 So.2d 997 (Ala.Cr.App. 1986).

25. *Garrett v. State,* 682 S.W.2d 301 (Tex.Cr.App. 1984). See also *Boggs v. Commonwealth,* 331 S.E.2d 407 (Va. 1985).

26. *State v. Isa,* 850 S.W.2d 876 (Mo. 1993).

27. *State v. Holmes,* 609 S.W.2d 132 (Mo. 1980).

28. *Brown v. State,* 410 A.2d 17 (Md.App. 1979).

29. *Smith v. State,* 398 A.2d 426 (Md.App. 1979).

30. *Young v. State,* 579 So.2d 721 (Fla. 1991).

31. *Askew v. State,* 439 N.E.2d 1350 (Ind. 1982).

32. *State v. Harden,* 384 So.2d 52 (Fla.App. 1980). See also *Boles v. State,* 598 S.W.2d 274 (Tex.Cr.App. 1980).

33. *Vaughn v. State,* 607 S.W.2d 914 (Tex.Cr.App. 1980).

34. *Nelson v. State,* 573 S.W.2d 9 (Tex.Cr.App. 1978).

35. *State v. Woods,* 297 S.E.2d 574 (N.C. 1982).

36. *State v. Frazier,* 574 N.E.2d 483 (Ohio 1991).

37. *Kearse v. State,* 662 So.2d 677 (Fla. 1995).

38. *State v. Rice,* 757 P.2d 889 (Wash. 1988).

39. *Myers v. State,* 510 N.E.2d 1360 (Ind. 1987).

40. *Lambert v. State,* 888 P.2d 494 (Okl.Cr. 1994).

41. *State v. Hartz,* 828 P.2d 618 (Wash.App. 1992).

42. *Alford v. State,* 906 P.2d 714 (Nev. 1995).

43. *People v. Hickman,* 684 P.2d 228 (Colo. 1984).

44. *People v. Johnson*, 284 Cal.Rptr. 579 (1991).

45. *Alford v. State*, 906 P.2d 714 (Nev. 1995).

46. *Matter of St. Pierre*, 823 P.2d 492 (Wash. 1992).

47. *Richie v. State*, 908 P.2d 268 (Okl.Cr. 1995). In accord, *Allen v. State*, 874 P.2d 60 (Okl.Cr. 1994).

48. *State v. Wilson*, 731 P.2d 306 (Kan. 1987).

49. *Givens v. Housewright*, 786 F.3d 1378 (9th Cir. 1986).

50. *Morris v. State*, 603 P.2d 1157 (Okl.Cr. 1979).

51. *People v. Diaz*, 834 P.2d 1171 (Cal. 1992). See also *People v. Maxwell*, 592 N.E.2d 960 (Ill. 1992).

52. *State v. King*, 634 P.2d 755 (Okl.Cr. 1981).

53. *Calderon v. Prunty*, 59 F.3d 1005 (9th Cir. 1995).

54. *Burris v. Farley*, 51 F.3d 655 (7th Cir. 1995).

55. *Averhart v. State*, 470 N.E.2d 666 (Ind. 1984). See also *State v. Reese*, 687 S.W.2d 635 (Mo.App. 1985).

56. *Tapia v. Tansy*, 926 F.2d 1554 (10th Cir. 1991).

57. *Short v. State*, 634 P.2d 755 (Okl.Cr. 1981).

58. *Clemens v. State*, 610 N.E.2d 236 (Ind. 1993).

59. *State v. Garcia*, 763 P.2d 585 (Kan. 1988).

60. *State v. Lane*, 629 S.W.2d 343 (Mo. 1982).

61. *State v. Harley*, 543 S.W.2d 288 (Mo.App. 1976).

CHAPTER 6

1. Kansas, Maryland, New Hampshire, New York, South Carolina, Tennessee, Washington, and the federal system.

2. For a discussion of pretrial notice of the death penalty, see Daniel S. Reinberg, "The Constitutionality of the Illinois Death Penalty Statute: The Right to Pretrial Notice of the State's Intention to Seek the Death Penalty," 85 *Nw. U. L. Rev.* 272 (1990).

3. For a discussion of this case, see Christopher M. Wilson, "Criminal Procedure—Death Penalty—A Convicted Criminal Must Be Adequately Notified That the Death Penalty May Be Imposed as a Sentence—Lankford v. Idaho," 22 *Seton Hall L. Rev.* 974 (1992).

4. California, Georgia, Kentucky, Maryland, New Hampshire, New York, Ohio, Oklahoma, Pennsylvania, Tennessee, and the federal system.

5. For a discussion of California's approach to pretrial disclosure generally, see Michael Alden Miller, "The Reciprocal Pretrial Discovery Provisions of Proposition 115 Apply to Both Guilt Phase and Penalty Phase Evidence— Nevertheless the Courts May Exercise Discretion Under Appropriate Circumstances and Postpone Disclosure of the Defendant's Penalty Phase Evidence Until the Guilt Phase Has Concluded," 21 *Pepp. L. Rev.* 1016 (1994).

6. See *Cargle v. State*, 909 P.2d 806 (Okl.Cr. 1995); *Richie v. State*, 908 P.2d 268 (Okl.Cr. 1995).

7. Delaware, Indiana, Nevada, and New Jersey.

CHAPTER 7

1. *Givens v. State*, 749 S.W.2d 954 (Tex.App.-Fort Worth 1988). See *State v. Holmes*, 388 So.2d 722 (La. 1980), holding that to sustain a prosecution for murder of a nontriggerman it is necessary to show defendant actively desired the death of the victim or great bodily harm thereto; *Shelton v. State*, 699 S.W.2d 728 (Ark. 1985), holding that it is not necessary that a defendant take an active part in a homicide to be prosecuted if he or she accompanies another who actually commits the murder and assists in some manner.

2. *State v. McAllister*, 366 So.2d 1340 (La. 1978). See also *Coxwell v. State*, 397 So.2d 355 (Fla.App. 1981); *People v. Steele*, 563 P.3d 6 (Colo. 1977); *State v. Wilder*, 608 P.2d 270 (Wash.App. 1980); *Daugherty v. State*, 640 P.2d 558 (Okl.Cr. 1982).

3. *Bryant v. State*, 412 So.2d 347 (Fla. 1982).

4. *Walsh v. State*, 658 S.W.2d 285 (Tex.App. 2 Dist. 1983).

5. *State v. Lindsey*, 543 So.2d 886 (La. 1989).

6. *Spears v. State*, 900 P.2d 431 (Okl.Cr. 1995).

7. *State v. Smith*, 563 A.2d 671 (Conn. 1989).

8. *State v. DePriest*, 907 P.2d 868 (Kan. 1995). See also *United States v. Wilson*, 665 F.2d 825 (8th Cir. 1981); *State v. Sonnier*, 402 So.2d 650 (La. 1981); *State v. White*, 622 S.W.2d 939 (Mo. 1981); *Ned v. State*, 654 S.W.2d 732 (Tex.App. 14 Dist. 1983); *Spears v. State*, 900 P.2d 431 (Okl.Cr. 1995). But see *Strickler v. Commonwealth*, 404 S.E.2d 227 (Va. 1991), holding that a defendant who is present and aids and abets actual killing but does not perform the killing may not be prosecuted for capital murder.

9. *People v. Hammond*, 226 Cal.Rptr. 475 (1986).

10. *Lockett v. Ohio*, 438 U.S. 586 (1978).

11. *State v. Ryan*, 534 N.W.2d 766 (Neb. 1995).

12. *United States v. Van Scoy*, 654 F.2d 257 (3rd Cir. 1981).

13. *Apostoledes v. State*, 593 A.2d 1117 (Md. 1991).

14. *State v. Willis*, 420 S.E.2d 158 (N.C. 1992).

15. *Fratello v. State*, 496 So.2d 903 (Fla.App. 4 Dist. 1986). See also *Nelson v. State*, 528 N.E.2d 453 (Ind. 1988).

16. *Contreras v. State*, 745 S.W.2d 59 (Tex.App.-San Antonio 1987). See also *State v. Davison*, 601 S.W.2d 623 (Mo. 1979).

17. *Berkeley v. Commonwealth*, 451 S.E.2d 41 (Va.App. 1994).

18. *People v. Esquivel*, 34 Cal.Rptr.2d 324 (1994).

19. *State v. Williamson*, 382 A.2d 588 (Md. 1978). But see *Cheng v. Com-*

monwealth, 393 S.E.2d 599 (Va. 1990), holding that an accessory before the fact may not be prosecuted for capital murder.

20. *State v. Johnson*, 455 S.E.2d 644 (N.C. 1995). See also *State v. Smith*, 447 S.E.2d 175 (S.C. 1993); *State v. Suites*, 427 S.E.2d 318 (N.C.App. 1993).

21. *State v. Malone*, 671 A.2d 1321 (Conn.App. 1996).

22. *State v. Marr*, 440 S.E.2d 275 (N.C.App. 1994).

23. *State v. Lattimore*, 456 S.E.2d 789 (N.C. 1995).

24. *United States v. Reavis*, 48 F.3d 763 (4th Cir. 1995). See also *People v. Priest*, 672 P.2d 539 (Colo.App. 1983); *State v. Toomey*, 690 P.2d 1175 (Wash.App. 1984).

25. *State v. Furr*, 235 S.E.2d 193 (N.C. 1977).

26. *State v. Barnes*, 447 S.E.2d 478 (N.C.App. 1994).

27. *Butler v. State*, 643 A. 2d 389 (Md. 1994).

28. *Thomas v. State*, 847 S.W.2d 695 (Ark. 1993).

29. *People v. Gil*, 608 N.E.2d 197 (Ill.App. 1 Dist. 1992). But see *Commonwealth v. Gaynor*, 612 A.2d 1010 (Pa.Super. 1992), holding that specific intent to kill is required for both principal and accomplice); *Lawton v. State*, 913 S.W.2d 542 (Tex.Cr.App. 1995), to hold a defendant liable for capital murder premised on accomplice liability, it must be shown that the defendant had the specific intent to promote or assist in the commission of murder.

30. *State v. Apodaca*, 887 P.2d 756 (N. M. 1994).

31. *State v. Dulany*, 781 S.W.2d 52 (Mo. 1989).

32. *Commonwealth v. Bachert*, 453 A.2d 931 (Pa. 1982).

33. *State v. Hunter*, 782 S.W.2d 95 (Mo.App. 1989).

34. See also *State v. DePriest*, 907 P.2d 868 (Kan. 1995), holding that when a solicited person murders a victim, the solicitor may be prosecuted for murder. But see *Bowie v. State*, 816 P.2d 1143 (Okl. Cr. 1991), holding that mere knowledge that defendant offered money to anyone who would kill victim would not make a person an accomplice to the actual murder.

35. *People v. Calvillo*, 524 N.E.2d 1054 (Ill.App. 1 Dist. 1988).

36. *People v. Rodriquez*, 627 N.E.2d 209 (Ill.App. 1 Dist. 1993).

37. *People v. Smith*, 368 N.E.2d 561 (Ill.App. 1977).

38. *People v. Chavez*, 592 N.E.2d 69 (Ill.App. 1 Dist. 1992).

39. *People v. Stanciel*, 589 N.E.2d 557 (Ill.App. 1 Dist. 1991).

40. *People v. McClain*, 645 N.E.2d 585 (Ill.App. 4 Dist. 1995).

41. *Richardson v. State*, 879 S.W.2d 874 (Tex.Cr.App. 1993).

42. *People v. Montes*, 549 N.E.2d 700 (Ill.App. 1 Dist. 1989).

43. *People v. Taylor*, 557 N.E.2d 917 (Ill.App. 4 Dist. 1990).

44. *Bryant v. State*, 412 So.2d 347 (Fla. 1982).

45. *Andrews v. State*, 744 S.W.2d 40 (Tex.Cr.App. 1987).

46. *State v. Martin*, 308 S.E.2d 277 (N.C. 1983). See also *People v. Luparelle*, 231 Cal.Rptr. 832 (1986).

47. *People v. Bustos*, 29 Cal.Rptr.2d 112 (1994).

48. *State v. Nguyen*, 833 P.2d 937 (Kan. 1992). See also *Sands v. State*, 418 S.E.2d 55 (Ga. 1992). However, in *Kuenzl v. State*, 577 So.2d 474 (Ala.Cr.App. 1990), it was said that a capital felony-murder conviction will stand against a confederate only if the defendant was an accomplice in the intentional killing of the victim, not merely an accomplice to the underlying felony. Further, in *State v. Reese*, 353 S.E.2d 352 (N.C. 1987), it was said that in a felony-murder prosecution of a defendant, the premeditation and deliberation of a co-felon who actually inflicted a victim's fatal injury could not be imputed to the defendant by reason of his or her participation in the underlying felony. It was also determined in *Hite v. State*, 364 So.2d 771 (Ala.App. 1978), that a defendant who was not present at the scene of a felony he or she participated in planning, which results in a victim being killed, may not be prosecuted for capital felony-murder.

49. *Rivers v. Commonwealth*, 464 S.E.2d 549 (Va.App. 1995).

50. But see *People v. Hoard*, 618 N.E.2d 808 (Ill.App. 1 Dist. 1993), holding that pursuant to the common design rule, an accomplice may be held liable for murder without a showing of intent to kill.

51. *People v. Novy*, 597 N.E.2d 273 (Ill.App. 5 Dist. 1992).

52. *Commonwealth v. Chipman*, 635 N.E.2d 1204 (Mass. 1994).

53. *Commonwealth v. Young*, 621 N.E.2d 1180 (Mass.App. 1993).

54. *Richard v. Commonwealth*, 415 N.E.2d 201 (Mass. 1981).

55. *Commonwealth v. Gilliard*, 629 N.E.2d 349 (Mass.App. 1994).

56. *Commonwealth v. Cook*, 644 N.E.2d 203 (Mass. 1994). See also *Commonwealth v. White*, 663 N.E.2d 834 (Mass. 1996), holding that under felony-murder joint venture theory, the prosecutor must show that the defendant was present at the crime scene with knowledge that the principal intended to commit a crime and by agreement was willing and available to help the principal if necessary.

57. *Commonwealth v. Semedo*, 665 N.E.2d 638 (Mass. 1996). See also *Stewart v. Coalter*, 855 F.Supp. 464 (D.Mass. 1994), holding that as an aider or abettor, a joint venturer to murder must intend that the victim be killed or know that there is a substantial likelihood of the victim being killed.

58. *Commonwealth v. Green*, 652 N.E.2d 572 (Mass. 1995).

59. *Commonwealth v. Nichypor*, 643 N.E.2d 452 (Mass. 1994).

CHAPTER 8

1. In addition to the right against self-incrimination and the right to trial by jury, a capital offender also has a constitutional right to confront his or her accusers and the right to compulsory process for obtaining witnesses in his or her favor. See *Boykin v. Alabama*, 395 U.S. 238 (1969); *Brady v. United States*, 397 U.S. 742 (1970).

2. Delaware, Florida, Idaho, Ohio, Oklahoma, and Oregon.

3. Alabama, Arizona, Arkansas, California, Colorado, Connecticut, Delaware, Florida, Georgia, Idaho, Illinois, Indiana, Louisiana, Maryland, Mississippi, Montana, Nebraska, Nevada, New Hampshire, New Jersey, New Mexico, North Carolina, Ohio, Oklahoma, Oregon, Pennsylvania, South Carolina, South Dakota, Utah, Washington, Wyoming, and the federal system.

4. A bench trial is deemed a privilege because there is no constitutional right to trial by the court. See *Singer v. United States*, 380 U.S. 24 (1965).

5. For a general discussion of a capital felon's right to trial by jury, see Welsh S. White, "Fact-finding and the Death Penalty: The Scope of a Capital Defendant's Right to Jury Trial," 65 *Notre Dame L. Rev.* 1 (1989).

6. For a general discussion of death-qualified juries, see Barbara J. Whisler, "Sixth Amendment—Death Qualification of the Jury: Process Is Permissible Where Defendant Does Not Face Death Penalty," 78 *J. Crim. L. & Criminology* 954 (1988); John A. Wasleff, "Lockhart v. McCree: Death Qualification as a Determinant of the Impartiality and Representativeness of a Jury in Death Penalty Cases," 72 *Cornell L. Rev.* 1075 (1987); William S. Geimer and Jonathan Amsterdam, "Why Jurors Vote Life or Death: Operative Factors in Ten Florida Death Penalty Cases," 15 *Am. J. Crim. L.* 1 (1988); Patrick J. Callans, "Sixth Amendment—Assembling a Jury Willing to Impose the Death Penalty: A New Disregard for a Capital Defendant's Rights," 76 *J. Crim. L. & Criminology* 1027 (1985); Jaye Mendros, "Criminal Procedure: Morgan v. Illinois Takes a Step Toward Eliminating Hanging Juries in Capital Cases," 46 *Okla. L. Rev.* 729 (1993).

7. For a discussion of capital juries, see Patrick E. Higginbotham, "Juries and the Death Penalty," 41 *Case W. Res. L. Rev.* 1047 (1991).

8. See *United States v. Walker*, 910 F.Supp. 837 (N.D.N.Y. 1995), holding that a capital felon is not entitled to have a non–death-qualified jury for the guilt phase and a separate death-qualified jury for the penalty phase.

CHAPTER 9

1. It will be noted that about five months prior to the *Furman* decision, the court in *People v. Anderson*, 493 P.2d 880 (Cal. 1972) held that the death penalty violated the constitution of the state of California.

2. For a discussion of issues involved in carrying out the death penalty, see Stephen R. Mcallister, "The Problem of Implementing a Constitutional System of Capital Punishment," 43 *U. Kan. L. Rev.* 1039 (1995).

3. For discussion of leniency in capital sentencing, see Paul Whitlock Cobb, Jr., "Reviving Mercy in the Structure of Capital Punishment," 99 *Yale L.J.* 389 (1989).

4. Justices who voted in favor of the *Furman* decision were Justice Douglas, Justice Brennan, Justice Stewart, Justice White, and Justice Marshall.

The dissenting justices were Chief Justice Burger, Justice Blackmun, Justice Powell, and Justice Rehnquist.

5. For a discussion of nonjudicial views on the death penalty, see William J. Bowers, Margaret Vandiver, and Patricia H. Dugan, "A New Look at Public Opinion on Capital Punishment: What Citizens and Legislators Prefer," 22 *Am. J. Crim. L.* 77 (1994). See also Samuel Cameron, "The Demand for Capital Punishment," 13 *Int'l Rev. L. & Econ.* 47 (1993).

6. Georgia's penalty phase scheme was patterned along the lines of a proposal created by the American Bar Association.

7. For a discussion of the period between the guilt phase and penalty phase, see Robin E. Abrams, "A Capital Defendant's Right to a Continuance Between the Two Phases of a Death Penalty Trial," 64 *N.Y.U. L. Rev.* 579 (1989).

8. A few jurisdictions permit the capital felon to give the opening statement first.

9. A few jurisdictions permit the capital felon to present his or her case-in-chief first.

10. *People v. Avena*, 916 P.2d 1000 (Cal. 1996). The defendant's case-in-chief encompasses rebuttal evidence. In the event that the prosecutor brings out a matter during its rebuttal that was not addressed during the defendant's case-in-chief, the trial court has discretion to allow surrebuttal by the defendant.

11. *State v. Sepulvado*, 672 So.2d 158 (La. 1996).

12. See *Commonwealth v. Wharton*, 665 A.2d 458 (Pa. 1995).

13. New Hampshire, North Carolina, Pennsylvania, and South Carolina.

14. For further discussion of penalty phase juries, see Marla Sandys, "Cross-overs—Capital Jurors Who Change Their Minds About the Punishment: A Litmus Test for Sentencing Guidelines," 70 *Ind. L.J.* 1183 (1995); Christopher Slobogin, "Should Juries and the Death Penalty Mix?: A Prediction About the Supreme Court's Answer," 70 *Ind. L.J.* 1249 (1995).

15. Alabama, Arkansas, California, Colorado, Connecticut, Delaware, Florida, Georgia, Illinois, Indiana, Kansas, Kentucky, Louisiana, Maryland, Mississippi, Missouri, Nevada, New Hampshire, New Jersey, New Mexico, New York, North Carolina, Ohio, Oklahoma, Oregon, Pennsylvania, South Carolina, South Dakota, Tennessee, Texas, Utah, Virginia, Washington, Wyoming, and the federal system.

16. See *State v. Weaver*, 912 S.W.2d 499 (Mo. 1995).

17. Arkansas, California, Colorado, Connecticut, Delaware, Georgia, Illinois, Indiana, Kansas, Kentucky, Louisiana, Maryland, Mississippi, Missouri, Nevada, New Hampshire, New Jersey, New Mexico, New York, North Carolina, Ohio, Oklahoma, Oregon, Pennsylvania, South Carolina, South Dakota, Tennessee, Texas, Utah, Virginia, Washington, Wyoming, and the federal system.

18. Arkansas, California, Colorado, Connecticut, Delaware, Florida, Georgia, Illinois, Kansas, Kentucky, Louisiana, Maryland, Mississippi, Missouri, New Hampshire, New Jersey, New Mexico, New York, North Carolina, Ohio, Oklahoma, Oregon, Pennsylvania, South Carolina, South Dakota, Tennessee, Texas, Utah, Virginia, Washington, Wyoming, and the federal system.

19. For a discussion of jury override, see Amy D. Ronner, "When Judges Impose the Death Penalty After the Jury Recommends Life: Harris v. Alabama as the Excision of the Tympanic Membrane in an Augmentedly Death-biased Procedure," 23 *Hastings Conts. L.Q.* 217 (1995); Katheryn K. Russell, "The Constitutionality of Jury Override in Alabama Death Penalty Cases," 46 *Ala. L. Rev.* 5 (1994).

20. Arkansas, California, Colorado, Connecticut, Georgia, Illinois, Kansas, Kentucky, Louisiana, Maryland, Mississippi, Missouri, Nevada, New Hampshire, New Jersey, New Mexico, New York, North Carolina, Oklahoma, Oregon, Pennsylvania, South Carolina, South Dakota, Tennessee, Texas, Utah, Virginia, Washington, Wyoming, and the federal system.

21. Alabama, Delaware, Florida, Indiana, and Ohio.

22. Arizona, Idaho, Montana, and Nebraska. See *State v. Gallegos*, 916 P.2d 1056 (Ariz. 1996), holding that a defendant is not denied equal protection because of a denial of a jury penalty phase proceeding.

23. Colorado, Indiana, Kentucky, New Mexico, Oklahoma, and Wyoming.

24. For a general discussion of a capital felon's right to have effective assistance of counsel, see Ronald J. Tabak, "Report: Ineffective Assistance of Counsel and Lack of Due Process in Death Penalty Cases," 22 *Hum. Rts.* 36 (Wtr. 1995); Gary Goodpaster, "The Trial for Life: Effective Assistance of Counsel in Death Penalty Cases," 58 *N.Y.U. L. Rev.* 299 (1983).

25. This discretionary authority is exercised in the first instance during the guilt phase and continues through the penalty phase.

26. See *Bell v. Watkins*, 692 F.2d 999 (5th Cir. 1982); *Riley v. Snyder*, 840 F.Supp. 1012 (D.Del. 1993): *State v. Burke*, 463 S.E.2d 212 (N.C. 1995); *People v. Padilla*, 906 P.2d 388 (Cal. 1995).

27. *People v. Simms*, 659 N.E.2d 922 (Ill. 1995).

28. For a general discussion, see Robert Alan Kelly, "Applicability of the Rules of Evidence to the Capital Sentencing Proceeding: Theoretical & Practical Support for Open Admissibility of Mitigating Evidence," 60 *UMKC L. Rev.* 411 (1992).

29. California, Colorado, Delaware, Georgia, Idaho, Indiana, Kentucky, Maryland, Montana, Nebraska, New Hampshire, New Mexico, North Carolina, Ohio, Pennsylvania, South Dakota, Utah, Washington, Wyoming, and the federal system.

30. Arizona, Arkansas, Connecticut, Illinois, New Jersey, New York, and Virginia.

31. Louisiana and Missouri.

32. Alabama, Florida, Kansas, Mississippi, Nevada, Oklahoma, Oregon, South Carolina, Tennessee, and Texas.

33. But see *Commonwealth v. Wharton*, 665 A.2d 458 (Pa. 1995), holding that a photograph of victims before they were murdered was admissible.

34. See *People v. Simms*, 659 N.E.2d 922 (Ill. 1995), holding that hearsay evidence of other crimes by defendant is admissible if it is relevant and reliable, even if the crime was never prosecuted.

35. See *State v. McLaughlin*, 462 S.E.2d 1 (N.C. 1995), holding that tape-recorded testimony of a codefendant given at guilt phase was properly admitted during the defendant's penalty phase hearing.

CHAPTER 10

1. Congress has delegated authority to the president to create aggravating circumstances for military death penalty offenses. See *Loving v. United States*, 116 S.Ct. 1737 (1996), in which the Supreme Court approved of delegation of such authority to the president. For a general discussion, see Annamary Sullivan, "The President's Power to Promulgate Death Penalty Standards," 125 *Mil. L. Rev.* 143 (1989).

2. For a discussion of *Tuilaepa*'s impact, see David Hesseltine, "The Evolution of the Capital Punishment Jurisprudence of the United States Supreme Court and the Impact of Tuilaepa v. California on That Evolution," 32 *San Diego L. Rev.* 593 (1995).

3. For a discussion in this area, see Kathleen D. Weron, "Rethinking Utah's Death Penalty Statute: A Constitutional Requirement for the Substantive Narrowing of Aggravating Circumstances," 1994 *Utah L. Rev. 1107 (1994)*.

4. For a discussion in this area, see Kenneth S. Gallant, "Ex Post Facto Judicial Clarification of a Vague Aggravating Circumstance in a Capital Punishment Statute," 59 *UMKC L. Rev.* 125 (1990).

5. California, Louisiana, New York, and Virginia.

6. Oregon, Texas, Utah, and Washington.

7. Alabama, California, Colorado, Delaware, Florida, Idaho, Illinois, Indiana, Kentucky, Louisiana, Maryland, Mississippi, Missouri, Montana, Nevada, New Jersey, New York, North Carolina, Ohio, Pennsylvania (its statute provides that all felony offenses are statutory aggravators), South Carolina, Tennessee, Texas, Utah, Virginia, Washington, and Wyoming.

8. Alabama, California, Colorado, Delaware, Florida, Idaho, Illinois, Indiana, Kentucky, Louisiana, Maryland, Mississippi, Missouri, Nevada, New Jersey, New York, North Carolina, Ohio, Pennsylvania (its statute provides that all felony offenses are statutory aggravators), South Carolina, Tennessee, Texas, Utah, Virginia, Washington, and Wyoming.

9. Alabama, California, Colorado, Delaware, Florida, Georgia, Idaho, Illinois, Indiana, Kentucky, Louisiana, Mississippi, Montana, Nevada, New Jersey, New York, North Carolina, Ohio, Pennsylvania (its statute provides that all felony offenses are statutory aggravators), South Carolina, Tennessee, Texas, Utah, Washington, and Wyoming.

10. Alabama, California, Colorado, Delaware, Florida, Georgia, Idaho, Illinois, Indiana, Louisiana, Maryland, Mississippi, Missouri, Montana, Nevada, New Jersey, New Mexico, New York, North Carolina, Ohio, Pennsylvania (its statute provides that all felony offenses are statutory aggravators), South Carolina, Tennessee, Texas, Utah, Virginia, Washington, Wyoming, and the federal system.

11. California, Colorado, Delaware, Florida, Georgia, Idaho, Illinois, Indiana, Kentucky, Louisiana, Maryland, Mississippi, Nevada, New Jersey, New York, North Carolina, Ohio, Pennsylvania (its statute provides that all felony offenses are statutory aggravators), Tennessee, Texas, Utah, Washington, and Wyoming.

12. Alabama, Arkansas, California, Colorado, Delaware, Florida, Georgia, Louisiana, Maryland, Mississippi, Montana, Nevada, New Hampshire, New Jersey, New Mexico, New York, North Carolina, Oklahoma, Oregon, Pennsylvania (its statute provides that all felony offenses are statutory aggravators), South Dakota, Tennessee, Texas, Utah, Washington, and Wyoming.

13. California and the federal system.

14. California, Illinois, Indiana, and Maryland.

15. Florida, Illinois, Mississippi, Missouri, North Carolina, Pennsylvania, Tennessee, Utah, Wyoming, and the federal system.

16. Illinois, Missouri, and Utah.

17. Georgia and Virginia.

18. Illinois and Missouri.

19. Illinois and Missouri.

20. Florida, Illinois, Indiana, Louisiana, Pennsylvania, South Carolina, South Dakota, and the federal system.

21. Delaware, Georgia, Illinois, Indiana, Kentucky, Louisiana, Missouri, Nebraska, New Mexico, North Carolina, Oklahoma, Oregon, Pennsylvania, South Carolina, South Dakota, Tennessee, Texas, Utah, and Washington.

22. Arizona, California, Colorado, Delaware, Florida, Georgia, Idaho, Illinois, Indiana, Kentucky, Louisiana, Maryland, Missouri, Montana, Nebraska, Nevada, New Mexico, New York, North Carolina, Ohio, Oklahoma, Oregon, Pennsylvania, South Carolina, South Dakota, Tennessee, Texas, Utah, Virginia, Washington, and Wyoming.

23. California, Colorado, Delaware, Illinois, Indiana, Louisiana, Missouri, Nevada, North Carolina, South Carolina, South Dakota, Tennessee, Texas, Utah, and Washington.

24. California, Colorado, Delaware, Idaho, Illinois, Indiana, Louisiana,

Missouri, New Mexico, New York, North Carolina, Ohio, Oregon, Pennsylvania, Utah, and Washington.

25. California, Delaware, Georgia, Idaho, Louisiana, Missouri, North Carolina, Pennsylvania, South Carolina, South Dakota, Tennessee, Utah, Washington, and Wyoming.

26. California, Colorado, Delaware, Georgia, Idaho, Illinois, Indiana, Louisiana, Missouri, New York, North Carolina, Oregon, Pennsylvania, South Carolina, South Dakota, Tennessee, Utah, Washington, and Wyoming.

27. Texas.

28. Colorado, Florida, Illinois, Indiana, Louisiana, Pennsylvania, South Carolina, and Tennessee.

29. New Jersey.

30. Arizona and Delaware.

31. Wyoming.

32. Delaware.

33. Louisiana.

34. Wyoming.

35. Arizona.

36. Indiana, Louisiana, Maryland, New York, Oregon, Utah, and Washington.

37. Delaware.

38. California, Louisiana, North Carolina, Oregon, Utah, Washington, and Wyoming.

39. Delaware and Pennsylvania.

40. California, Colorado, Florida, Kentucky, Missouri, Ohio, Pennsylvania, Utah, and the federal system.

41. The victim of this incident was named Leon Klinghoffer. The family of Mr. Klinghoffer eventually brought a civil suit against those allegedly responsible for his death. See *Klinghoffer v. S.N.C. Achille Lauro*, 739 F.Supp. 854 (S.D.N.Y.), aff'd, 921 F.2d 21 (2d Cir. 1990). For a discussion of the murder, see Gerald P. McGinley, "The Achille Lauro Affair—Implications for International Law," 52 *Tenn. L. Rev.* 691 (1985); George R. Constantinople, "Towards a New Definition of Piracy: The Achille Lauro Incident," 26 *Va. J Int'l. L.* 723 (1986); Gregory V. Gooding, "Fighting Terrorism in the 1980's: The Interception of the Achille Lauro Hijackers," 21 *Yale J. Int'l. L.* 158 (1987).

42. Delaware, New Hampshire, and Wyoming.

43. California and Delaware.

44. *Zant v. Stephens*, 462 U.S. 862 (1983).

45. Alabama, Arizona, Arkansas, California, Colorado, Connecticut, Florida, Idaho, Kansas, Louisiana, Mississippi, Nebraska, North Carolina, Oklahoma, Tennessee, Utah, Wyoming, and the federal system.

46. Arizona, Arkansas, California, Colorado, Delaware, Idaho, Kentucky, Maryland, Missouri, Nebraska, Nevada, New York, North Carolina, Ohio, Ore-

gon, South Carolina, Tennessee, Texas, Utah, Virginia, Washington, Wyoming, and the federal system.

47. Alabama, Arizona, Arkansas, Colorado, Connecticut, Florida, Georgia, Idaho, Kansas, Kentucky, Louisiana, Mississippi, Missouri, Nebraska, Nevada, New Hampshire, New Jersey, North Carolina, Oklahoma, Pennsylvania, South Carolina, South Dakota, Tennessee, Utah, Wyoming, and the federal system.

48. Alabama, Arizona, Arkansas, Colorado, Delaware, Florida, Illinois, Indiana, Kansas, Kentucky, Louisiana, Maryland, Mississippi, Montana, Nevada, New Mexico, New York, North Carolina, Ohio, Oklahoma, Oregon, Tennessee, Texas, Utah, Virginia, Washington, Wyoming, and the federal system.

49. Alabama, Arizona, Arkansas, California, Colorado, Connecticut, Delaware, Florida, Georgia, Idaho, Illinois, Indiana, Kansas, Kentucky, Louisiana, Mississippi, Missouri, Montana, Nebraska, Nevada, New Hampshire, New Jersey, North Carolina, Ohio, Oklahoma, Oregon, Pennsylvania, South Carolina, South Dakota, Tennessee, Utah, Wyoming, and the federal system.

50. Arkansas, California, Colorado, Delaware, Florida, Indiana, Mississippi, North Carolina, Oregon, Tennessee, Utah, Wyoming, and the federal system.

51. California, Delaware, Georgia, Illinois, Missouri, Montana, Nevada, New Jersey, New York, Oregon, Pennsylvania, South Carolina, South Dakota, and Virginia.

52. Alabama, Arkansas, Florida, Mississippi, Nebraska, North Carolina, and Utah.

53. This distinction has been blurred somewhat because of the sentencing trend involving "split-sentencing." Under split-sentencing a defendant is actually incarcerated for a brief period, usually not longer than six months, and released to probation after serving the confinement.

54. Indiana and Wyoming.

55. Arizona, Indiana, Washington, and Wyoming.

56. Arizona, Arkansas, and Washington.

57. Connecticut.

58. California, Illinois, Indiana, Louisiana, and Washington.

59. Delaware, Georgia, Illinois, Kansas, Missouri, New Jersey, South Carolina, and South Dakota.

60. California, Colorado, Indiana, and Montana.

CHAPTER 11

1. For a general discussion, see Gary Joseph Vyneman, "Irreconcilable Differences: The Role of Mitigating Circumstances in Capital Punishment

Sentencing Schemes," 13 *Whittier L. Rev.* 763 (1992); Mark Andrew Stafford, "State v. Barts: North Carolina Relaxes Foundation Requirements for Mitigating Evidence in Capital Sentencing Hearings," 66 *N.C. L. Rev.* 1221 (1988).

2. A defendant is not precluded from presenting aggravating circumstance evidence, but in most instances defendants do not present such evidence. There are rare occasions when a defendant wants to be executed. It is during such rare occasions that aggravating circumstance evidence will be presented by a defendant.

3. For a discussion of *Lockett* and its meaning, see Louis D. Bilionis, "Moral Appropriateness, Capital Punishment, and the Lockett Doctrine," 82 *J. Crim. L. & Criminology* 283 (1991).

4. See *Martin v. Wainwright*, 770 F.2d 918 (11th Cir. 1985), modified en banc on other grounds, 781 F.2d 185 (11th Cir. 1985), upholding exclusion of testimony on the deterrent effect of capital punishment on mentally ill defendants.

5. For a discussion, see Christopher Grafflin Browning, Jr., "State v. Huffstetler: Denying Mitigating Instructions in Capital Cases on Grounds of Relevancy," 63 *N.C. L. Rev.* 1122 (1985).

6. For further discussion, see David W. Doyle, "Life or Death in Florida: What Mitigating Evidence Will the Judge Consider in Capital Cases?" 4 *Cooley L. Rev.* 693 (1987); Joshua N. Sondheimer, "A Continuing Source of Aggravation: The Improper Consideration of Mitigating Factors in Death Penalty Sentencing," 41 *Hastings L.J.* 409 (1990).

7. For further discussion of *Delo*, see Wm. Scott Sims, "Eighth and Fourteenth Amendment Capital Sentencing Jurisprudence—Jury Instruction Regarding a Mitigating Factor Upon Which a Criminal Defendant Has Presented No Evidence—Delo v. Lashley," 61 *Tenn. L. Rev.* 1029 (1994).

8. The mitigating circumstance evidence in *Penry*, which had a two-edged sword effect, was the evidence involving the defendant's mental problem. This evidence had the potential of diminishing the defendant's responsibility for his crime, but it also had the potential for being interpreted as revealing his future dangerousness, which was a special statutory issue.

9. See *Graham v. Collins*, 113 S.Ct. 892 (1993), and *Johnson v. Texas*, 113 S.Ct. 2658 (1993).

10. For a discussion of the impact of *Penry*, see Peggy M. Tobolowsky, "What Hath Penry Wrought? Mitigating Circumstances and the Texas Death Penalty," 19 *Am. J. Crim. L.* 345 (1992). See also Ellen Fels Berkman, "Mental Illness as an Aggravating Circumstance in Capital Sentencing," 89 *Colum. L. Rev.* 291 (1989).

11. Capital punishment jurisdictions without statutory mitigating circumstances are Delaware, Georgia, Idaho, Oklahoma, South Dakota, Texas, and Washington.

12. Alabama, Arkansas, California, Colorado, Florida, Illinois, Indiana, Kansas, Kentucky, Louisiana, Maryland, Mississippi, Missouri, Montana,

Nebraska, Nevada, New Hampshire, New Jersey, New Mexico, New York, North Carolina, Ohio, Oklahoma, Oregon, Pennsylvania, South Carolina, Tennessee, Utah, Virginia, Wyoming, and the federal system.

13. For a discussion of the use of a prior criminal record at the penalty phase, see Max J. Burbach, "Prior Criminal Activity and Death Sentencing: State v. Reeves," 24 *Creighton L. Rev.* 547 (1991).

14. Alabama, Arkansas, California, Colorado, Florida, Illinois, Indiana, Kansas, Kentucky, Louisiana, Mississippi, Missouri, Montana, Nebraska, Nevada, New Hampshire, New Jersey, New Mexico, New York, North Carolina, Oregon, Pennsylvania, South Carolina, Tennessee, Utah, Virginia, Wyoming, and the federal system.

15. A few jurisdictions such as New York specifically provide that the mental or emotional disturbance cannot rise to the level of a defense to prosecution.

16. Alabama, California, Florida, Illinois, Indiana, Kansas, Kentucky, Maryland, Mississippi, Missouri, Montana, Nebraska, Nevada, New Hampshire, New Jersey, New Mexico, North Carolina, Ohio, Pennsylvania, South Carolina, Tennessee, Virginia, Wyoming, and the federal system.

17. Alabama, Arizona, Arkansas, California, Colorado, Connecticut, Florida, Illinois, Indiana, Kansas, Kentucky, Louisiana, Mississippi, Missouri, Montana, Nebraska, Nevada, New Hampshire, New York, Ohio, Pennsylvania, South Carolina, Tennessee, Utah, Wyoming, and the federal system.

18. Alabama, Arizona, Arkansas, California, Colorado, Connecticut, Florida, Illinois, Indiana, Kansas, Kentucky, Montana, Nebraska, Nevada, New Hampshire, New Jersey, New Mexico, New York, North Carolina, Ohio, Pennsylvania, South Carolina, Utah, Wyoming, and the federal system.

19. Alabama, Arizona, Arkansas, California, Colorado, Connecticut, Florida, Indiana, Kansas, Kentucky, Louisiana, Maryland, Mississippi, Missouri, Montana, Nebraska, New Hampshire, New Jersey, New Mexico, New York, North Carolina, Ohio, Pennsylvania, South Carolina, Tennessee, Utah, Virginia, Wyoming, and the federal system.

20. Arizona, Arkansas, California, Colorado, Florida, Kansas, Kentucky, Louisiana, Maryland, Mississippi, Missouri, Nebraska, Nevada, New Hampshire, New Mexico, North Carolina, Ohio, Oregon, Pennsylvania, South Carolina, Tennessee, Utah, Virginia, and Wyoming.

21. Connecticut, Indiana, Montana, and South Carolina.

22. Massachusetts.

23. Arizona, Colorado, and Connecticut.

24. California, Colorado, Kentucky, Louisiana, New Mexico, and Tennessee.

25. Colorado, New Jersey, New Mexico, and North Carolina.

26. *State v. Compton*, 726 P.2d 837 (N.M. 1986). See also *State v. Guzman*, 676 P.2d 1321 (N.M. 1984).

27. Colorado, Maryland, and New Mexico.

28. For a discussion of this statutory mitigating circumstance, see Debra D. Burke and Mary Anne Nixon, "Post-traumatic Stress Disorder and the Death Penalty," 38 *How. L.J.* 183 (1994).

29. Kansas.

30. Maryland.

31. Massachusetts.

32. New Hampshire and the federal system.

33. For a discussion of this statutory mitigating circumstance, see Thomas Criswell, "Death Penalty: Rios Grande: The Texas Court of Criminal Appeals Examines Mental Retardation as a Mitigating Factor in Rios v. Texas," 47 *Okla. L. Rev.* 373 (1994).

34. New York, South Carolina, and Virginia.

CHAPTER 12

1. Some special circumstances are duplicated as statutory aggravating circumstances. When this duplication occurs, the statutory aggravating circumstance is actually proven to exist at the guilt phase as a special circumstance. The Supreme Court held in *Lowenfield v. Phelps*, 484 U.S. 231 (1988), that the Constitution does not require proving the existence of a statutory aggravating circumstance at the penalty phase when its existence has been proven at the guilt phase as a special circumstance. See also *Jurek v. Texas*, 428 U.S. 262 (1976).

2. Alabama, Arizona, Arkansas, Colorado, Connecticut, Delaware, Florida, Georgia, Idaho, Illinois, Indiana, Kansas, Kentucky, Louisiana, Maryland, Mississippi, Missouri, Montana, Nebraska, Nevada, New Hampshire, New Jersey, New Mexico, New York, North Carolina, Ohio, Oklahoma, Pennsylvania, South Carolina, South Dakota, Tennessee, Wyoming, and the federal system.

3. See *People v. Davenport*, 221 *Cal.Rptr.* 794 (1985).

4. The position taken by California is not derelict. California is one of the jurisdictions that duplicate all of their statutory aggravating circumstances as special circumstances, but California allows the statutory aggravating circumstances to be litigated at the penalty phase.

5. For a discussion of the decision in *Mills*, see Miranda B. Strassmann, "Mills v. Maryland: The Supreme Court Guarantees the Consideration of Mitigating Circumstances Pursuant to Lockett v. Ohio," 38 *Cath. U. L. Rev.* 907 (1989).

6. See also *Rivera v. Delaware*, 429 U.S. 877 (1976).

7. Arizona, Connecticut, Florida, Maryland, New Hampshire, New York, Pennsylvania, Wyoming, and the federal system. At least four jurisdictions provide the same standard of proof based upon judicial decisions: Delaware, Indiana, North Carolina, and Ohio.

8. Arkansas, California, Georgia, Idaho, Illinois, Kansas, Kentucky, Louisiana, Mississippi, Missouri, Montana, Nebraska, Nevada, New Jersey, New Mexico, Oklahoma, Oregon, South Carolina, South Dakota, Tennessee, Texas, Utah, Virginia, Washington, Wyoming, and the federal system.

9. Alabama.

10. For a critique of the weighing process, see Marcia A. Widder, "Hanging Life in the Balance: The Supreme Court and the Metaphor of Weighing in the Penalty Phase of the Capital Trial," 68 *Tul. L. Rev.* 1341 (1994).

11. For a discussion of *Harris* and its implications, see Abe Muallem, "Harris v. Alabama: Is the Death Penalty in America Entering a Fourth Phase?" 22 *J. Legis.* 85 (1996).

12. Alabama, California, Indiana, Louisiana, Montana, Nebraska, New Hampshire, Pennsylvania, and the federal system.

13. Arizona, Colorado, Florida, Idaho, Illinois, Kansas, Kentucky, Mississippi, Nevada, New Mexico, North Carolina, and Oklahoma.

14. Delaware and Maryland.

15. Arkansas, New Jersey, New York, Ohio, Tennessee, and Utah.

16. For further discussion of the distinction between weighing and non-weighing, see Srikanth Srinivasan, "Capital Sentencing Doctrine and the Weighing-Nonweighing Distinction," 47 *Stan. L. Rev.* 1347 (1995).

17. Connecticut, Georgia, Montana, Oregon, South Carolina, South Dakota, Virginia, Washington, and Wyoming.

18. Georgia, Missouri, Oregon, South Carolina, South Dakota, Virginia, and Wyoming.

19. Washington.

20. Connecticut.

21. A weighing or sufficiency determination that is favorable to the defendant means that the death penalty will not be imposed.

22. Alabama, Arizona, California, Delaware, Idaho, Illinois, Indiana, Kansas, Maryland, New Jersey, New Mexico, Ohio, Oklahoma, Pennsylvania, Tennessee, Texas, and Wyoming.

23. Connecticut, Oregon, and Washington.

24. Colorado, Florida, Kentucky, Louisiana, Mississippi, Missouri, Montana, Nebraska, Nevada, New Hampshire, New York, North Carolina, and the federal system.

25. Arkansas and Utah.

26. Georgia, South Carolina, South Dakota, and Virginia.

CHAPTER 13

1. For a general discussion in this area, see Joseph M. Giarratano, "To the Best of Our Knowledge We Have Never Been Wrong: Fallibility vs. Finality in Capital Punishment," 100 *Yale L.J.* 1005 (1991).

2. For a discussion of "harmless" error analysis in death penalty cases, see C. Elliot Kessler, "Death and Harmlessness: Application of the Harmless Error Rule by the Bird and Lucas Courts in Death Penalty Cases—A Comparison & Critique," 26 *U.S.F. L. Rev.* 41 (1991); Linda E. Carter, "Harmless Error in the Penalty Phase of a Capital Case: A Doctrine Misunderstood and Misapplied," 28 *Ga. L. Rev.* 125 (1993).

3. See also *Franz v. State*, 754 S.W.2d 839 (Ark. 1988).

4. For a general discussion of appellate review, see Ira P. Robbins, "Toward a More Just and Effective System of Review in State Death Penalty Cases," 40 *Am. U. L. Rev.* 1 (1990).

5. Connecticut, Georgia, Idaho, Maryland, Missouri, Nevada, Oklahoma, South Carolina, South Dakota, Virginia, Washington, and the federal system.

6. Alabama, California, Delaware, Idaho, Illinois, Indiana, Kansas, Kentucky, Maryland, Mississippi, Missouri, Montana, Nevada, New Jersey, North Carolina, Oklahoma, Oregon, Virginia, Washington, and Wyoming.

7. For a discussion of the waiver issue, see Tim Kaine, "Capital Punishment and the Waiver of Sentence Review," 18 *Harv. C.R.C.L. L. Rev.* 483 (1983).

8. The seven jurisdictions are California, Florida, Illinois, Indiana, New Jersey, Oregon, and Texas.

9. Alabama, Arizona, Arkansas, Kansas, Montana, New York, Washington, and Wyoming.

10. Alabama, Arizona, Colorado, Connecticut, Delaware, Georgia, Idaho, Kansas, Kentucky, Louisiana, Maryland, Mississippi, Missouri, Montana, Nevada, New Hampshire, New Mexico, New York, North Carolina, Oklahoma, Pennsylvania, South Carolina, South Dakota, Tennessee, Virginia, Washington, Wyoming, and the federal system.

11. In *People v. McLain*, 757 P.2d 564 (Cal. 1988), and *State v. Eaton*, 524 So.2d 1194 (La. 1988), both appellate courts held that a death sentence is not necessarily disproportionate merely because a defendant in a factually similar case received a life sentence. For a discussion of comparative sentencing, see Gregory Michael Stein, "Distinguishing Among Murders When Assessing the Proportionality of the Death Penalty," 85 *Colum. L. Rev.* 1786 (1985).

12. Alabama, Arizona, Connecticut, Delaware, Georgia, Idaho, Kentucky, Louisiana, Mississippi, Missouri, Montana, Nebraska, Nevada, New Hampshire, New Jersey, New Mexico, New York, North Carolina, Ohio, Pennsylvania, South Carolina, South Dakota, Tennessee, Virginia, and Washington.

13. For a discussion of comparative review of death penalty cases, see W. Ward Morrison, Jr., "Washington's Comparative Proportionality Review: Toward Effective Appellate Review of Death Penalty Cases Under the Washington State Constitution," 60 *Wash. L. Rev.* 111 (1989).

14. Alabama, Arizona, Maryland, New Mexico, New York, Ohio, and Tennessee.

15. Alabama, Arizona, Delaware, Georgia, Idaho, Kentucky, Maryland, Mississippi, Missouri, Nevada, New Hampshire, New Mexico, New York, North Carolina, Oklahoma, Oregon, Pennsylvania, South Carolina, South Dakota, Utah, Virginia, Wyoming, and the federal system.

16. Alabama, Connecticut, Maryland, and Pennsylvania.

17. Alabama, Arizona, Missouri, Nevada, Tennessee, Virginia, and Wyoming.

CHAPTER 14

1. *Capital Punishment 1994*, Bureau of Justice Statistics, p. 8, Table 7 (February 1996).

2. Gary Knell, "Capital Punishment: Its Administration in Relation to Juvenile Offenders in the Nineteenth Century and Its Possible Administration in the Eighteenth," 5 *Brit. J. Crim.* 198 (1965).

3. Victor Streib, "Death Penalty for Children: The American Experience with Capital Punishment for Crimes Committed While Under Age Eighteen," 36 *Okl. L. Rev.* 613 (1983).

4. For a discussion of capital punishment and youth, see Cele Hancock, "The Incompatibility of the Juvenile Death Penalty and the United Nations Convention on the Rights of the Child: Domestic and International Concerns," 12 *Ariz. J Int'l & Comp. L.* 699 (1995); Norman J. Finkel, "Prestidigitation, Statistical Magic, and Supreme Court Numerology in Juvenile Death Penalty Cases," 1 *Psychol. Pub. Pol'y & L.* 612 (1995); Suzanne D. Strater, "The Juvenile Death Penalty: In the Best Interests of the Child?" 26 *Loy. U. Chi. L.J.* 147 (1995); Bruce L. Brown, "The Juvenile Death Penalty in Washington: A State Constitutional Analysis," 15 *U. Puget Sound L. Rev.* 361 (1992).

5. For a specific discussion of imposing the death penalty on female youth, see Victor L. Streib and Lynn Sametz, "Executing Female Juveniles," 22 *Conn. L. Rev.* 3 (1989).

6. For a discussion of this case, see T. Shawn Lanier, "Juvenile Offenders and the Death Penalty: An Analysis of Stanford v. Kentucky," 45 *Mercer L. Rev.* 1097 (1994); Etta J. Mullin, "At What Age Should They Die? The United States Supreme Court Decision with Respect to Juvenile Offenders and the Death Penalty Stanford v. Kentucky and Wilkins v. Missouri," 16 *T. Marshall L. Rev.* 161 (1990).

7. Advisory Committee on Criminal Law, "Women Defendants and Prisoners: Who and Where They Are," 67 *S. Calif. L. Rev.* 919 (1994).

8. *Capital Punishment* 1994, Bureau of Justice Statistics, p. 1 (February 1996).

9. For a general discussion of capital punishment and female capital felons, see Elizabeth Rapaport, "Some Questions About Gender and the Death Penalty," 20 *Golden Gate U. L. Rev.* 501 (1990); Victor Streib, "Death Penalty for Female Offenders," 58 *U. Cin. L. Rev.* 845 (1990).

10. Alabama, Arizona, California, Florida, Georgia, Idaho, Indiana, Kansas, Kentucky, Louisiana, Mississippi, Missouri, Montana, Nebraska, Nevada, New Hampshire, New Jersey, New Mexico, New York, Ohio, Oklahoma, South Dakota, Utah, Wyoming, and the federal system.

11. For a general discussion of insanity and capital felons, see Jonathan L. Entin, "Psychiatry, Insanity, and the Death Penalty: A Note on Implementing Supreme Court Decisions," 79 *Crim. L. & Criminology* 218 (1988).

12. Alabama, Arizona, Arkansas, California, Connecticut, Florida, Georgia, Kansas, Kentucky, Maryland, Mississippi, Missouri, Montana, Nebraska, Nevada, New Mexico, New York, Ohio, Oklahoma, South Dakota, Utah, Wyoming, and the federal system.

13. For a general discussion of the death penalty and mental disabilities, see Michael L. Perlin, "The Sanist Lives of Jurors in Death Penalty Cases: The Puzzling Role of Mitigating Mental Disability Evidence," 8 *Notre Dame J.L. Ethics & Pub. Pol'y* 239 (1994); Van W. Ellis, "Guilty but Mentally Ill and the Death Penalty: Punishment Full of Sound and Fury, Signifying Nothing," 43 *Duke L.J.* 87 (1993).

14. For a discussion of *Penry* and its impact, see Robert L. Hayman, "Beyond Penry: The Remedial Use of the Mentally Retarded Label in Death Penalty Sentencing," 59 *UMKC L. Rev.* 17 (1990); J. Dwight Carmichael, "Penry v. Lynaugh: Texas Death Penalty Procedure Unconstitutionally Precludes Jury Consideration of Mitigating Evidence," 42 *Baylor L. Rev.* 347 (1990).

15. *Capital Punishment 1994*, Bureau of Justice Statistics, p. 10, table 11 (February 1996).

16. For further discussion, see Gerald Kirven, "Capital Crime and Punishment: Shortening the Time Between Them," 42 *Fed. Law.* 20 (1995).

17. Alabama, Arizona, California, Colorado, Florida, Georgia, Illinois, Indiana, Louisiana, Maryland, Missouri, New Jersey, New Mexico, New York, North Carolina, Ohio, Oklahoma, Oregon, Pennsylvania, Tennessee, Texas, Washington, and the federal system.

18. The defendant could remain in the state system by starting state habeas corpus proceedings.

19. The defendant can begin by filing a federal habeas corpus petition in a federal district court.

20. For a critical discussion of habeas corpus, see Alan W. Clarke, "Procedural Labyrinths and the Injustice of Death: A Critique of Death Penalty Habeas Corpus," 30 *U. Rich. L. Rev.* 303 (1996).

21. The defendant can appeal to the Supreme Court the denial of habeas

corpus relief by the state's highest court, but this is not the normal course by defendants.

22. For a discussion of federal habeas corpus issues, see Joseph L. Hoffman, "Is Innocent Sufficient? An Essay on the U.S. Supreme Court's Continuing Problems with Federal Habeas Corpus and the Death Penalty," 68 *Ind. L.J.* 817 (1993); Stephanie O. Joy, "A Claim of Newly Discovered Evidence of Actual Innocence Does Not Entitle Death Penalty Claimant to Federal Habeas Corpus Relief," 4 *Seton Hall Const. L.J.* 361 (1993).

23. One of the more recent Supreme Court decisions limiting habeas corpus petitions in federal court is *McCleskey v. Zant*, 111 S.Ct. 1454 (1991). For a discussion of this case and its impact, see Cheryl R. Sweeney, "McCleskey v. Zant: The Cause and Prejudice Standard in Capital Punishment Cases," 24 *U. Tol. L. Rev.* 231 (1992); Martha Hallisey, "To Habe or Not to Habe: Curtailing the Writ of Habeas Corpus in McCleskey v. Zant," 19 *New Eng. J. on Crim. & Civ. Confinement* 397 (1993).

24. *Capital Punishment 1994*, Bureau of Justice Statistics, p. 12, Appendix Table 1 (February 1996).

25. For a discussion of executive clemency, see Daniel Lim, "State Due Process Guarantees for Meaningful Death Penalty Clemency Proceedings," 28 *Colum. J.L. & Soc. Probs.* 47 (1994); Bruce Ledewitz and Scott Staples, "The Role of Executive Clemency in Modern Death Penalty Cases," 27 *U. Rich. L. Rev.* 227 (1993).

26. For discussion of commutation see, Victoria J. Palacios, "Faith in Fantasy: The Supreme Court's Reliance on Commutation to Ensure Justice in Death Penalty Cases," 49 *Vand. L. Rev.* 311 (1996); Daniel T. Kobil, "Due Process in Death Penalty Commutations: Life, Liberty, and the Pursuit of Clemency," 27 *U. Rich. L. Rev.* 201 (1993).

CHAPTER 15

1. See generally Hugo Adam Bedau, *The Death Penalty in America* (3d ed. 1982).

2. See Steven A. Blum, "Public Executions: Understanding the Cruel and Unusual Punishments Clause," 19 *Hastings Con. L. Q.* 413 (1992).

3. Reported in David Sternbach, "Hanging Pictures: Photographic Theory and the Framing of Images of Execution," 70 *N.Y.U. L. Rev.* 1100 (1995).

4. Id.

5. The following jurisdictions have not set out any statutory guidelines for conducting executions: Arkansas, Idaho, and the federal system. The state of Delaware lists only two factors.

6. Delaware and Louisiana.

7. Ohio.

8. Washington.

9. Indiana and Wyoming.

10. Alabama, Arizona, California, Missouri, New Mexico, Oklahoma, Oregon, South Dakota, Texas, and Utah.

11. New York.

12. Connecticut, Kansas, Kentucky, Nebraska, and Ohio.

13. Mississippi.

14. Georgia, New Hampshire, North Carolina, Tennessee, and Washington.

15. Alabama and Connecticut.

16. Mississippi.

17. Kentucky, Mississippi, South Carolina, and Tennessee.

18. Arizona, California, Colorado, Delaware, Florida, Georgia, Illinois, Kansas, Louisiana, New Hampshire, New Jersey, New Mexico, New York, North Carolina, Pennsylvania, South Carolina, South Dakota, and Virginia.

19. Delaware authorizes the presiding trial judge to determine who shall attend the execution as witnesses.

20. Alabama, Missouri, Ohio, and Texas.

21. Indiana, Kentucky, and Wyoming.

22. Alabama and Texas.

23. Connecticut, Indiana, Kansas, Kentucky, Louisiana, Maryland, Nebraska, Pennsylvania, South Carolina, Tennessee, Texas, and Virginia.

24. Arizona, California, Mississippi, Missouri, New Jersey, New Mexico, New York, Oklahoma, Oregon, and South Dakota.

25. Alabama, Florida, Georgia, New Hampshire, North Carolina, Ohio, Utah, and Wyoming.

26. For a brief review of a book critical of physician participation in executions, see John Kaisersatt, "Capital Punishment: Physicians Executioners?" 22 *Am. J. Crim. L.* 317 (1994).

27. For a general discussion of the role of physicians in capital punishment cases, see David J. Rothman, "Physicians and the Death Penalty," 4 *J.L. & Pol'y* 151 (1995).

28. Arizona, Colorado, Connecticut, Florida, Kentucky, Nevada, New Hampshire, New Mexico, North Carolina, Oklahoma, Pennsylvania, Tennessee, Utah, and Virginia.

29. Alabama, California, Georgia, Indiana, Louisiana, Mississippi, New Jersey, Texas, and Wyoming.

30. Kansas.

31. New York, Ohio, and Oregon.

32. Arizona, California, Louisiana, New Mexico, New York, South Dakota, and Utah.

33. Missouri and Nevada.

34. Florida, Georgia, Maryland, New York, North Carolina, South Carolina, Virginia, and Washington.

35. Arizona, California, Missouri, New Hampshire, New Mexico, Oregon, South Dakota, and Utah.

36. New York, Oklahoma, South Dakota, Utah, and Washington.

37. New York, South Dakota, Texas, and Washington.

CHAPTER 16

1. California, Missouri, Montana, North Carolina, Ohio, South Carolina, Utah, Virginia, and Washington. It will be noted that Missouri sets out two statutory methods of execution but fails to say whether the capital felon may select between the two methods. Because of the statutory silence, the presumption is that the capital felon makes the determination.

2. California's statute previously provided that lethal gas was the default method of execution. However, as a result of a federal court of appeals ruling on lethal gas in *Fierro v. Gomez*, 77 F.3d (9th Cir. 1996), reversed, 117 S.Ct. 285 (1996), finding lethal gas unconstitutional, California amended its statute so that lethal injection is now the default method of execution. North Carolina has not changed its default method of execution. In fact, subsequent to the decision by the federal court of appeals in *Fierro*, but prior to the reversal of that decision, the North Carolina Supreme Court ruled in the case of *State v. Boyd*, 473 N.E.2d 327 (N.C. 1996), that death by lethal gas was constitutional.

3. The defendant in *Campbell v. Wood*, 18 F.3d 662 (9th Cir. 1994), argued that it was unconstitutional for the state of Washington to allow him to select between hanging and lethal injection as the method of his execution. The court in that case addressed the issue as follows:

> Campbell claims that his First and Eighth Amendment rights are violated by the statutory provision that allows him to elect death by lethal injection rather than by hanging....
>
> Campbell's First Amendment challenge is premised on the Free Exercise Clause. He contends that his religious beliefs preclude him from participating at any level in his own execution, and that these beliefs are infringed upon by [the statute] which allows him to elect lethal injection and avoid death by judicial hanging.
>
> We see no infringement upon Campbell's free exercise of his religious beliefs. We agree with Campbell that a statute providing for a choice between two methods of execution, one constitutional and the other unconstitutional, might place an impermissible burden on the free exercise of the asserted beliefs. This is not, however, the situation here.
>
> First, Campbell is not required to make any choice or to participate in the selection of the method to be employed in his execution. He may remain absolutely silent and refuse to participate in any election. The statute provides for imposition of the death penalty by hanging, and does not require him to choose the method of his execution.... The statute

does not compel Campbell to compromise one constitutional right to avoid the infringement of another.

Campbell also argues that the statutory provision of an option for death by lethal injection constitutes cruel and unusual punishment.... Campbell faces a heavy burden in attempting to show that the existence of an option related to his execution is cruel and unusual. We cannot say the State descends to inhuman depths by allowing the condemned to exercise such an election. We believe that benefits to prisoners who may choose to exercise the option and who may feel relieved that they can elect lethal injection outweigh the emotional costs for those who find the mere existence of an option objectionable[.]

4. Arkansas, California, Delaware, Idaho, Illinois, Mississippi, New Hampshire, Ohio, Oklahoma, South Carolina, and Wyoming.

5. See Roderick C. Patrick, "Hiding Death," 18 *New Eng. J. on Crim. & Civ. Confinement* 117 (1992). See also Norman Mailer, *The Executioner's Song* (3d ed., 1979).

6. For a general discussion on the humaneness of execution methods see, Brian Hill, "Judicial Response to Changing Societal Values on the Death Penalty: Must the Method Chosen Be the Most Humane," 7 *St. Thomas L. Rev.* 409 (1995).

7. See *Andrew v. Shulsen*, 802 F.2d 1256 (10th Cir. 1986).

8. See V.A.C. Gatrell, *The Hanging Tree: Execution and the English People 1770–1868* (1994).

9. For a critical discussion of hanging and lethal gas, see Allen Huang, "Hanging, Cyanide Gas, and the Evolving Standards of Decency: The Ninth Circuit's Misapplication of the Cruel and Unusual Clause of the Eighth Amendment," 74 *Or. L. Rev.* 995 (1995).

10. Montana and Washington.

11. Delaware and New Hampshire.

12. Oklahoma.

13. California, Missouri, Montana, North Carolina, Ohio, South Carolina, Utah, Virginia, and Washington. Missouri does not indicate in its statute whether the capital felon actually chooses between the two methods of execution.

14. California, South Carolina, Utah, and Virginia.

15. Arizona, Arkansas, Colorado, Delaware, Idaho, Illinois, Indiana, Kansas, Louisiana, Maryland, Mississippi, Nevada, New Hampshire, New Jersey, New Mexico, New York, Oklahoma, Oregon, Pennsylvania, South Dakota, Texas, and Wyoming.

16. See *State v. Moen*, 786 P.2d 111 (Or. 1990), holding lethal injection not cruel and unusual; *Hopkinson v. State*, 798 P.2d 1186 (Wyo. 1990), holding lethal injection constitutional; *People v. Stewart*, 520 N.E.2d 348 (Ill. 1988), lethal injection not unconstitutional.

17. For a critical discussion on the use of electrocution to impose death, see Lonny J. Hoffman, "The Madness of the Method: The Use of Electrocution and the Death Penalty," 70 *Tex. L. Rev.* 1039 (1992); Deborah W. Denno, "Is Electrocution an Unconstitutional Method of Execution? The Engineering of Death Over the Century," 35 *Wm. & Mary L. Rev.* 551 (1994); Philip R. Nugent, "Pulling the Plug on the Electric Chair: The Unconstitutionality of Electrocution," 2 *Wm. & Mary Bill Rts. J.* 185 (1993).

18. Ohio, South Carolina, and Virginia.

19. Arkansas and Illinois.

20. Oklahoma.

21. Alabama, Connecticut, Florida, Georgia, Kentucky, Nebraska, and Tennessee.

22. California, Missouri, and North Carolina.

23. Mississippi and Wyoming. California utilizes both of its methods of execution as a single fallback option.

24. See also *Duisen v. State*, 441 S.W.2d 688 (Mo. 1969); *Calhoun v. State*, 468 A.2d 45 (Md. 1983); and *State v. Boyd*, 473 N.E.2d 327 (N.C. 1996), all of which hold that lethal gas is not cruel and unusual punishment.

25. It should be kept in mind that the dispositions brought out here are limited to what is contained in the death penalty statutes of jurisdictions that addressed the issue in their death penalty statutes.

26. Alabama, Connecticut, Florida, Georgia, Kentucky, Mississippi, New Jersey, New York, North Carolina, Ohio, Pennsylvania, South Carolina, South Dakota, Texas, Virginia, and Wyoming.

27. Alabama, Connecticut, Georgia, Kentucky, Ohio, and South Carolina.

28. Alabama, Connecticut, Georgia, Kentucky, Mississippi, New Jersey, New York, North Carolina, Ohio, Texas, and Wyoming.

29. Alabama and Kansas.

30. Mississippi, New Jersey, New York, Pennsylvania, and Texas.

31. Alabama, Connecticut, Florida, Georgia, Kentucky, Mississippi, New Jersey, New York, North Carolina, Ohio, Pennsylvania, South Carolina, South Dakota, Texas, and Wyoming.

Bibliography

Death Penalty Sentencing Statutes

Ala. Code § 13A-5-38 et seq. (1995)
Ariz. Rev. Stat. Ann. § 13-703 et seq. (Supp. 1996)
Ark. Code Ann. § 5-4-601 et seq. (1993)
Cal. Penal Code § 190 et seq. (1988)
Colo. Rev. Stat. § 16-11-103 et seq. (Supp. 1996)
Conn. Gen. Stat. Ann. § 53a-46a et seq. (1994)
Del. Code Ann. tit. 11, § 4209 (1995)
Fla. Stat. Ann. § 921.141 et seq. (Supp. 1997)
Ga. Code Ann. § 17-10-30 et seq. (1990)
Idaho Code § 19-2515 (1987)
Ill. Comp. Stat. Ann. ch. 720, § 5/9-1 (1993)
Ind. Code Ann. § 35-50-2-9 (1994)
Kan. Stat. Ann. § 21-4622 et seq. (1995)
Ky. Rev. Stat. Ann. § 532.025 et seq. (1990)
La. Code Crim. Proc. art. 905 et seq. (1984)
Md. Ann. Code art. 27, § 412 et seq. (1996)
Miss. Code Ann. § 99-19-101 et seq. (1994)
Mo. Rev. Stat. § 565.032 et seq. (1996)
Mont. Code Ann. § 46-18-301 et seq. (1995)
Neb. Rev. Stat. § 29-2519 et seq. (1989)
Nev. Rev. Stat. § 175.552 et seq. and § 200.033 et seq. (1991)
N.H. Rev. Stat. Ann. § 630:1 et seq. (1986)
N.J. Stat. Ann. § 2C:11-3 (1995)
N.M. Stat. Ann. § 31-20A-1 et seq. (1994)
N.Y. Crim. Proc. Law § 400.27 (1994)
N.C. Gen Stat. § 15A-2000 (1988)
Ohio Rev. Code Ann. § 2929.03 et seq. (1993)
Okla. Stat. Ann. tit. 21, § 701.10 et seq. (1983)
Or. Rev. Stat. § 163.150 (1993)
Pa. Stat. Ann. tit. 42 § 9711 (Supp. 1996)

S.C. Code Ann. § 16-3-20 (1996)
S.D. Codified Laws Ann. § 23A-27A-1 et seq. (1988)
Tenn. Code Ann. § 39-13-202 et seq. (1991)
Tex. Crim. Proc. Code Ann. art. 37.071 (1981)
Utah Code Ann. § 76-3-207 (1995)
Va. Code Ann. § 19.2-264.4 (1988)
Wash. Rev. Code § 10.95.020 et seq. (1990)
Wyo. Stat. Ann. § 6-2-101 et seq. (1988)
18 U.S.C.A. 3591 et seq. (Supp. 1996)

BOOKS

Anderson, B. *The Death Penalty and Public Opinion: The Example of the State of Iowa* (San Francisco: Austin and Winfield, 1995).
Bedau, H. *The Case Against the Death Penalty* (New York: ACLU, 1985).
_____. *The Death Penalty in America*, 3d ed. (New York: Oxford University Press, 1982).
Black, C. *Capital Punishment: The Inevitability of Caprice and Mistake* (New York: Norton, 1981).
Cabana, D. *Death at Midnight: The Confession of an Executioner* (Boston: Northeastern University Press, 1996).
Carrington, F. *Neither Cruel Nor Unusual* (New Rochelle, N.Y.: Arlington House, 1978).
Coyne, R. *Capital Punishment and the Judicial Process* (Durham, N.C.: Carolina Academic Press, 1994).
Duker, W. F. *A Constitutional History of Habeas Corpus* (Westport, Conn: Greenwood, 1980).
Finalason, W. F. *Reeves' History of the English Law*, vols. I, III (Philadelphia: M. Murphy, 1879).
Garland, D. *Punishment and Modern Society* (Chicago: University of Chicago Press, 1990).
Gatrell, V. A. C. *The Hanging Tree: Execution and the English People 1770–1868* (New York: Oxford University Press, 1994).
Gettinger, S. *Sentenced to Die: The People, the Crimes and the Controversy* (New York: Macmillan, 1979).
Gorecki, J. *Capital Punishment: Criminal Law and Social Evolution* (New York: Columbia University Press, 1983).
Holdsworth, W. *A History of English Law*, vols. II, III, VI, VII, IX, XI, XIII (London: Methuen & Co., reprints 1971, 1973, 1971, 1973, 1966, 1966, 1971).
Jackson, B., and Christian D. *Death Row* (Boston: Beacon Press, 1980).
Kadish, S. H. *Encyclopedia of Crime and Justice*, vol. 3 (New York: Macmillan, 1983).

Kronenwerter, M. *Capital Punishment: A Reference Handbook* (Santa Barbara, Calif.: ABC-CLIO, 1993).

Loeb, R. *Crime and Capital Punishment* (New York: F. Watts, 1978).

Mailer, N. *The Executioner's Song* (Boston: Little, Brown, 1979).

Miller, K., and Radelet, M. *Executing the Mentally Ill* (Newberry Park, Calif.: Sage Publications, 1993).

Neubauer, D. *America's Courts and the Criminal Justice System* (North Scituate, Mass.: Duxbury Press, 1979).

Newman, G. *Just and Painful: A Case for the Corporal Punishment of Criminals* (New York: Free Press, 1983).

Pannick, D. *Toward a Comparative Jurisprudence on Capital Punishment Judicial Review of the Death Penalty* (London: Duckworth, 1982).

Pollock, F., and Maitland, F. *The History of English Law*, vol. I (Cambridge: Cambridge University Press, 1968).

Potter, H. *Hanging in Judgment: Religion and the Death Penalty in England from the Bloody Code to Abolition* (New York: Continuum, 1993).

Pound, R. *Criminal Justice in America* (New York: Da Capo Press, 1975).

Radelet, M., Bedau, H., and Putnam, C. *In Spite of Innocence: Erroneous Convictions in Capital Cases* (Boston: Northeastern University Press, 1992).

Robbins, I. P. *Toward a More Just and Effective System of Review in State Death Penalty Cases* (Chicago: ABA, 1990).

Singer, R. *Just Deserts: Sentencing Based on Equality and Desert* (Cambridge: Ballinger Publishing Company, 1979).

Stafford, S. *Clemency: Legal Authority, Procedure and Structure* (Williamsburg, Va.: National Center for State Courts, 1977).

Streib, V. L. *Death Penalty for Juveniles* (Bloomington: Indiana University Press, 1987).

Stubben, D. *#555 Death Row* (Amarillo, Tex.: Tri State Promotions, 1981).

Van den Haag, E. and Conrad, J. *The Death Penalty: A Debate* (New York: Plenum, 1983).

White, W. S. *The Death Penalty in the Nineties: An Examination of the Modern System of Capital Punishment* (Ann Arbor: University of Michigan Press, 1991).

ARTICLES (IN REVERSE CHRONOLOGICAL ORDER)

Louis J. Palmer, Jr., "Capital Punishment: A Utilitarian Proposal for Recycling Transplantable Organs as Part of a Capital Felon's Death Sentence," 29 *U. West L.A.L. Rev.* 1 (1998).

Phyllis L. Crocker, "Concepts of Culpability and Deathworthiness: Differentiating Between Guilt and Punishment in Death Penalty Cases," 66 *Fordham L. Rev.* 21 (1997).

Christopher J. Meade, "Reading Death Sentences: The Narrative Construction of Capital Punishment," 71 *N.Y.U. L. Rev.* 732 (1996).

Abe Muallem, "Harris v. Alabama: Is the Death Penalty in America Entering a Fourth Phase?" 22 *J. Legis.* 85 (1996).

Richard Klein, "Constitutional Concerns About Capital Punishment: The Death Penalty Statute in New York State," 11 *J. Suffolk Acad. L.* 1 (1996).

Damien P. Horigan, "Of Compassion and Capital Punishment: A Buddhist Perspective on the Death Penalty," 41 *Am. J. Juris.* 271 (1996).

Victoria J. Palacios, "Faith in Fantasy: The Supreme Court's Reliance on Commutation to Ensure Justice in Death Penalty Cases," 49 *Vand. L. Rev.* 311 (1996).

Alan W. Clarke, "Procedural Labyrinths and the Injustice of Death: A Critique of Death Penalty Habeas Corpus," 30 *U. Rich. L. Rev.* 303 (1996).

John J. Farmer, "The Evolution of Death-Eligibility in New Jersey," 26 *Seton Hall L. Rev.* 1573 (1996).

Daniel A. Rudolph, "The Misguided Reliance in American Jurisprudence on Jewish Law to Support the Moral Legitimacy of Capital Punishment," 33 *Am. Crim. L. Rev.* 437 (1996).

Randall Coyne, "Marking the Progress of Humane Justice: Harry Blackmun's Death Penalty Epiphany," 43 *U. Kan. L. Rev.* 367 (1995).

David Sternbach, "Hanging Pictures: Photographic Theory and the Framing of Images of Execution," 70 *N.Y.U. L. Rev.* 1100 (1995).

Srikanth Srinivasan, "Capital Sentencing Doctrine and the Weighing-Nonweighing Distinction," 47 *Stan. L. Rev.* 1347 (1995).

Stephen R. Mcallister, "The Problem of Implementing a Constitutional System of Capital Punishment," 43 *U. Kan. L. Rev.* 1039 (1995).

Marla Sandys, "Cross-overs—Capital Jurors Who Change Their Minds About the Punishment: A Litmus Test for Sentencing Guidelines," 70 *Ind. L.J.* 1183 (1995).

Christopher Slobogin, "Should Juries and the Death Penalty Mix?: A Prediction About the Supreme Court's Answer," 70 *Ind. L.J.* 1249 (1995).

Helen Prejean, "Capital Punishment: The Humanistic and Moral Issues," 27 *St. Mary's L.J.* 1 (1995).

Amy D. Ronner, "When Judges Impose the Death Penalty After the Jury Recommends Life: Harris v. Alabama as the Excision of the Tympanic Membrane in an Augmentedly Death-biased Procedure," 23 *Hastings Conts. L.Q.* 217 (1995).

David Hesseltine, "The Evolution of the Capital Punishment Jurisprudence of the United States Supreme Court and the Impact of Tuilaepa v. California on That Evolution," 32 *San Diego L. Rev.* 593 (1995).

Ronald J. Tabak, "Report: Ineffective Assistance of Counsel and Lack of Due Process in Death Penalty Cases," 22 *Hum. Rts.* 36 (1995).

Gerald Kirven, "Capital Crime and Punishment: Shortening the Time Between Them," 42 *Fed. Law.* 20 (1995).

Cele Hancock, "The Incompatibility of the Juvenile Death Penalty and the United Nations Convention on the Rights of the Child: Domestic and International Concerns," 12 *Ariz. J. Int'l & Comp. L.* 699 (1995).

Allen Huang, "Hanging, Cyanide Gas, and the Evolving Standards of Decency: The Ninth Circuit's Misapplication of the Cruel and Unusual Clause of the Eighth Amendment," 74 *Or. L. Rev.* 995 (1995).

David J. Rothman, "Physicians and the Death Penalty," 4 *J.L. & Pol'y* 151 (1995).

Norman J. Finkel, "Prestidigitation, Statistical Magic, and Supreme Court Numerology in Juvenile Death Penalty Cases," 1 *Psychol. Pub. Pol'y & L.* 612 (1995).

Suzanne D. Strater, "The Juvenile Death Penalty: In the Best Interests of the Child?" 26 *Loy. U. Chi. L.J.* 147 (1995).

Brian Hill, "Judicial Response to Changing Societal Values on the Death Penalty: Must the Method Chosen Be the Most Humane," 7 *St. Thomas L. Rev.* 409 (1995).

Kathleen D. Weron, "Rethinking Utah's Death Penalty Statute: A Constitutional Requirement for the Substantive Narrowing of Aggravating Circumstances," 1994 *Utah L. Rev.* 1107 (1994).

Katheryn K. Russell, "The Constitutionality of Jury Override in Alabama Death Penalty Cases," 46 *Ala. L. Rev.* 5 (1994).

Alan I. Bigel, "Justices William J. Brennan, Jr. and Thurgood Marshall on Capital Punishment: Its Constitutionality, Morality, Deterrent Effect, and Interpretation by the Court," 8 *Notre Dame J.L. Ethics & Pub. Pol'y* 11 (1994).

John Kaisersatt, "Capital Punishment: Physicians Executioners?" 22 *Am. J. Crim. L.* 317 (1994).

Marcia A. Widder, "Hanging Life in the Balance: The Supreme Court and the Metaphor of Weighing in the Penalty Phase of the Capital Trial," 68 *Tul. L. Rev.* 1341 (1994).

Michael Alden Miller, "The Reciprocal Pretrial Discovery Provisions of Proposition 115 Apply to Both Guilt Phase and Penalty Phase Evidence— Nevertheless the Courts May Exercise Discretion Under Appropriate Circumstances and Postpone Disclosure of the Defendant's Penalty Phase Evidence Until the Guilt Phase Has Concluded," 21 *Pepp. L. Rev.* 1016 (1994).

Paul J. Arougheti, "Imposing Homicide Liability on Gun Battle Participants for the Deaths of Innocent Bystanders," 27 *Colum. J.L. & Soc. Probs.* 467 (1994).

Wm. Scott Sims, "Eighth and Fourteenth Amendment Capital Sentencing Jurisprudence—Jury Instruction Regarding a Mitigating Factor Upon

Which a Criminal Defendant Has Presented No Evidence—Delo v. Lashley," 61 *Tenn. L. Rev.* 1029 (1994).

Michael L. Perlin, "The Sanist Lives of Jurors in Death Penalty Cases: The Puzzling Role of Mitigating Mental Disability Evidence," 8 *Notre Dame J.L. Ethics & Pub. Pol'y* 239 (1994).

Debra D. Burke and Mary Anne Nixon, "Post-traumatic Stress Disorder and the Death Penalty," 38 *How. L.J.* 183 (1994).

T. Shawn Lanier, "Juvenile Offenders and the Death Penalty: An Analysis of Stanford v. Kentucky," 45 *Mercer L. Rev.* 1097 (1994).

Thomas Criswell, "Death Penalty: Rios Grande: The Texas Court of Criminal Appeals Examines Mental Retardation as a Mitigating Factor in Rios v. Texas," 47 *Okla. L. Rev.* 373 (1994).

William J. Bowers, Margaret Vandiver & Patricia H. Dugan, "A New Look at Public Opinion on Capital Punishment: What Citizens and Legislators Prefer," 22 *Am. J. Crim. L.* 77 (1994).

Daniel Lim, "State Due Process Guarantees for Meaningful Death Penalty Clemency Proceedings," 28 Colum. *J.L. & Soc. Probs.* 47 (1994).

Deborah W. Denno, "Is Electrocution an Unconstitutional Method of Execution? The Engineering of Death Over the Century," 35 *Wm. & Mary L. Rev.* 551 (1994).

Philip R. Nugent, "Pulling the Plug on the Electric Chair: The Unconstitutionality of Electrocution," 2 *Wm. & Mary Bill Rts. J.* 185 (1993).

Bruce Ledewitz and Scott Staples, "The Role of Executive Clemency in Modern Death Penalty Cases," 27 *U. Rich. L. Rev.* 227 (1993).

Samuel Cameron, "The Demand for Capital Punishment," 13 *Int'l Rev. L. & Econ.* 47 (1993).

Brian Serr, "Of Crime and Punishment, Kingpins and Footsoldiers, Life and Death: The Drug War and the Federal Death Penalty Provision—Problems of Interpretation and Constitutionality," 25 *Ariz. St. L.J.* 895 (1993).

Van W. Ellis, "Guilty but Mentally Ill and the Death Penalty: Punishment Full of Sound and Fury, Signifying Nothing," 43 *Duke L.J.* 87 (1993).

Joseph L. Hoffman, "Is Innocent Sufficient? An Essay on the U.S. Supreme Court's Continuing Problems with Federal Habeas Corpus and the Death Penalty," 68 *Ind. L.J.* 817 (1993).

Stephanie O. Joy, "A Claim of Newly Discovered Evidence of Actual Innocence Does Not Entitle Death Penalty Claimant to Federal Habeas Corpus Relief," 4 *Seton Hall Const. L.J.* 361 (1993).

Jaye Mendros, "Criminal Procedure: Morgan v. Illinois Takes a Step Toward Eliminating Hanging Juries in Capital Cases," 46 *Okla. L. Rev.* 729 (1993).

Martha Hallisey, "To Habe or Not to Habe: Curtailing the Writ of Habeas Corpus in McCleskey v. Zant," 19 *New Eng. J. on Crim. & Civ. Confinement* 397 (1993).

Katharyne C. Johnson, "Sentencing and Punishment: Permit Judicial Consideration of Certain Evidence and Testimony in Cases in Which the Death Penalty May Be Imposed," 10 *Ga. St. U.L. Rev.* 113 (1993).

Bruce Ledewitz, "Could the Death Penalty Be a Cruel Punishment?" 3 *Widener J. Pub. L.* 121 (1993).

Linda E. Carter, "Harmless Error in the Penalty Phase of a Capital Case: A Doctrine Misunderstood and Misapplied," 28 *Ga. L. Rev.* 125 (1993).

Daniel T. Kobil, "Due Process in Death Penalty Commutations: Life, Liberty, and the Pursuit of Clemency," 27 *U. Rich. L. Rev.* 201 (1993).

Lonny J. Hoffman, "The Madness of the Method: The Use of Electrocution and the Death Penalty," 70 *Tex. L. Rev.* 1039 (1992).

Steven A. Blum, "Public Executions: Understanding the Cruel and Unusual Punishments Clause," 19 *Hastings Con. L. Q.* 413 (1992).

Ronald J. Mann, "The Individualized Consideration Principles and the Death Penalty as Cruel and Unusual Punishment," 29 *Hous. L. Rev.* 493 (1992).

Peggy M. Tobolowsky, "Drugs and Death: Congress Authorizes the Death Penalty for Certain Drug-related Murders," 18 *J. Contemp. L.* 47 (1992).

Michael A. Dawson, "Popular Sovereignty, Double Jeopardy, and the Dual Sovereignty Doctrine," 102 *Yale L.J.* 281 (1992).

Cheryl R. Sweeney, "McCleskey v. Zant: The Cause and Prejudice Standard in Capital Punishment Cases," 24 *U. Tol. L. Rev.* 231 (1992).

Roderick C. Patrick, "Hiding Death," 18 *New Eng. J. on Crim. & Civ. Confinement* 117 (1992).

Kenneth Melilli, "Prosecutorial Discretion in an Adversary System," 1992 *B.Y.U.L. Rev.* 669 (1992).

Stan Robin Gregory, "Capital Punishment and Equal Protection: Constitutional Problems, Race and the Death Penalty," 5 *St. Thomas L. Rev.* 257 (1992).

Christopher M. Wilson, "Criminal Procedure—Death Penalty—A Convicted Criminal Must Be Adequately Notified That the Death Penalty May Be Imposed as a Sentence—Lankford v. Idaho," 22 *Seton Hall L. Rev.* 974 (1992).

Robert Alan Kelly, "Applicability of the Rules of Evidence to the Capital Sentencing Proceeding: Theoretical & Practical Support for Open Admissibility of Mitigating Evidence," 60 *UMKC L. Rev.* 411 (1992).

Bruce L. Brown, "The Juvenile Death Penalty in Washington: A State Constitutional Analysis," 15 *U. Puget Sound L. Rev.* 361 (1992).

Peggy M. Tobolowsky, "What Hath Penry Wrought? Mitigating Circumstances and the Texas Death Penalty," 19 *Am. J. Crim. L.* 345 (1992).

Gary Joseph Vyneman, "Irreconcilable Differences: The Role of Mitigating Circumstances in Capital Punishment Sentencing Schemes," 13 *Whittier L. Rev.* 763 (1992).

Linda Andre-Wells, "Imposing the Death Penalty Upon Juvenile Offenders:

A Current Application of the Eighth Amendment's Prohibition Against Cruel and Unusual Punishment," 21 *N.M. L. Rev.* 373 (1991).

Louis D. Bilionis, "Moral Appropriateness, Capital Punishment and the Lockett Doctrine," 82 *J. Crim. L. & Criminology* 283 (1991).

Joseph M. Giarratano, "To the Best of Our Knowledge We Have Never Been Wrong: Fallibility vs. Finality in Capital Punishment," 100 *Yale L.J.* 1005 (1991).

C. Elliot Kessler, "Death and Harmlessness: Application of the Harmless Error Rule by the Bird and Lucas Courts in Death Penalty Cases—A Comparison & Critique," 26 *U.S.F. L. Rev.* 41 (1991).

Patrick E. Higginbotham, "Juries and the Death Penalty," 41 *Case W. Res. L. Rev.* 1047 (1991).

Hugo Bedau, "How to Argue About the Death Penalty," 25 *Israel L. Rev.* 466 (1991).

Mark V. Tushnet, "The Politics of Executing the Innocent: The Death Penalty in the Next Century," 53 *U. Pitt. L. Rev.* 261 (1991).

Max J. Burbach, "Prior Criminal Activity and Death Sentencing: State v. Reeves," 24 *Creighton L. Rev.* 547 (1991).

Glenn M. Bieler, "Death Be Not Proud: A Note on Juvenile Capital Punishment," 7 *N.Y.L. Sch. J. Hum. Rts.* 179 (1990).

Daniel S. Reinberg, "The Constitutionality of the Illinois Death Penalty Statute: The Right to Pretrial Notice of the State's Intention to Seek the Death Penalty," 85 *Nw. U. L. Rev.* 272 (1990).

Sandra R. Acosta, "Imposing the Death Penalty Upon Drug Kingpins," 27 *Harv. J. on Legis.* 596 (1990).

Richard A. Rosen, "Felony Murder and the Eighth Amendment Jurisprudence of Death," 31 *B.C. L. Rev.* 1103 (1990).

Robert L. Hayman, "Beyond Penry: The Remedial Use of the Mentally Retarded Label in Death Penalty Sentencing," 59 *UMKC L. Rev.* 17 (1990).

J. Dwight Carmichael, "Penry v. Lynaugh: Texas Death Penalty Procedure Unconstitutionally Precludes Jury Consideration of Mitigating Evidence," 42 *Baylor L. Rev.* 347 (1990).

Etta J. Mullin, "At What Age Should They Die? The United States Supreme Court Decision with Respect to Juvenile Offenders and the Death Penalty Stanford v. Kentucky and Wilkins v. Missouri," 16 *T. Marshall L. Rev.* 161 (1990).

Wayne Logan, "A Proposed Check on the Charging Discretion of Wisconsin Prosecutors," 1990 *Wis. L. Rev.* 1695 (1990).

Kenneth S. Gallant, "Ex Post Facto Judicial Clarification of a Vague Aggravating Circumstance in a Capital Punishment Statute," 59 *UMKC L. Rev.* 125 (1990).

Russell Leblang, "Controlling Prosecutorial Discretion Under State Rico," 24 *Suffolk U.L. Rev.* 79 (1990).

Norman J. Finkel, "Capital Felony-Murder, Objective Indicia, and Community Sentiment," 32 *Ariz. L. Rev.* 819 (1990).

Victor L. Streib, "Death Penalty for Female Offenders," 58 *U. Cin. L. Rev.* 845 (1990).

Elizabeth Rapaport, "Some Questions About Gender and the Death Penalty," 20 *Golden Gate U. L. Rev.* 501 (1990).

John W. Poulos, "The Lucas Court and Capital Punishment: The Original Understanding of the Special Circumstances," 30 *Santa Clara L. Rev.* 333 (1990).

Joshua N. Sondheimer, "A Continuing Source of Aggravation: The Improper Consideration of Mitigating Factors in Death Penalty Sentencing," 41 *Hastings L.J.* 409 (1990).

Ira P. Robbins, "Toward a More Just and Effective System of Review in State Death Penalty Cases," 40 *Am. U. L. Rev.* 1 (1990).

Andrew H. Friedman, "Tison v. Arizona: The Death Penalty and the Non-triggerman: The Scales of Justice Are Broken," 75 *Cornell L. Rev.* 123 (1989).

Miranda B. Strassmann, "Mills v. Maryland: The Supreme Court Guarantees the Consideration of Mitigating Circumstances Pursuant to Lockett v. Ohio," 38 *Cath. U. L. Rev.* 907 (1989).

Annamary Sullivan, "The President's Power to Promulgate Death Penalty Standards," 125 *Mil. L. Rev.* 143 (1989).

Ellen Fels Berkman, "Mental Illness as an Aggravating Circumstance in Capital Sentencing," 89 *Colum. L. Rev.* 291 (1989).

Robin E. Abrams, "A Capital Defendant's Right to a Continuance Between the Two Phases of a Death Penalty Trial," 64 *N.Y.U. L. Rev.* 579 (1989).

Paul Whitlock Cobb, Jr., "Reviving Mercy in the Structure of Capital Punishment," 99 *Yale L.J.* 389 (1989).

Welsh S. White, "Fact-finding and the Death Penalty: The Scope of a Capital Defendant's Right to Jury Trial," 65 *Notre Dame L. Rev.* 1 (1989).

Victor L. Streib and Lynn Sametz, "Executing Female Juveniles," 22 *Conn. L. Rev.* 3 (1989).

W. Ward Morrison, Jr., "Washington's Comparative Proportionality Review: Toward Effective Appellate Review of Death Penalty Cases Under the Washington State Constitution," 60 *Wash. L. Rev.* 111 (1989).

Lynn D. Wittenbrink, "Overstepping Precedent? Tison v. Arizona Imposes the Death Penalty on Felony Murder Accomplices," 66 *N.C. L. Rev.* 817 (1988).

Jonathan L. Entin, "Psychiatry, Insanity, and the Death Penalty: A Note on Implementing Supreme Court Decisions," 79 *Crim. L. & Criminology* 218 (1988).

Mark Andrew Stafford, "State v. Barts: North Carolina Relaxes Foundation Requirements for Mitigating Evidence in Capital Sentencing Hearings," 66 *N.C. L. Rev.* 1221 (1988).

James J. Holman, "Redefining a Culpable Mental State for a Non-trigger-man—Tison v. Arizona," 33 *Vill. L. Rev.* 367 (1988).

Barbara J. Whisler, "Sixth Amendment—Death Qualification of the Jury: Process Is Permissible Where Defendant Does Not Face Death Penalty," 78 *J. Crim. L. & Criminology* 954 (1988).

William S. Geimer and Jonathan Amsterdam, "Why Jurors Vote Life or Death: Operative Factors in Ten Florida Death Penalty Cases," 15 *Am. J. Crim. L.* 1 (1988).

Karen M. Quinn, "A Reckless Indifference to Human Life Is Sufficient Evidence to Prove Culpability in a Felony-Murder Case and Therefore Imposition of the Death Penalty Is Not a Violation of the Eighth Amendment—Tison v. Arizona," 37 *Drake L. Rev.* 767 (1988).

John A. Wasleff, "Lockhart v. McCree: Death Qualification as a Determinant of the Impartiality and Representativeness of a Jury in Death Penalty Cases," 72 *Cornell L. Rev.* 1075 (1987).

Stephen Taylor, "Cruel and Unusual Punishment—Imposition of the Death Penalty on a Non-triggerman—Tison v. Arizona," 13 *T. Marshall L. Rev.* 211 (1987).

David W. Doyle, "Life or Death in Florida: What Mitigating Evidence Will the Judge Consider in Capital Cases?" 4 *Cooley L. Rev.* 693 (1987).

Franklin E. Zimring and Gordon Hawkins, "A Punishment in Search of a Crime: Standards for Capital Punishment in the Law of Criminal Homicide," 46 *Md. L. Rev.* 115 (1986).

Stephen Nathanson, "Does It Matter If Death Penalty Is Arbitrarily Administered," 14 *Phil. & Pub. Aff.* 149 (1985).

Christopher Grafflin Browning, Jr., "State v. Huffstetler: Denying Mitigating Instructions in Capital Cases on Grounds of Relevancy," 63 *N.C. L. Rev.* 1122 (1985).

Patrick J. Callans, "Sixth Amendment—Assembling a Jury Willing to Impose the Death Penalty: A New Disregard for a Capital Defendant's Rights," 76 *J. Crim. L. & Criminology* 1027 (1985).

Gregory Michael Stein, "Distinguishing Among Murders When Assessing the Proportionality of the Death Penalty," 85 *Colum. L. Rev.* 1786 (1985).

Victor Streib, "Death Penalty for Children: The American Experience with Capital Punishment for Crimes Committed While Under Age Eighteen," 36 *Okl. L. Rev.* 613 (1983).

Gary Goodpaster, "The Trial for Life: Effective Assistance of Counsel in Death Penalty Cases," 58 *N.Y.U. L. Rev.* 299 (1983).

Tim Kaine, "Capital Punishment and the Waiver of Sentence Review," 18 *Harv. C.R.C.L. L. Rev.* 483 (1983).

Richard O. Lempert, "Desert and Deterrence: An Assessment of the Moral Bases of the Case for Capital Punishment," 79 *Mich. L. Rev.* 1177 (1981).

William J. Bowers & Glenn L. Pierce, "Deterrence or Brutalization: What Is the Effect of Executions?" 26 *Crime & Delinq.* 453 (1980).

Douglas Noll, "Controlling a Prosecutor's Screening Discretion Through Fuller Enforcement," 29 *Syracuse L. Rev.* 697 (1978).

Ernest van den Haag, "In Defense of the Death Penalty: A Legal-Practical-Moral Analysis," 14 *Crim. L. Bull.* 51 (1978).

Charles Bubany and Frank Skillern, "Taming the Dragon: An Administrative Law for Prosecutorial Decisionmaking," 13 *Am. Cr. L. Rev.* 473 (1976).

James Vorenberg, "Narrowing the Discretion of Criminal Justice Officials," 1976 *Duke L.J.* 651 (1976).

Anthony F. Granucci, "Nor Cruel and Unusual Punishments Inflicted: The Original Meaning," 57 *Cal. L. Rev.* 839 (1969).

Gary Knell, "Capital Punishment: Its Administration in Relation to Juvenile Offenders in the Nineteenth Century and Its Possible Administration in the Eighteenth," 5 *Brit. J. Crim.* 198 (1965).

W. Scott Van Alstyne, Jr., "The District Attorney—A Historical Puzzle," 1952 *Wis. L. Rev.* 125 (1952).

CASES

Ake v. Oklahoma, 470 U.S. 68 (1985)
Alford v. State, 906 P.2d 714 (Nev. 1995)
Armstrong v. State, 642 So.2d 730 (Fla. 1994)
Baal v. State, 787 P.2d 391 (Nev. 1990)
Baldwin v. Alabama, 472 U.S. 372 (1985)
Baldwin v. New York, 399 U.S. 66 (1970)
Ballenger v. State, 667 So.2d 1242 (Miss. 1995)
Ballew v. Georgia, 435 U.S. 223 (1978)
Barbour v. State, 673 So.2d 461 (Ala.Cr.App. 1994)
Barclay v. Florida, 463 U.S. 939 (1983)
Battles v. State, 420 S.E.2d 303 (Ga. 1992)
Beathard v. State, 767 S.W.2d 423 (Tex.Cr.App. 1989)
Bloom v. California, 774 P.2d 698 (Cal. 1989)
Borrego v. State, 800 S.W.2d 373 (Tex.App.-Corpus Christi 1990)
Boyde v. California, 494 U.S. 370 (1990)
Brecht v. Abrahamson, 944 F.2d 1363 (7th Cir. 1991)
Brown v. State, 410 A.2d 17 (Md.App. 1979)
Buford v. State, 403 So.2d 943 (Fla. 1981)
Bullington v. Missouri, 451 U.S. 430 (1981)
Burch v. Louisiana, 441 U.S. 130 (1979)
Bush v. State, 461 So.2d 936 (Fla. 1984)
California v. Brown, 479 U.S. 538 (1987)
Campbell v. Blodgett, 1993 U.S.App. LEXIS 1036 (9th Cir., 1/25/93)

Campbell v. State, 571 So.2d 415 (Fla. 1990)

Campbell v. Wood, 18 F.3d 662 (1994)

Cargle v. State, 909 P.2d 806 (Okl.Cr. 1995)

Cave v. State, 660 So.2d 705 (Fla. 1995)

Chavez v. State, 657 S.W.2d 146 (Tex.Cr.App. 1983)

Clemons v. Mississippi, 494 U.S. 738 (1990)

Codispoti v. Pennsylvania, 418 U.S. 506 (1974)

Coker v. Georgia, 433 U.S. 584 (1977)

Coker v. State, 911 S.W.2d 357 (Tenn. 1995)

Commonwealth v. Lacava, 666 A.2d 221 (Pa. 1995)

Commonwealth v. Stevens, 670 A.2d 623 (Pa. 1996)

Commonwealth v. Williams, 650 A.2d 420 (Pa. 1994)

Cook v. State, 251 S.E.2d 230 (Ga. 1978)

Crawford v. State, 632 S.W.2d 800 (Tex.App. 14 Dist. 1982)

Crawford v. State, 863 S.W.2d 152 (Tex.App.-Houston 1993)

Crossley v. State, 420 So.2d 1376 (Miss. 1982)

Darden v. State, 758 S.W.2d 264 (Tex.Cr.App. 1988)

Davis v. State, 782 S.W.2d 211 (Tex.Cr.App. 1989)

DeAngelo v. State, 616 So.2d 440 (Fla. 1993)

Delo v. Lashley, 113 S.Ct. 1222 (1993)

Duncan v. Louisiana, 391 U.S. 145 (1968)

Dunn v. State, 434 S.E.2d 60 (Ga. 1993)

Enmund v. Florida, 458 U.S. 782 (1982)

Ex Parte Granviel, 561 S.W.2d 503 (Tex.Cr.App. 1978)

Ex Parte May, 717 S.W.2d 84 (Tex.Cr.App. 1986)

Ex Parte Simmons, 649 So.2d 1282 (Ala. 1994)

Ex Parte Wilson, 571 So.2d 1251 (Ala. 1990)

Fairchild v. State, 459 So.2d 793 (Miss. 1984)

Fierro v. Gomez, 1993 U.S.Dist. LEXIS 14445 (N.D.Cal., 10/13/93)

Fierro v. Gomez, 77 F.3d 301 (9th Cir. 1996), reversed, 117 S.Ct. 285 (1996)

Ford v. Wainwright, 477 U.S. 399 (1986)

Francis v. Resweber, 329 U.S. 459 (1947)

Furman v. Georgia, 408 U.S. 238 (1972)

Garrett v. Estelle, 556 F.2d 1274 (5th Cir. 1977)

Gideon v. Wainwright, 372 U.S. 335 (1963)

Grandison v. State, 670 A.2d 398 (Md. 1995)

Gray v. Lucas, 710 F.2d 1048 (5th Cir. 1983)

Gray v. State, 441 A.2d 209 (Del. 1981)

Greene v. State, 469 S.E.2d 129 (Ga. 1996)

Gregg v. Georgia, 428 U.S. 153 (1976)

Hagood v. State, 588 So.2d 526 (Ala.Cr.App. 1991)

Halquist v. Dept. of Corrections, 783 P.2d 1065 (Wash. 1989)

Harmelin v. Michigan, 501 U.S. 957 (1991)

Harris v. Alabama, 115 S.Ct. 1031 (1995)

Harrison v. State, 644 N.E.2d 1243 (Ind. 1995)

Hatch v. Oklahoma, 58 F.3d 1447 (10th Cir. 1995)

Hays v. State, 599 So.2d 1230 (Ala.Cr.App. 1992)

Heath v. Alabama, 474 U.S. 82 (1985)

Heckler v. Chaney, 470 U.S. 821 (1985)

Hildwin v. Florida, 490 U.S. 638 (1989)

Hogue v. State, 711 S.W.2d 9 (Tex.Cr.App. 1986)

Holden v. Minnesota, 137 U.S. 483 (1890)

Hunt v. Nuth, 57 F.3d 1327 (4th Cir. 1995)

Hunt v. State, 659 So.2d 933 (Ala.Cr.App. 1994)

Hurtado v. California, 110 U.S. 516 (1884)

In re Gault, 387 U.S. 1 (1967)

In re Kemmler, 136 U.S. 436 (1890)

In re Oliver, 333 U.S. 257 (1948)

Jackson v. Virginia, 413 U.S. 307 (1979)

Janecka v. State, 823 S.W.2d 232 (Tex.Cr.App. 1990)

Jenkins v. State, 912 S.W.2d 793 (Tex.Cr.App. 1993)

Johnson v. Estelle, 704 F.2d 232 (5th Cir. 1983)

Johnson v. Louisiana, 406 U.S. 356 (1972)

Johnson v. State, 815 S.W.2d 707 (Tex.Cr.App. 1991)

Johnson v. State, 660 So.2d 637 (Fla. 1995)

Jurek v. Texas, 428 U.S. 262 (1976)

King v. State, 594 S.W.2d 425 (Tex.Cr.App. 1980)

Koehler v. State, 653 S.W.2d 617 (Tex.App. 4 Dist. 1983)

KQED v. Vasquez, No. C-90-1383 (N.D.Cal. August 6, 1991)

Lankford v. Idaho, 500 U.S. 110 (1991)

Leatherwood v. State, 548 So.2d 389 (Miss. 1989)

Leland v. Oregon, 343 U.S. 790 (1952)

Lindsey v. Smith, 820 F.2d 1137 (11th Cir. 1987)

Lockett v. Ohio, 438 U.S. 586 (1978)

Long v. State, 820 S.W.2d 888 (Tex.App.-Houston 1991)

McCall v. State, 501 So.2d 496 (Ala.Cr.App. 1986)

McClellan v. Commonwealth, 715 S.W.2d 464 (Ky. 1986)

McCleskey v. Kemp, 481 U.S. 279 (1987)

McKane v. Durston, 153 U.S. 684 (1894)

McKenna v. McDaniel, 65 F.3d 1483 (9th Cir. 1995)

McKoy v. North Carolina, 494 U.S. 433 (1990)

Manna v. State, 440 N.E.2d 473 (Ind. 1982)

Mempa v. Rhay, 389 U.S. 128 (1967)

Miles v. State, 918 S.W.2d 511 (Tex.Cr.App. 1996)

Mills v. Maryland, 486 U.S. 367 (1988)

Miranda v. Arizona, 384 U.S. 436 (1966)

Moore v. Clarke, 951 F.2d 895 (8th Cir. 1991)

Morgan v. Illinois, 112 S.Ct. 2222 (1992)

Morrison v. State, 500 So.2d 36 (Ala. 1985)

Newman v. United States, 382 F.2d 479 (D.C. Cir. 1967)

North Carolina v. Alford, 400 U.S. 25 (1970)

Nunley v. State, 660 P.2d 1052 (Okla. 1983)

Odle v. Calderon, 919 F.Supp. 1367 (N.D.Cal. 1996)

Parker v. State, 610 So.2d 1181 (Ala. 1992)

Peck v. State, 923 S.W.2d 839 (Tex.App.-Tyler 1996)

Penick v. State, 659 N.E.2d 484 (Ind. 1995)

Pennington v. State, 913 P.2d 1356 (Okl.Cr. 1995)

Penry v. Lynaugh, 492 U.S. 302 (1989)

People v. Arellano, 524 P.2d 305 (Colo. 1974)

People v. Arias, 913 P.2d 980 (Cal. 1996)

People v. Belmontes, 755 P.2d 310 (Cal. 1988)

People v. Bounds, 662 N.E.2d 1168 (Ill. 1995)

People v. Bunyard, 756 P.2d 795 (Cal. 1988)

People v. Casseus, 606 N.Y.S.2d 21 (1993)

People v. Christiansen, 506 N.E.2d 1253 (Ill. 1987)

People v. Crews, 522 N.E.2d 1167 (Ill. 1988)

People v. Davenport, 906 P.2d 1068 (Cal. 1995)

People v. Davis, 794 P.2d 159 (Colo. 1990)

People v. Deason, 584 N.E.2d 829 (Ill.App. 4 Dist. 1991)

People v. Douglas, 788 P.2d 640 (Cal. 1990)

People v. Edelbacher, 766 P.2d 1 (Cal. 1989)

People v. Edwards, 819 P.2d 436 (Cal. 1991)

People v. Grant, 755 P.2d 894 (Cal. 1988)

People v. Guzman, 755 P.2d 917 (Cal. 1988)

People v. Hayes, 564 N.E.2d 803 (Ill. 1990)

People v. Lucas, 907 P.2d 373 (Cal. 1995)

People v. McDonald, 660 N.E.2d 832 (Ill. 1995)

People v. Medina, 906 P.2d 2 (Cal. 1995)

People v. Membro, 905 P.2d 1305 (Cal. 1995)

People v. Memro, 47 Cal.Rptr. 219 (1996)

People v. Moore, 662 N.E.2d 1215 (Ill. 1996)

People v. Nitz, 610 N.E.2d 1289 (Ill.App. 5 Dist. 1993)

People v. Pock, 23 Cal.Rptr.2d 900 (1993)

People v. Pride, 833 P.2d 643 (Cal. 1992)

People v. Richards, 413 N.E.2d 5 (Ill.App. 1980)

People v. Sims, 20 Cal.Rptr. 537 (1993)

People v. Taylor, 646 N.E.2d 567 (Ill. 1995)

People v. Van Ronk, 217 Cal.Rptr. 581 (1985)

People v. Vernon, 152 Cal.Rptr. 765 (1979)

People v. Watts, 525 N.E.2d 233 (Ill.App. 4 Dist. 1988)
People v. West, 560 N.E.2d 594 (Ill. 1990)
People v. Wilkins, 31 Cal.Rptr. 764 (1994)
People v. Young, 538 N.E.2d 461 (Ill. 1989)
Petition of Thomas, 155 F.R.D. 124 (D.Md. 1994)
Pickens v. State, 783 S.W.2d 341 (Ark. 1990)
Price v. State, 362 So.2d 204 (Miss. 1978)
Purifoy v. State, 822 S.W.2d 374 (Ark. 1991)
Ridgely v. State, 756 S.W.2d 870 (Tex.App.-Fort Worth 1988)
Roberts v. State, 314 S.E.2d 83 (Ga. 1984)
Robison v. Maynard, 943 F.2d 1216 (10th Cir. 1991)
Rogers v. Commonwealth, 410 S.E.2d 621 (Va. 1991)
Rougeau v. State, 738 S.W.2d 651 (Tex.Cr.App. 1987)
Rupe v. Wood, 863 F.Supp. 1307 (W.D.Wash. 1994)
Russell v. State, 670 So.2d 816 (Miss. 1995)
Smith v. Farley, 59 F.3d 659 (7th Cir. 1995)
Spaziano v. Florida, 468 U.S. 447 (1984)
Stanford v. Kentucky, 492 U.S. 361 (1989)
State ex rel. Maurer v. Steward, 644 N.E.2d 369 (Ohio 1994)
State v. Apelt, 861 P.2d 654 (Ariz. 1993)
State v. Bacon, 390 S.E.2d 327 (N.C. 1990)
State v. Barrett, 469 S.E.2d 888 (N.C. 1996)
State v. Bellamy, 359 S.E.2d 63 (S.C. 1987)
State v. Blankenship, 447 S.E.2d 727 (N.C. 1994)
State v. Bockorny, 866 P.2d 1230 (Or.App. 1993)
State v. Brown, 651 A.2d 19 (N.J. 1994)
State v. Clemmons, 682 S.W.2d 843 (Mo.App. 1984)
State v. Commer, 799 P.2d 333 (Ariz. 1990)
State v. Cooey, 544 N.E.2d 895 (Ohio 1989)
State v. Copeland, 300 S.E.2d 63 (S.C. 1983)
State v. Cotton, 381 N.E.2d 190 (Ohio 1978)
State v. Crowder, 123 S.E.2d 42 (W.Va. 1961)
State v. Cummings, 404 S.E.2d 849 (N.C. 1991)
State v. Dees, 916 S.W.2d 287 (Mo.App. 1995)
State v. Dickerson, 543 N.E.2d 1250 (Ohio 1989)
State v. DiFrisco, 662 A.2d 442 (N.J. 1995)
State v. Fierro, 804 P.2d 72 (Ariz. 1990)
State v. Flanders, 572 A.2d 983 (Conn. 1990)
State v. Forrest, 356 So.2d 945 (La. 1978)
State v. Gandy, 324 S.E.2d 65 (S.C. 1984)
State v. Gee Jon, 211 P. 676 (Nev. 1923)
State v. Golson, 658 So.2d 225 (La.App. 2 Cir. 1995)
State v. Gordon, 915 S.W.2d 393 (Mo.App. 1996)

State v. Hightower, 577 A.2d 99 (N.J. 1990)
State v. Hines, 919 S.W.2d 573 (Tenn. 1995)
State v. Johnson, 365 So.2d 1267 (La. 1978)
State v. Jones, 475 A.2d 1087 (Conn. 1984)
State v. Kolbe, 838 P.2d 612 (Ore. 1992)
State v. Langford, 837 P.2d 1037 (Wash.App. Div. 3 1992)
State v. Lavers, 814 P.2d 333 (Ariz. 1991)
State v. Littlejohn, 459 S.E.2d 629 (N.C. 1995)
State v. Martin, 702 S.W.2d 560 (Tenn. 1985)
State v. McConnaughey, 311 S.E.2d 26 (N.C.App. 1984)
State v. McLoughlin, 679 P.2d 504 (Ariz. 1984)
State v. Murray, 906 P.2d 542 (Ariz. 1995)
State v. Pizzuto, 810 P.2d 680 (Idaho 1989)
State v. Raines, 606 A.2d 265 (Md. 1992)
State v. Ramseur, 524 A.2d 188 (N.J. 1987)
State v. Roscoe, 910 P.2d 635 (Ariz. 1996)
State v. Sepulvado, 672 So.2d 158 (La. 1996)
State v. Simpson, 462 S.E.2d 191 (N.C. 1995)
State v. Sivak, 806 P.2d 413 (Idaho 1990)
State v. Smith, 381 S.E.2d 724 (S.C. 1989)
State v. Stuard, 863 P.2d 881 (Ariz. 1993)
State v. Thomas, 595 S.W.2d 325 (Mo.App. 1980)
State v. Wallace, 773 P.2d 983 (Ariz. 1989)
State v. West, 388 N.W.2d 823 (Neb. 1986)
State v. Williams, 292 S.E.2d 243 (N.C. 1982)
State v. Williams, 468 S.E.2d 626 (S.C. 1996)
State v. Wood, 648 P.2d 71 (Utah 1981)
Stephens v. Borg, 59 F.3d 932 (9th Cir. 1995)
Stephenson v. State, 593 So.2d 160 (Ala.Cr.App. 1991)
Stevenson v. State, 404 So.2d 111 (Ala.Cr.App. 1981)
Strickler v. Commonwealth, 404 S.E.2d 227 (Va. 1991)
Stroud v. United States, 251 U.S. 15 (1919)
Thompson v. Oklahoma, 487 U.S. 815 (1988)
Tison v. Arizona, 481 U.S. 137 (1987)
Townes v. Commonwealth, 362 S.E.2d 650 (Va. 1987)
Trest v. State, 409 So.2d 906 (Fla.Cr.App. 1981)
Trop v. Dulles, 356 U.S. 86 (1958)
Tuilaepa v. California, 114 S.Ct. 2630 (1994)
Turner v. State, 406 So.2d 1066 (Ala.Cr.App. 1981)
Underwood v. State, 535 N.E.2d 507 (Ind. 1989)
United States v. Chandler, 996 F.2d 1083 (11th Cir. 1993)
United States v. Darden, 70 F.3d 1507 (8th Cir. 1995)
United States v. Walker, 910 F.Supp. 837 (N.D.N.Y. 1995)

United States v. Yunis, 681 F.Supp. 896 (D.D.C. 1988)
Upshaw v. State, 350 So.2d 1358 (Miss. 1977)
Wainwright v. Witt, 469 U.S. 412 (1985)
Wallace v. Lockart, 701 F.2d 719 (8th Cir. 1983)
Walton v. Arizona, 497 U.S. 639 (1990)
Wayte v. United States, 470 U.S. 598 (1985)
Weaver v. State, 407 So.2d 568 (Ala.Cr.App. 1981)
Welch v. State, 331 S.E.2d 573 (Ga. 1985)
Whittlesey v. State, 665 A.2d 223 (Md. 1995)
Wilcher v. Hargett, 978 F.2d 872 (5th Cir. 1992)
Wilkerson v. Utah, 99 U.S. 130 (1878)
Williams v. Collins, 16 F.3d 626 (5th Cir. 1994)
Williams v. Florida, 399 U.S. 78 (1970)
Witherspoon v. Illinois, 391 U.S. 510 (1968)
Wood v. State, 547 N.E.2d 772 (Ind. 1989)
Woodson v. North Carolina, 428 U.S. 280 (1976)
Woratzeck v. Lewis, 863 F.Supp. 1079 (D.Ariz. 1994)
Zant v. Stephens, 462 U.S. 862 (1983)

Index

Pride see *People v. Pride*
prosecutorial discretion 45–52, 49–50
psychological disorder 122
public executions: last public execution 168; origin of 167–168
public prosecutor: American colonies 47–48; Dutch colonies 48–49; modern day 49
Purifoy v. State 72

quash 55

Raines see *State v. Raines*
Ramseur see *State v. Ramseur*
relevant mitigators 117
reprieve 165
requesting death 140–141
respite 165
retrial of penalty phase 89
retribution 13–14, 140
Richards see *People v. Richards*
Ridgely v. State 62
right to jury, waiving of 81, 92
rights, to: allocution 141; counsel 92–93; co-counsel 93; psychiatrist 118–119; self-representation 139–140
Roberts v. State 60
Robison v. Maynard 117
Rogers, Don 30
Rogers v. Commonwealth 73
Roscoe see *State v. Roscoe*
Rougeau v. State 62
Ruiz, Alejandro Gilbert 171
rules of evidence 93–94
Rupe v. Wood 182
Russell v. State 96

schout 48–49
sentencing errors 137–139
Sepulvado see *State v. Sepulvado*
Simpson see *State v. Simpson*
Simpson, O.J. 102, 105, 108
Sims see *People v. Sims*
Sivak see *State v. Sivak*
Sixth Amendment 81, 83, 91–92, 139
Smith see *State v. Smith*
Smith v. Farley 72
sodium thiopental 185–186
sovereignty 52–54
Spaziano v. Florida 90, 92
Stanford v. Kentucky 155
state attorney 49
State ex rel. Maurer v. Steward 165–166
State v. Apelt 122

State v. Bacon 124
State v. Barrett 88
State v. Bellamy 132
State v. Blankenship 77
State v. Bockorny 61
State v. Brown 62
State v. Clemmons 61
State v. Commer 143–144
State v. Cooey 122
State v. Copeland 34
State v. Cotton 27
State v. Crowder 37
State v. Cummings 145–146
State v. Dees 75
State v. Dickerson 145
State v. DiFrisco 30
State v. Fierro 36, 143
State v. Flanders 61
State v. Forrest 72
State v. Gandy 27
State v. Gee Jon 189
State v. Golson 24
State v. Gordon 75
State v. Hightower 141
State v. Hines 87
State v. Johnson 77
State v. Jones 60
State v. Kolbe 30
State v. Langford 75
State v. Lavers 34
State v. Littlejohn 77
State v. Martin 25
State v. McConnaughey 24
State v. McLoughlin 28
State v. Murray 88
State v. Pizzuto 34
State v. Raines 73
State v. Ramseur 122
State v. Roscoe 89
State v. Sepulvado 88, 96
State v. Simpson 40–41
State v. Sivak 129
State v. Smith 142
State v. Stuard 122
State v. Thomas 72
State v. Wallace 145
State v. West 25
State v. Williams 60, 95
State v. Wood 130
statutory aggravating circumstances: aggravators distinguished 99–100; meaning of 97; not element of offense 128
statutory issue, special: meaning of 99